# Disneyland Politics

In the series *Urban Life, Landscape, and Policy*,
edited by David Stradling, Larry Bennett, and Davarian Baldwin.
Founding editor, Zane L. Miller.

ALSO IN THIS SERIES:

A list of additional titles in this series appears at the back of this book.

PETER F. BURNS, MATTHEW O. THOMAS, AND MAX R. BIEGANSKI

# Disneyland Politics

*How a Medium-Size City
and Corporate Giant Coexist*

T

TEMPLE UNIVERSITY PRESS
*Philadelphia* • *Rome* • *Tokyo*

TEMPLE UNIVERSITY PRESS
Philadelphia, Pennsylvania 19122
tupress.temple.edu

Library of Congress Cataloging-in-Publication Data

Names: Burns, Peter F., author. | Thomas, Matthew O., author. | Bieganski,
Max R., 1994– author.
Title: Disneyland politics : how a medium-size city and corporate giant
coexist / Peter F. Burns, Matthew O. Thomas, and Max R. Bieganski.
Other titles: Urban life, landscape, and policy.
Description: Philadelphia : Temple University Press, 2026. | Series: Urban
life, landscape, and policy | Includes bibliographical references and
index. | Summary: "Uses a case study of Disneyland in Anaheim,
California, to examine the relationship between government and private
capital in a medium-size city"— Provided by publisher.
Identifiers: LCCN 2025036795 (print) | LCCN 2025036796 (ebook) | ISBN
9781439926857 (cloth) | ISBN 9781439926864 (paperback) | ISBN
9781439926871 (pdf)
Subjects: LCSH: Corporations—Political activity—California—Anaheim—Case
studies. | Public-private sector cooperation—California—Anaheim—Case
studies. | Countervailing power—California—Anaheim—Case studies. |
Disneyland (Calif.)—Political activity—California—Anaheim—Case
studies. | Anaheim (Calif.)—Politics and government.
Classification: LCC HD2798.5.A3 B87 2026 (print) | LCC HD2798.5.A3 (ebook)
LC record available at https://lccn.loc.gov/2025036795
LC ebook record available at https://lccn.loc.gov/2025036796

The manufacturer's authorized representative in the EU for product safety is
Temple University Rome, Via di San Sebastianello, 16, 00187 Rome RM, Italy
(https://rome.temple.edu/).
tempress@temple.edu

Printed in the United States of America

9  8  7  6  5  4  3  2  1

# Contents

## PART III  THERE, AND BACK AGAIN

# Acknowledgments

Peter Burns thanks his research assistants over the course of this book project. The research assistants were Max Bieganski, Ana Schugurensky, Kaitlyn Haibel, Akemi Terukina, Aska Wurtz, Valentina Ferreira Einsfeld, and Mili Fukada. He thanks Soka University and its administrators for providing a sabbatical, research assistants, and financial assistance to conduct research. The administrators include Ed Feasel, Michael Weiner, Bryan Penprase, and Robert Hamersley. Special thanks to Esther Chang, the Social and Behavioral Sciences concentration at Soka, and Teri Chester. Peter Burns also thanks Clarence Stone, Chris Wiseman, and John Erlingheuser for help with the book. Thanks to Matt Thomas and Max Bieganski, who are great friends and colleagues, and thanks also to my parents, my sister Patty, brother-in-law Ed, and my favorite niece, Holly.

Matt Thomas thanks his colleagues in the Department of Political Science and Criminal Justice as well as the College of Behavioral and Social Sciences at California State University, Chico. Special thanks to Clarence Stone for an academic lifetime of support and guidance and to Peter Burns for his collaboration and friendship. Finally, thanks to my wife Kristen and sons Zachary and Liam for their support and love.

Max Bieganski thanks Soka University of America and his mentors there for making his contributions to this book possible. They include Peter Burns, Daniel Habuki, Hyon Moon, Michael Golden, Monika Calef, Phat Vu, Danielle Denardo, Kristi Wilson, Tomas Crowder-Taraborelli, George Busenberg, Bryan Penprase, Tomoko Takahashi, John Heffron, Karen Moran Jackson,

Edward Feasel, and the Class of 2019. Max thanks his mother, Nancy Bieganski, for her enduring support and examples of tenacity and optimism during the course of this project. Finally, Max expresses his deepest gratitude to his life mentor, Daisaku Ikeda, Buddhist philosopher, peacebuilder, and founder of SUA, for embodying the qualities of a global citizen that shine as a beacon of hope for the twenty-first century.

Peter, Matt, and Max thank Aaron Javsicas for his stewardship of this project. They are also in debt to Larry Bennett, who provided countless helpful suggestions and mentoring. Aaron and Larry greatly improved this book.

# Disneyland Politics

# Introduction

*Power in a Medium-Size City*

## Choices

Walt Disney claimed that the idea for Disneyland "came about when my daughters were very young. . . . I'd take 'em to the merry-go-round and different places. And as I'd sit there on a bench, you know, eating peanuts while they rode the merry-go-round and did all these things, I felt that there should be some kind of an amusement enterprise built, where parents and their children could have fun together. So that's how Disneyland started."[1] Disneyland's origins also took root in the letters Walt received from fans who wanted to visit their favorite characters at the company's studios in Burbank, California.[2] Walt knew that, when visitors arrived at his studios, the children and their parents would see men operating cameras and not much else. In 1939, Disney purchased property across the street from his studios in Burbank.[3] On Sundays, he sat in that weed-filled lot and dreamed of a small park with picnic tables, grass, and trees along with singing waterfalls and statues of Disney characters.[4] Disney wanted to monetize consumer passion for his products, and this little park, which would be ringed by railroad tracks and a train, provided one way to do it.

The city of Burbank needed to agree to make this place, which he named Mickey Mouse Park, a reality. Burbank's Board of Parks and Recreation approved Disneyland, which would take up sixteen acres and cost $1.5 million; Disney needed the Burbank City Council to do the same.[5] Walt and Harper Goff, who drew the designs for Disneyland, made a presentation before the city council, but that legislative body rejected the project.[6] One member of the council argued, "We don't want a carny atmosphere in Burbank. We don't want people falling in the river, or merry-go-rounds squawking all day long." Goff believed that the Burbank City Council had "sneered at us." Walt Disney said nothing, and they left. He knew they lacked the power to change the council's mind.

Burbank's City Council made a choice. It exercised its land-use power to reject Disney and development. If the council had approved this Disney park, the area around the studios—and the city itself—would be much different. Today, this site includes green space, running trails, and equestrian areas. A Disney park would have brought hotels, tourists, restaurants, stores, and a variety of other businesses and activities, in addition to various problems such as traffic, which would have transformed this quaint area. Walt went to a Plan B.

Like the leaders in Burbank, the city administrator and an official with the chamber of commerce in Anaheim, California, made a choice that produced consequences for their locality. They wanted to grow the city's industrial and economic base and jumped at the chance to build Disneyland in their town. Once Walt Disney decided to locate his park in Anaheim, that city had to figure out how to coexist with this company. On which terms would Anaheim coexist with the Walt Disney Company and Disneyland? Under which conditions would those terms change? Disneyland presented a puzzle for Anaheim's government. How would the city balance the interests of private control of investment against those of the citizenry when the two conflict? This public-private relationship, which now spans seventy years, allows us to see how Anaheim, Disney, and various other actors attempted to solve this puzzle. According to one political leader, the tension between citizenry and private capital "is extreme in Anaheim, but every city has it."[7]

## The Disneyland Imperative

This book is about power. The urban power debate has centered on whether city officials possess power over their constituents or if they must create the power to govern.[8] *Disneyland Politics* takes a new path, one that shows several types of power in competition. Power comes in many forms in a capitalistic and republican society, and not all kinds of power are equal. *Disneyland Politics* shows that the varieties of power possessed by Disneyland make balance difficult to achieve and harder to sustain. We conclude that Anaheim has pursued a Disneyland Imperative, one that has favored the company over competing concerns, because the corporate giant controls and exercises many kinds of power. This book shows Disney's power in action and how those who pursue alternative agendas attempt to get their way. Over time, however, Disney has had to mobilize more power even as its grip over the city's agenda has loosened. For Disney, victories in city politics have come at a much greater cost in recent years. Those who fought for a more balanced public policy agenda changed the terms of coexistence to be less in the favor of Disneyland over time.

According to sociologist Max Weber, "Within a social relationship, power is any chance (regardless of the basis of this chance) to carry through one's own will (even against resistance)." *Disneyland Politics* unpacks power and describes various types of power and how they are formed and exercised. What are the various kinds of power, and how do they work? Political scientist Clarence N. Stone concludes, "Power can derive from relationships."[9] Entities, whether they are groups, individuals, or institutions, possess *relational power* when they form deep and broad partnerships with others who possess money, authority, or access to large amounts of other kinds of resources. Reputation also produces power. Entities exercise *reputational power* when they get their way because others perceive that they have power. Fear can be an important element of reputational power because some may act because they are afraid of what reputed power will do to them.

*Institutional capacity* plays a key role in the kind of power that Disney possesses. It includes the amount of land the company owns, the number of people it employs in the city and area, and the size of Disney's tax revenues. Disney's *financial power*, which consists of the sheer amount of the company's financial contributions to the city and elected officials, makes it impossible for Anaheim to ignore it. Disney doesn't get its way simply because it is large.

Despite its prominence in Anaheim, Disney must still participate in an uncertain politics to get its way. Disney has built and exercised relational power in Anaheim and the region since before it constructed the park. From the start, Disney relied on strong bonds with Anaheim's city manager, city council, others with authority over land-use, planning, and taxation decisions, and the most prominent businesspeople in Anaheim and Orange County. Disney continues to work hard to build and exercise power to maintain a public policy imperative that favors its business.

The city of Anaheim also exercises power, particularly in the areas of land use and taxation. *Governmental power* consists of taxing, control over land use, and authority. The Walt Disney Company needed the city of Anaheim to do the things that only a local government could do, such as zoning, infrastructure, and taxation (or the lack thereof). Despite the context of scarce resources faced by most cities, urban governments exercise financial power. They allocate hundreds of millions of dollars. Disneyland asked every level of government to spend money and provide it with infrastructure such as a parking garage and roads, freeways, and exit ramps.

*People power* exists. People can increase their power by developing co-operative relationships with others. They can also achieve influence when they organize, spend their resources, and vote. People can put pressure on government and businesses when they organize. In a democracy, government and corporations can fear the power of the people and make decisions accordingly.

Power dynamics are present in every city and jurisdiction to one degree or another, and the Disney-Anaheim relationship provides a window into how to understand power. Power is not one thing but many. Entities throughout a city wield various kinds of power. In this book, we show that Disney exerted all kinds of power to get its way. The Walt Disney Company exercised reputational power, relational power, financial power, and even people power. These forms of power helped Disney secure significant policy victories, but its success was far from guaranteed. It competed in the political arena with others who exercised power. In most instances, Disney created relational power by having strong bonds with government and other elites in the city. In a few instances, this company could not rely on this kind of partnership.

It is vital to note that government and people, even the most marginalized, exercise power. In many instances, Disney's level and breadth of resources won out. The pages of this book illustrate how actors in society wield power and the results of the exercise of that power.

We do not refer to alternative agendas as anti-Disney, because some of the advocates for policy change believe that Disneyland should play a prominent role in the city. Opponents of the Disneyland Imperative face an interesting puzzle in Anaheim. Many of them believe a prosperous resort helps the city. They do not want Disneyland to leave or the Disney Company to invest less in the parks. We refer to these groups as pro-balance because they want the city to maintain Disneyland but focus attention to neighborhoods and other issues as well. Under the terms of coexistence between the park and the city, over the decades, the pro-balance group has seen an imbalance that favors Disneyland and hurts them. Advocates for change want greater focus on issues that affect neighborhoods and service workers. Those with alternative agendas have used marches, protests, demonstrations, and other forms of people power to protest the actions of city government and the Disney Company. They exercised voting power to elect a pro-balance majority on the city council and enact a living wage ordinance in Anaheim. Democracy is not enough. It does not allow those with alternative agendas to compete against Disney on a regular basis. People and voting power work in some cases, but they are not enough to sustain an urban agenda. More power is needed, like the kind Disney exercises.

## The Conversation on Urban Power: The Public, Private, and Partnership Perspectives

The current thinking on urban politics, power, and economic development needs a better and updated understanding of the relationship between corporate giants and cities, the effects of this relationship, and how this relationship can change over time. Political scientists Hank Savitch and Paul Kantor argue that certain conditions provide more discretion to local officials to shape business development.[10] Local officials have more discretion when the city economy is strong, a centralized intergovernmental system regulates the marketplace, and people have channels to express their preferences and hold elites accountable. Business has a bargaining advantage when the local economy is weak, the intergovernmental system is decentralized, and voters and residents lack popular controls over local decisions. Bargaining advantages are cumulative. Cities in the strongest positions can have an advantage in terms of imposing costs on business.

Savitch and Kantor studied only major large global cities, which included the U.S. cities of New York, San Francisco, Washington, DC, and Detroit. New York had favorable market conditions, ranked in the middle regarding systems of popular control, and operated in a decentralized intergovernmental system. San Francisco scored in the middle in terms of market conditions and had strong popular control systems but existed in a decentralized intergovernmental system. Washington, DC, faced an average strength market and popular control systems in a dispersed intergovernmental system. Detroit scored at the bottom for each category, and, consequently, officials there face the weakest bargaining position.

In their article titled "Can Politicians Bargain with Business," Kantor and Savitch refer to the relationship between Walt Disney World and local governments in Florida. At first, they argue, Disney held the advantage and won concessions like political autonomy, tax advantages, and free infrastructure. "With huge sunk investments [over time,] Disney executives had little choice but to accommodate the public sector."[11]

Kantor and Savitch focus on some of the largest cities in the United States. They do not study medium-size cities but do write, "Aside from major cities, there are smaller communities that do not seek to compete for capital investment such as suburban areas and middle-size cities that after years of expansion, now face environmental degradation."[12] Our work examines a medium-size city that must coexist with a large and dominant corporate interest over an extended period. In the next sections, we discuss the private, public, and partnership perspectives, which have dominated the discussion of urban economic development politics over the past forty or fifty years.

## Private Perspective

Political scientist Paul Peterson's *City Limits*, which we refer to as the private perspective, argues that cities must pursue large-scale economic development projects because they compete with other urban areas for scarce financial resources.[13] The private perspective contends that elected officials don't have much choice when it comes to what occupies their public agenda. They must develop their urban cores to get the financial resources necessary to run their cities. For Peterson, the day-to-day urban politics were trivial in contrast to the consequential matter of developmental decision-making.

This book provides an alternative to the private perspective of *City Limits*. Peterson's work deals with issues that overlap the ones examined in this book, especially when it comes to intercity competition. It is not strictly comparative to this book, because it was published forty years ago and focused on the nation's largest cities. Our book shows how discordant interests come to understand not only the uneven effects of development policy but the ways in which it is possible to fight back against a powerful corporation. It illustrates how corporate giants exercise various kinds of power to ensure that their agenda continues. Development is often, but not always, the giant's policy goal. Politics and power, which need more attention from Peterson, form the spine of this book. *City Limits* also provides no way to understand change, while this book shows the conditions under which change occurs.

## Public Perspective

Law professor Richard Schragger's view, which we refer to as the public perspective, contends that cities can and should redistribute wealth. According to Schragger and others, evidence does not support the claims either that economic development policies, particularly convention centers and sports stadiums and arenas, help cities or that redistributive policies hurt them.[14] The public perspective proposes that corporations wield disproportionate power in urban America. Cities' decisions to promulgate developmental policies arise not from the demonstrated benefits of growth but from persistent exercises of corporate power. Interlocal competition remains a factor.

Schragger infers that large corporations like Disney threaten democracy: "Decision-making appears to be migrating away from democratic institutions to global markets, leaving many to ask whether citizens have any role to play in the governance of their political communities."[15] A new politics has emerged in cities, one in which communities, residents, and low-wage workers have taken up the fight against global capitalism. This resistance reinforces democracy because it provides a means for citizens to take control of their local economies.

The public perspective does not explain what happens when advocates of redistributive policies, or any agenda that does not put development first, attempt to execute public policy alternatives. This book shows what happens next; it provides a more complete picture of this so-called new politics, how the corporate giant reacts to it, and the circumstances that produce and prevent change over time. The current conversation lacks this kind of analysis of practical politics.

### Partnership Perspective

The partnership perspective, advanced by sociologist Leland Saito, shows a middle ground between Peterson and Schragger.[16] He argues that cities can balance corporate demands with resident interests. Developmental politics in cities has changed.[17] In large cities, growth coalitions lost power while labor, environmental, slow-growth, faith-based, and community organizations gained strength through coalitions.[18] Growth interests, Los Angeles Alliance for a New Economy (LAANE), Strategic Actions for a Just Economy (SAJE), and low-income residents built a coalition that created a Community Benefits Agreement (CBA) around LA Live, an entertainment district with the Staples Center sports arena as its home. Saito found that three factors led to the changes in Los Angeles and, in particular, to the successful negotiation of this CBA. First, Los Angeles's growth interests fragmented and weakened over time. Next, LAANE and SAJE provided resources, such as expertise on development, to those groups excluded or punished by development. Finally, given that Los Angeles is a prime real estate market, developers there are more amenable to enter a CBA, with government subsidies providing a further incentive to do so.

The Los Angeles story suggests that a large city can balance the interests of developers and of groups excluded by developmental policies. An analysis of Los Angeles cannot tell us whether the same kind of balance is possible in smaller cities, which may depend more on mobile capital than the nation's biggest urban centers. *Disneyland Politics* fills this intellectual gap and does so for a much longer period than studied by Saito in Los Angeles. It shows that while Disney may have lost some control over Anaheim's agenda over time, its power did not fragment, and it hardly formed a partnership with new coalitions that pursued alternative agendas. Corporate giants are more powerful and a greater threat to democracy in medium-size cities than in large urban centers.

## Politics and Political Order

This book is also about politics and change. Political scientists, geographers, anthropologists, sociologists, and planners offer different definitions of politics.[19] Even within disciplines, scholars disagree over how to define politics. Political scientist Harold Lasswell referred to politics as who gets what, when, and how.[20] This definition provides a good start, but it's static and incomplete. Those who do not get what they want often oppose the current agenda. Some of them do so in active ways. Politics is, therefore, an ongoing process characterized by competing interests and power dynamics.

To examine urban politics and change over time, we use our concept of political order, which highlights the importance of changes in governance and holds that governing coalitions are as often dynamic political interrelationships as stable long-term regimes.[21] The political order framework overcomes the criticism that regime theory does not account for political change or the roles played by excluded actors or the marginalized.[22] Political order incorporates the possibility of multiple political arrangements (coalitions) and differing levels of agenda fidelity and can encompass cases that range from a city dominated by, for example, a pro-growth coalition with strong agenda fidelity to a city composed of diffuse arrangements with little agreement among them. The concept of political order provides a framework with which to analyze cities as their governing arrangements change. The process of change indicates where power lies.

The theoretical framework behind the concept of a political order considers the process of governance as a multitiered phenomenon and incorporates seemingly disparate elements of the urban sphere that range from elites to marginalized groups. We can illustrate the multitiered nature of political order with a series of concentric circles arranged around a central set of inner core actors, as in Figure I.1. The more distant the urban sphere element is from the core, the less the dominant governing arrangement serves it. The agenda setters occupy the center of the political order. They dictate which policies the city pursues and which ones the government avoids. Actors that occupy the space next to the center of a city's political order work to support and benefit from the status quo. Coalitions that advance alternative agendas make up the next ring.[23] Marginalized groups of society lie at the outermost ring of the order.

When change occurs in city politics, the components of the political order, as illustrated earlier, are shuffled. Political order analysis integrates these actors into a cohesive but dynamic system in which they may collaborate or collide, nonetheless participating in the process of city governance.[24] This approach provides a foundation for understanding both major and minor changes in a city through time.

The outer-core actors that once supported the central agenda may pursue policies at some variance from those promoted by the inner core. The outermost ring of actors encompass a variety of interests. When the center of the order neglects and marginalizes groups, it has difficulty drawing on outer

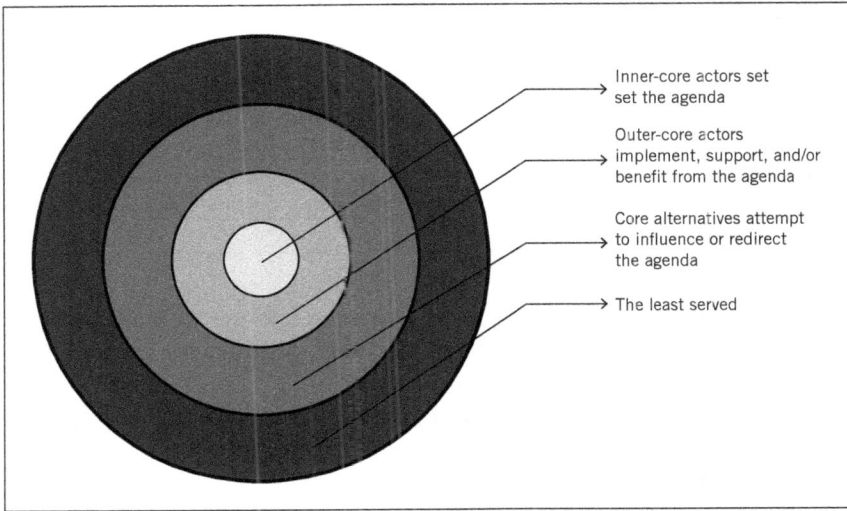

Inner-core actors set set the agenda

Outer-core actors implement, support, and/or benefit from the agenda

Core alternatives attempt to influence or redirect the agenda

The least served

**Figure I.1** Illustration of a generic political order.

actors when a crisis affects all components of the order. Alienated and marginalized parts of the city hold consequences for all.

As political scientists Stone, Stephen J. McGovern, and Neil Kraus in addition to the sociologist Louise Seamster argue, urban political theories have paid little attention to those who do not benefit from city policies.[25] Political scientists Kathy Cohen, Jamila Michener, and Michael Jones-Correa and Diane Wong, in their book and articles, respectively, have shown how marginalized groups, particularly people of color and the poor, can marshal political power.[26] The political order concept enables us to consider how city politics affects the marginalized and racial and ethnic minorities.

The concentration of a city's political arrangements, and the degree to which core actors can shape a desired agenda, known as agenda fidelity, is another attribute of political orders. Political arrangements are condensed or diffuse based on whether they incorporate fewer or more numerous groups of discrete interests. Strong arrangements yield executable agendas; ineffective arrangements struggle to shape coherent policy. Table I.1 shows how combinations of different political arrangements and degrees of agenda fidelity lead to various political orders. In previous research we conducted in New Orleans, we demonstrated that multiple political arrangements had pursued conflicting agendas in the pre-Katrina era.[27] The opposite of this state is one in which a city possesses unified political arrangements with strong agenda fidelity. Under these conditions, the city's various coalitions support and execute a shared agenda. If a city's political order falls between these extremes, it may indicate a transition in governance. Such a transition would entail move-

| TABLE I.1 POLITICAL ORDER | | Policy agenda fidelity | |
|---|---|---|---|
| | | Strong | Weak |
| Political arrangement(s) | Concentrated | • Concentrated & strong<br>• Single arrangement | • Concentrated & weak<br>• Single arrangement |
| | Diffuse | • Diffuse & strong<br>• Multiple arrangements | • Diffuse & weak<br>• Multiple arrangements |
| Adapted from Burns and Thomas, *Reforming New Orleans*. | | | |

ment from one corner of the Table I.1 matrix to another, perhaps through an intermediate state that consists of a diffuse political arrangement with strong agenda fidelity, or vice versa.

In this book, we trace the evolution of the political order in Anaheim. We specify who set and supported the agenda, the alternative agendas, and who the order marginalized from the founding of Disneyland to the present. We also identify the various coalitions (the arrangement) that supported an agenda and the extent to which the core could enact its preferred policies. Political order analysis attempts to address McGovern's call for scholars to move beyond elite-centric studies of urban politics and focus on the lives of ordinary people.[28] We view political orders as specific to individual jurisdictions.[29] Those who oppose the agendas and policies produced by the order sometimes win but often do not. Opponents who secure a victory or two still do so within the dominant order. To be the dominant force within the order, a core needs to set the city's agenda. For the most part, Disney has held this position in Anaheim during the past seventy years. In recent years, Disney lost control of the political order for a brief time, and the city's policy agenda changed, but, by applying the political order concept, we demonstrate that, even as Disney's power diminished over time, the company retained its position as the chief agenda setter in the city. Despite its ability to continue to set the agenda, Disney did have to work harder to do so and was not as dominant or successful at it as it once was.

In this book, we argue that what we term social learning and social education help explain both allegiance to the status quo and calls for change. Using a standard definition of learning, we define social learning as the acquisition of knowledge about society through experience and education. Citizens experience social learning in many ways, via the media, day-to-day contacts and conversations, and sometimes through programmed corporate communications. Social education is the process of providing information about the world in which we live. Entities that support the status quo and those that advocate change try to educate and convince the public at large that their version of reality is correct. In this book, we argue that change accelerated when people came to understand that Disney's social education, which emphasized that what was good for Disneyland was also good for the city, did not conform to their social learning. Disney broadcasted the notion that its investments in the theme park invariably helped the city, but residents saw problems worsen as Disney prospered. This change in social learning was not enough. Forces for change also had to engage in political learning, a process of acquiring and applying knowledge about how to defeat defenders of the status quo. A desire for change was not enough; people had to learn how to access and wield power. That lesson was hard but produced some victories. In the end, Disney also learned what it could and could not do politically, and it further learned how to use its power to win in new contexts.

## Power, City Size, and Anaheim, California

Political science tends to overlook medium-size cities and what these urban areas teach about power, politics, and policy.[30] Some in the discipline have noticed this oversight. Political scientists Tanu Kumar and Matthew Stenberg conclude that political scientists who study urban areas focus upon the largest cities.[31] They argue that an emphasis on the largest cities hurts our understanding of cities because smaller cities (not in the nation's top ten in population) exhibit different economic, social, and political patterns than their larger counterparts. Smaller cities have less access to resources, weaker intergovernmental relations, and different citizen preferences and demographics than large cities. Kumar and Stenberg claim that larger cities do not have to rely on property taxes and they enjoy greater Foreign Direct Investment (FDI) than medium-size cities.

These political scientists also suggest that power dynamics may be different in larger cities than smaller ones. They write:

> Consider, for example, Bentonville, Arkansas in the United States, which is home to Walmart, the largest retail company in the world. The city has a population of just under 50,000. At the same time, over 14,000 people work for the company's corporate headquarters (Adler and Florida 2020). Given a worker's set of skills, a company like Walmart may be the sole or best employer in a small labor market. Such a monopsony is likely to give the company and its leadership disproportionate power in local and regional politics.[32]

Realistically, few would assume a medium-size city like Anaheim could stand up to the power of a corporation as large and significant as Disney.[33] One might expect a global city like Chicago or New York to look at Disney the same way they do all the other major employers in their cities. A city like Anaheim may lack the same leverage.

Kumar and Stenberg encourage political scientists to examine smaller cities because they tell a different story than a nation's largest urban areas. We take up that call. A study of Anaheim and Disneyland allows us to explore power relations in a city that has fewer resources and weaker relations with state government and other metro areas than Los Angeles and other large cities.

Anaheim isn't a company town in the strictest sense of the term, but the Disney Company is a major economic, social, and political presence in the city. A study of this company's influence provides insight into how dominant corporations and industries affect the lives of people in the medium-size cities that house these commercial powers. Kumar and Stenberg argue "that both focusing specifically on smaller cities and including them in larger empirical analyses will broaden and deepen our theories while simultaneously lending greater credibility to our findings."[34] Our study of Anaheim and Disneyland over time focuses on a medium-size Sunbelt city that experienced growth over time. It offers lessons about power and politics that studies of cities like New York, Los Angeles, Chicago, Houston, Phoenix, and others cannot.

Anaheim's size is important because smaller less affluent municipalities may be less able than larger cities and counties to push back against business demands. To understand power in a city, we argue that a longitudinal perspective that examines both public and private actors is needed. Coalition building, bargaining, agenda setting, and other factors connected with politics, power, and political order are highly dependent on historical dynamics, and a case study is the best tool to capture this detail.[35] A case study is also the best way to delve into the underlying activities of city policymakers over time.

By studying the Disney/Anaheim relationship, we develop an understanding of the kinds of power and leverage corporate giants possess over medium-size cities. Anaheim, California, a city of more than 350,000, was the fifty-fifth-largest city in the United States and tenth most populous in the state in 2019. Agriculture dominated the local economy until Disneyland transformed Anaheim into one of the world's top tourist destinations. A current local leader observed that Anaheim "would have been like Garden Grove, Orange, Fullerton, and other bedroom communities without Disneyland." According to *Governing Magazine,*

> Anaheim is a curiously shaped city. Imagine a bow tie twenty-two miles wide. In the west part of the city, there are flatlands filled with working-class Latino neighborhoods. The central portion of the city is anchored by the Anaheim Resort District [and Disneyland]. To the east, the city rises into the Anaheim Hills, the wealthy, largely white part of town.[36]

One political actor concluded that "Anaheim is so wide that Mother Teresa could be in West Anaheim and East Anaheim wouldn't know it."[37] Among local interviewees, we have found that Disney supporters and advocates of a more balanced approach describe Anaheim in different ways. Pro-Disney individuals describe Anaheim as "the largest, most important city in Orange County. It has the biggest economy centered on tourism and conventions. The economy drives the region." Another figure, who is not a fan of Disney, refers to Anaheim as "a city of promise for working-class families."

The city of Anaheim operates under a council-manager form of government. The city council currently includes six council members elected by district, and the mayor, who is elected at large, also sits on the city council.[38] Prior to the 2016 election, the city council numbered four at-large councillors and an at-large mayor. A 2012 lawsuit brought by the American Civil Liberties Union (ACLU) charged the city with violations under the California Voting Rights Act, alleging that the at-large council precluded Latino representation on the council (see Chapter 8).[39] In response to the suit, the city agreed to put forth two ballot measures: Measure L proposed moving to district elections for councillors, and Measure M proposed increasing the number of councillors from four to six, while continuing to elect an at-large mayor. Both measures passed in 2014, leading to the enlarged city council.

The city council serves as the legislative body for Anaheim, and appoints the nonpartisan city manager, who handles the day-to-day implementation of public policy. Policy is set by the council, which meets weekly in a public session. The city's planning commission is composed of seven members, each of whom is appointed by the city council to staggered four-year terms.[40] The commission meets twice a month in open meetings to review land-use and development proposals, and the meetings include the opportunity for public comment. Recommendations from the planning commission are sent to the city council, which may adopt or reject those recommendations. In addition, planning commission decisions may be appealed to the city council for additional consideration, allowing for an override of a rejection by the planning commission.[41]

In the decades since Disneyland opened, Anaheim has undergone a substantial shift in demographics, much like its neighbors in Orange County and the rest of Southern California.[42] Anaheim's Latino population has grown from 17.2% in 1980 to 55.7% in 2018.[43] Latinos in Anaheim have experienced discrimination over the years in the form of de jure segregated schools and public facilities, urban renewal that led to displacement, mistreatment and abuse by the police, and severe underrepresentation in public office (see Chapter 8 for more). The majority of Anaheim's electorate voted for Propositions 187 (1994) and 227 (2016), which sought, respectively, to "prevent illegal aliens in the United States from receiving benefits or public services in the state of California" and require that "all public school instruction be conducted in English."[44] In her research on the tension over the city's refusal to approve a liquor license for a Gigante Supermarket in the city, Stacy Anne Harwood described Anaheim as a place with a "history of anti-immigrant and anti-Mexican attitudes."[45]

The changing demographics have modified the power dynamic in Anaheim and highlighted the city's inequalities, best captured by the emergence of the so-called Two Anaheims. The Latino population in Anaheim is concentrated in the western and central areas of the city located close to the Disneyland Resort, whereas the eastern part of the city, known as Anaheim Hills, is home to much of Anaheim's high-income households.[46] Income and racial inequality have played a more significant role in Anaheim politics as the relationship between Disney and the city's authorities has changed.

Sociologist Robert E. Lang and his coauthors Jennifer B. LeFurgy and Patrick A. Simmons refer to Anaheim and other similar places as a boomburb, defined as a population of more than one hundred thousand, as not being the largest city in its Metropolitan Statistical Area (MSA), by rapid population growth over at least a decade, low density, and as lacking an identifiable business core.[47] These scholars contend that a boomburb "is urban in fact, but not feel."[48] In our view, Anaheim is much more city than boomburb. The density is greater in Anaheim than it is in Houston, Phoenix, Denver, San Antonio, San Diego, Dallas, Indianapolis, Detroit, Memphis, Milwaukee, Cleveland, Pittsburgh, St. Louis, or Buffalo.[49] Anaheim exhibits other characteristics of a city such as its social diversity, a struggling downtown, and several commercial cores located throughout the city and near Disneyland. Anaheim is home to more than fifteen thousand businesses, including one hundred manufacturing plants.[50] Anaheim may not be the largest city in the Los Angeles-Long Beach-Anaheim MSA, but it is the largest city in Orange County. Located twenty-six miles from Los Angeles and separated by the dense Southern California traffic, Anaheim is hardly a satellite of Los Angeles.

Despite Anaheim's prominence as the site of a worldwide cultural icon and phenomenon, scholars have not paid much attention to this city or the power that Disneyland wields within it. The authors of the edited volume *Tourist City* mention Anaheim only twice, once noting that Anaheim appeared in a list of cities with the largest convention trade in 1981.[51] Much of the research on Disneyland focuses on what happens inside the gates. Scholars have examined how Disneyland presents and sometimes misrepresents history, race, gender, middle-class values, morality, and reality.[52] According to historian Mike Wallace, "It's possible that Walt Disney has taught people more history, in a more memorable way, than they ever learned in school."[53] Researchers have also focused on the ways in which Disneyland valorizes and represents American myths, capitalism, colonialism, imperialism, and manifest destiny.[54]

Disneyland certainly holds implications for urban design, planning, and architecture.[55] During the keynote address at the Urban Design Conference at Harvard in 1963, renowned urban developer James W. Rouse, asserted:

> I hold a view that may be somewhat shocking to an audience as so-phisticated as this, that the greatest piece of urban design in the United States today is Disneyland. If you think about Disneyland and think of its performance in relationship to its purpose, its meaning to peo-ple—more than that, its meaning to the process of development—you will find it the outstanding piece of urban design in the United States. It took an area of activity—the amusement park—and lifted it to a standard so high in its performance, in its respect for people, in its functioning for people, that it really does become a brand-new thing.[56]

Yet, very little is known about what happens outside of Disneyland's gates and the role the company plays in city politics.[57]

Although the political relationship between Disneyland and Anaheim has yet to be studied in a systematic way, political scientist Richard Fogle-song has examined the effect of Walt Disney World on the Orlando, Florida, area. Of the Walt Disney World and Orlando relationship, Foglesong writes, "Seldom has the location decision of a single corporation so transformed a city."[58] The same can be said of Disneyland's presence in Anaheim. Disney-land predates Walt Disney World by more than sixteen years and is the only Disney theme park that Walt visited. In his book *Married to the Mouse*, Fogle-song characterizes the Walt Disney World/Orlando relationship as a mar-riage, one that went through many phases including serendipity, seduction, secrecy, growth, and conflict. Disney's power had made it difficult for local politicians to take a stand against Walt Disney World in Florida. Foglesong argued that institutional, political, and cultural path dependence limited Or-lando's opportunities to break away from Walt Disney World and tourism.

Significant differences exist between Disneyland in Anaheim and Walt Disney World in central Florida. The state of Florida had granted political autonomy to Disney World to secure the Disney Company's commitment to locate the theme park near Orlando. The Reedy Creek Improvement Dis-trict, the special purpose district governing Disney World, had fused public and private functions, allowing Disney to regulate land use and building codes without municipal or county government interference. The legislation that created this district even gave Disney the authority to build a nuclear power plant on its property if the company so desired. Throughout *Married to the Mouse*, Foglesong emphasizes that Walt Disney World's powers outstripped the authority and capacity of both the Orlando city government and other private developers.[59] By contrast, Anaheim exerts public authority over Disneyland. For example, in preparation for the recently developed Star Wars: Galaxy's Edge part of the park, Disneyland needed authorization to not only knock down the abandoned skyway station in Frontierland but also replace the old sign to Adventureland to expand the walkways in anticipation of increased foot traffic.

In 2022, Florida Governor Ron DeSantis, a Republican with presidential aspirations, championed and signed HB 1557, a bill named Parental Rights in Education. One part of the law "prohibits classroom discussion about sexual orientation or gender identity in certain grade levels [kindergarten through the 3rd grade.]"[60] Critics called this piece of legislation the "Don't Say Gay" law. Following initial silence on the matter and after internal and external pressures from LGBTQ employees and advocates, Disney CEO Bob Chapek publicly condemned the law and called DeSantis to express concerns that the law "could be used to unfairly target gay, lesbian, non-binary, and transgender kids and families."[61]

In response to Disney's opposition, Governor DeSantis championed and signed a bill into law that dissolved the Reedy Creek Improvement District and created the Central Florida Tourism Oversight District in its place.[62] The five-member panel, all appointed by the governor, subsumed the duties of the Reedy Creek Improvement District but without Disney's control. In March 2024, Disney agreed to drop its lawsuits against the Central Florida Tourism Oversight District and work with the new board to plan Walt Disney World's future.[63] A spokesperson for the governor wrote, "No corporation should be its own government. Moving forward, we stand ready to work with Disney and the District to help promote economic growth, family-friendly tourism, and accountable government in Central Florida."[64] Even with the change to the Reedy Creek Improvement District, Walt Disney World has enjoyed the kind of governmental autonomy never available to Disneyland.

The Walt Disney World Resort is not located within the municipal boundaries of Orlando, nor is it contained in a single jurisdiction. Its four theme parks are in Orange County, Florida, but the Walt Disney World property also extends into Osceola County, Florida. Bay Lake and Lake Buena Vista, Florida are home to the theme parks. Both municipalities are creatures of Disney; the Reedy Creek Improvement District created them to serve as a local governance buffer for the Walt Disney Company.[65] In contrast, all of Disneyland is in Anaheim and that city's government exercises authority over land-use decisions in that theme park.

Scale is another difference between Disneyland and Walt Disney World. The entire Disneyland property encompassed 160 acres when the theme park opened. The Walt Disney World property occupies 27,000 acres. This study of Disneyland in Anaheim answers the question of whether (and how) Disney can get its way without the benefits of Walt Disney World's private government. Anaheim serves as an excellent research site to examine a particular set of circumstances, one in which a city must grapple with the wants of those who control private investment, on the one hand, and the voters, on the other. In this instance, we have an opportunity to explore the relationship between a profit-seeking corporate giant and a medium-size city over time. This book provides insights into whether accommodation is possible between capital and representative democracy.

## Coexistence between Disneyland and Anaheim over Time

The pages of this book tell the story of the relationship between Disneyland and Anaheim in three parts. The first, Part I, which covers the initial three and a half decades of the relationship, shows how the city was strictly bound by the Disneyland Imperative. Disney provided a social education to Anaheim residents and the county that equated Disneyland's prosperity with success for the city, region, and state. During this period, Disney established a political arrangement that advanced company interests and yielded a Disneyland Political Order that dominated the city. Social education and social learning, in addition to a strong political alliance, produced results for Disney. In these first thirty-five years, the corporate giant received about everything it wanted from government, and most, but not all, public and private actors believed that what was good for the park was also good for them. Disney used relational, reputational, and financial power to establish the local political order and get what it wanted. Public officials exercised their land-use and taxing powers to support the Disneyland Imperative. Opponents of the Disneyland Imperative attempted to get their way via lawsuits or appeals to the planning commission or city council. In this era, their efforts were not successful.

Part II shows that the public's attitude toward Disneyland shifted from the 1990s to the 2010s. Social learning changed as more people came to understand that Disneyland produced negative consequences for them and the city. Many residents came to believe both that at least two Anaheims existed and that Disneyland prospered as neighborhoods declined. More people pushed back against this corporation and its supporters. These actors who wanted a more balanced public policy agenda lacked the power necessary to change the Disneyland Political Order. They mobilized but realized they didn't have the capacity to produce change at that moment. Despite greater resistance in this second era, Disney continued to benefit from public policies, including the construction of a parking garage, tax rebates, a ban on a gate tax to enter the park, and the creation of a special district. It once again relied on financial, reputational, and relational power to get its way, but its grip over Anaheim had loosened.

From the early 2010s until the present, covered in Part III, the pro-balance coalition wielded people, voting, and financial power to achieve victories that moved the city's political order away from a strict focus on pro-Disney policies. In this period, the government changed its views on public subsidies toward Disney, and, by the end of this era, the corporate giant did not ask for such benefits. Citizens also approved a living wage ordinance at this time. The pro-balance actors secured these various victories through a combination of lawsuits, initiatives and referenda, district elections, winning political office, and the inclusion of service unions in their coalition. After it lost at the polls, Disney regrouped, scaled back its demands on local government, and spent millions to get its candidates elected. When Disney's allies regained control of the mayor's office and city council, they emphasized that development projects needed to benefit the neighborhoods, but they still advanced the interests of the Disneyland Political Order. The terms had changed, Disney responded with a modified public approach but millions in campaign dollars, and the Disneyland Political Order continued to prevail. Ultimately, an FBI investigation toppled the pro-Disney mayoral administration and showed how Disney, the mayor, and the chamber of commerce worked together to promote the Disneyland Imperative.

The three parts of *Disneyland Politics* track the three eras of the Disney/Anaheim relationship. To tell this story, we have used a variety of sources, including archival research, news accounts, government and nonprofit reports, census data, and interviews with public and private leaders. News accounts from mainstream and independent sources allow us to lay out and keep track of the basic narrative. Anaheim does not have a daily newspaper, but the *Orange County Register* and the *Los Angeles Times*, as well as other local news outlets, cover the city's major issues. The interviews have allowed us to tap individuals' sense of their city and its political dynamics. Our narrative explains key interactions between Disney and the city of Anaheim from the time before the park opened to the present day. Our concluding chapter summarizes how the presence of the Disney Company has shaped the political order in Anaheim, and it outlines the broader implications of our research.

# I

# The Quiet Partnership

# Part I Introduction

Walt Disney dreamed of a theme park, and, in hindsight, the massive success of Disneyland can create an impression of inevitability, but the path to make the park a reality was far from linear. Several critical choices set the stage for Disneyland's eventual location, key among them were Anaheim leadership's choice to focus on industry—as opposed to becoming yet another Los Angeles bedroom community—and Walt Disney's choice of Anaheim for the theme park's site.

Walt Disney and his allies created a Disneyland Political Order that supported the company's efforts in Anaheim. They taught the city's civic and political leaders and residents that Disneyland would benefit them. This social education emphasized that Disneyland was the goose that laid the golden egg. Disney solidified its support through financial power in the form of trips, park tickets, and contributions to the city and area's most powerful political actors. Walt and company built relational power in this period by establishing strong ties with the most influential political and economic people in the city and region. They also threatened to allocate resources elsewhere if the city did not meet company demands. The city yielded to this kind of reputational power.

The city's land-use and taxing powers were crucial to Disney. The corporation used relational, financial, and reputational power to get what it wanted from those with authority in Anaheim. Some citizens opposed Disney with lawsuits or by taking their claims to the city council or planning commission, but Disney's variety of powers were too strong to overcome. Disney got its way, in part, because it wielded many of these kinds of power, whereas its opponents did not have access to the same power.

This Disneyland Political Order pursued a Disneyland Imperative, which placed the theme park and Disney above everything else, including other economic development projects. The Disneyland Imperative included favorable land-use decisions and taxing policies. The city council and planning commission, key actors in the Disneyland Political Order, held this power and helped secure these policies.

In a short time span, Disneyland went from just another industry to be recruited by Anaheim's civic leadership to the key piston that drove the economic engine of the city. The foundation of that relationship and the initial terms of coexistence are the focus of this section.

# 1

# The Kingdom Begins

The Gabrielino and Luiseño-Juaneño Native American tribes originally inhabited the land that is now part of Anaheim, and the first permanent European settlement in California was in 1769 at the Presidio in what is now a national park at the northern tip of San Francisco.[1] By the 1850s, the Ontiveros family owned the land that would become Anaheim, but legend has it that ranchero Juan Pacifico Ontiveros claimed that the land was so barren that it couldn't support a goat.[2] According to journalist and Anaheim resident Gustavo Arellano, "There is no record whatsoever that Ontiveros actually said this, but the myth has been repeated in Orange County history books and passed as fact ever since."[3] In 1857, Ontiveros sold the land for $2 an acre. Violinist Charles Kohler and flutist John Frohling, both German immigrants, purchased the property and turned the land into a vineyard that produced one hundred thousand gallons of wine per year.[4] They named the place Anaheim; Ana represented the Santa Ana River and *heim* is the German word for home.[5] Disease destroyed the vineyards in 1888, however, and citrus groves replaced the vines. By 1915, the city's chamber of commerce dubbed Anaheim the capital of the Valencia orange empire.[6] To build on the popularity of the fruit, the Anaheim Chamber of Commerce hosted the California Valencia Orange Show in town starting in 1921. Anaheim's other agricultural products included walnuts, sugar beets, lemons, apricots, and the American chili pepper.[7]

Anaheim's history, like many American cities, included a darker past as well; racism and immigrant exploitation are also important to understanding the city. Anaheim had earned the nickname Klanaheim because four of the five city councillors were members of the Ku Klux Klan in 1924.[8] After that election, close to three hundred members of the KKK lived in Anaheim, and the KKK patrolled the streets in robes and masks.[9] The city council fired municipal employees and replaced them with members of the KKK.[10] It also increased the size of the police by eleven people, and ten of the new officers were Klansmen. Banners that welcomed KKK members hung over city roads, the KKK council members painted KIGY (Klansmen I Greet You) over major city streets, and stores offered 20% discounts to the KKK.[11] The year the members of the KKK won elected office in the city, Anaheim was the site of the largest gathering of white supremacists in the history of California.[12] Anaheim was the hot spot of KKK activity in Orange County at the time and had a national reputation as a Klan city.[13] Less than a year after they were elected, the city's electorate recalled the four members of the KKK on the city council. One of those recalled, Mayor E. H. Metcalf, claimed that he and others were removed from office because of "ineligible Mexican" voters.[14] The so-called USA Club, a coalition of civic leaders that included the Orange County district attorney, led the recall effort. The discrimination against people of color and the openness with which Anaheim welcomed white supremacy proponents are important parts of the context in which Anaheim pursued postwar development.

By 1940, Anaheim was still an agricultural town with a population of more than eleven thousand people. One informant described Anaheim at that time as "a sleepy suburb." The city and region were about to change.

## Anaheim and Disney Recruit Each Other

In the post–World War II period, a triumvirate of white men made decisions that led Anaheim to industry and Disneyland; they helped establish the Disneyland Political Order.[15] Charles Pearson, owner of the largest trucking company in Orange County, took over as Anaheim's mayor in 1936. According to Anaheim historian and journalist John Wescott, "Pearson's contacts and skills made him the most influential leader in the city's history." Earne Moeller became the secretary of the Anaheim Chamber of Commerce in 1945. Moeller saw industry as the key to Anaheim's future, and he worked to ensure that the chamber would play a key role in the rapid economic expansion of the city. The third key actor, Keith Murdoch, held the city manager's position from 1950 until 1976. Murdoch's view of Anaheim's future is telling: "When I got there [in 1950], the rest of Orange County's cities thought they would go broke if they took a chance on industry. They wanted to be bedroom cities. But it's industry that pays the city's bills through taxes, and it's industry that provides for city residents."[16]

According to Westcott, "Pearson, Moeller, and Murdoch were determined to make Anaheim an industrial giant."[17] By virtue of their key positions in government and business, the triumvirate held substantial agenda-setting power and their choices had consequences. If Mayor Pearson, the chamber of commerce's Moeller, and city manager Murdoch hadn't chosen to pursue corporations that could generate revenue for the city, it's likely that homes would have dominated the Anaheim landscape because of the locality's proximity to Los Angeles. This scenario played out in most other Orange County municipalities, which chose to become bedroom communities to Los Angeles rather than focus on attracting large-scale businesses.

To pursue an industrial strategy, Anaheim took out ads in the *Wall Street Journal* and other national papers, and local officials, including the mayor, provided interested businesses with tours and pitches about why they should locate their businesses in the city.[18] Murdoch oversaw the planning department and created a so-called super stamp for building permits, whereby industries that chose Anaheim could begin construction at once. Businesses did not have to submit plans to the city. Murdoch wanted veterans returning from World War II to have a place to work in Anaheim; he highlighted Anaheim's proximity to the proposed Santa Ana Freeway, which connected key communities, including Anaheim, to Los Angeles.[19]

Kwikset, a key and lock company, was the first large industrial firm to locate in Anaheim.[20] It established a plant of eight hundred employees in the city in 1948.[21] The defense industry followed when companies like Northrop Nortronics, Rockwell International's Autonetics, and Boeing all moved into Anaheim.[22] As part of its industrial expansion, Anaheim also became home to businesses such as Robertshaw-Fulton Controls Company, the Essex Wire Company, and General Electric.[23]

Not everyone in Anaheim regarded the move toward industry as a universal benefit for the city. Some residents feared that industry would bring a smokestack image to Anaheim.[24] To counter these concerns, Murdoch arranged tours of Kwikset for city residents. The city also established "Industrial Education Days," in which high school teachers and local clergy visited different industries in the city. Citrus growers also protested the move toward an industrial city.[25] The move toward industry, as well as expanded production capacity in the Central Valley, killed the agricultural businesses in Anaheim. The one solace for growers was that the price of their land per acre increased from $2,750 in 1947 to $6,000 in 1954 to $20,000 in 1960.

In the 1950s, the Pearson, Moeller, and Murdoch triumvirate's industrial strategy succeeded, at least in one respect. Anaheim went from 27 industries that employed 1,400 in 1950 to 460 industries with 48,500 workers by 1968.[26] The industrial giant for whom Anaheim's leadership had looked was about to arrive in the early 1950s, and it would change the city and region forever.

## A Theme Park Instead of a Factory

After Burbank rejected the company's initial theme park concept, Disney's Mickey Mouse Park, Nat Winecoff—the vice president and secretary of WED Enterprises (named for Walter Elias Disney)—heard from colleagues that the Stanford Research Institute (SRI) might be able to help identify a location for Disneyland. Founded as a partnership between Stanford University and the business community, SRI aimed to stimulate and enhance economic development.[27] At SRI, the Disney Company worked with Cornelius Vanderbilt (C. V.) Wood, the future first general manager for Disneyland, and Harrison "Buzz" Price, an adviser to Walt Disney until Walt's death.[28] In June 1953, Walt commissioned Wood, Price, and SRI to find potential properties for Disneyland in Southern California.[29]

Walt Disney had a lengthy list of site preferences: inexpensive land, a single current owner, at least one hundred acres of flat land, easy access to a major highway, 360 degrees to expand, no oil fields nearby, away from land controlled by government, and a significant distance from the water so as to not "attract the barefoot beach crowd."[30] His dream of a theme park evolved from his original Burbank concept to something much larger and more comprehensive. The SRI team studied population trends and climate figures about rain, fog, humidity, and wind; it also considered the utility capacity because Walt Disney wanted to broadcast his television show from the park.[31] SRI used the burgeoning highway system as a key barometer for where to place Disneyland.[32]

Two factors drew Price's attention toward the Santa Ana area. First, regional population growth headed southeast, in the direction of Santa Ana. Second, the weather in that area was eight degrees cooler in the summer than the temperatures in Pomona or the San Fernando Valley. According to Price, "Eight degrees makes a big difference to an outdoor park."[33] In June 1954, Wood narrowed his search and led SRI to a five-mile radius around Anaheim.[34]

At least two sources mention Fred Wallich as a key figure in the decision to select Anaheim as the location for Disneyland.[35] According to the chamber of commerce's Moeller, Wallich sent SRI a note, which stated, "This site [in Anaheim] was not found in your search through Orange County records because there are 17 parcels involving many owners. I know many of the owners are considering selling to a housing subdivision."[36]

Price took his findings to Walt and Roy Disney, Walt's brother and business partner, and the Disneys did not hesitate.[37] A few days later, Walt, Winecoff, and Price visited the property, which Walt liked, and he immediately deposited $10,000 intending to secure it. In the following days, however, speculators bought property around this site, which prompted Walt to walk away because he felt that the price would be too high. Nonetheless, Disney still liked Anaheim and wanted to look for other sites in the city.

According to Disney historian Steven Watts, "Walt Disney never cared much for politics."[38] Disney was a political conservative who disliked the tax system. One source described Disney as "an anti-Semitic Hoover ally and Goldwater supporter."[39] Disney "was a man suspicious of government bureaucracy" and had a "well-known antipathy to blacks and Jews."[40] Moreover, Disney was anti-communist and anti-union.[41]

## A Relationship Makes a Dream Come True

Disneyland was a political enterprise that required Walt to get involved in local politics. While he may not have cared for politics, Walt Disney possessed perceptive political instincts. The Burbank incident convinced him that his park ventures needed local political support. He exercised relational power by creating partnerships with the most powerful public and private actors in Anaheim and the county. According to Richard Snow, "Disney decided to form an alliance with the city government sooner than he had planned." Disney and Anaheim recruited each other. Murdoch "looked at Disney as another industrial opportunity."[42] Walt Disney needed Murdoch and the city for their power over land use and ability to limit taxes.

In the postwar years, the city and chamber of commerce hosted an annual Halloween parade and invited executives from companies it pursued to send a representative to judge the parade. Employees from General Electric and Ford, among other companies, served in this capacity.[43] Murdoch and Moeller asked Disney to send a representative to do the same in Anaheim's 1953 Halloween parade. They had heard of Disney's interest in Southern California and wanted the company to consider Anaheim for its expansion opportunities. To foster a relationship with the city, Walt chose Nat Winecoff as his representative, with the knowledge that Price's study had already identified Anaheim properties as the place to build his park. Disney also had his employees design floats for the Fantasyland Division of the parade and sent Snow White, Peter Pan, and Pinocchio to march in the parade as well.[44] Murdoch would refer to the decision to involve Disney in the parade as a "good sales tool."[45] After the parade, Winecoff informed Moeller of his top secret project and Walt's desire to build Disneyland in Anaheim.[46] Moeller asked Winecoff if Murdoch could join the conversation and Winecoff agreed. Moeller went through the crowd to retrieve Murdoch, and the three men adjourned to a car in the alleyway outside the chamber of commerce offices, where Winecoff laid out Walt's vision for a theme park.

After Murdoch told him that Walt Disney was interested in building Disneyland in Anaheim, Mayor Pearson expressed reservations about the theme park. Like his colleagues in Burbank, Pearson wanted no honky-tonk enterprise in his city.[47] He feared that peanut shells would dominate city streets. Murdoch communicated the mayor's concerns to Walt Disney, who gave a presentation to Pearson and Murdoch to assure the mayor that Disneyland would provide family entertainment and would be far from honky-tonk—something Disney opposed as much as Pearson. To that end, Disneyland would not serve alcohol and even its peanuts would be shelled to maintain a clean environment. This presentation at the Disney Studios convinced Pearson, who, along with the chamber of commerce and Murdoch, would work their hardest to make Disneyland a reality.[48] Disneyland opened a year and a half after this meeting.[49]

A week after the Halloween conversation, Disney, Winecoff, Murdoch, and Moeller hopped into a station wagon and looked for properties in Anaheim.[50] The discussions among this group of local leaders and Disney representatives was the kernel of an emerging political order that has lasted to this day. After a failed attempt to secure property because speculators gobbled up the land, Disney saw the piece of land that Disneyland now occupies, at the intersection of Katella Avenue and South Harbor Boulevard. It met most of Walt's criteria, including easy access to the Santa Ana Freeway, but a public road ran through the property. Walt pointed to Cerritos Street on a map and asked Murdoch, "What are we gonna do with that street?"[51] Murdoch replied, "We've closed streets before for no reason. Why not close that one?" Walt concluded, "If you can close that street, we've got a deal." In a city that pursued industry to the utmost, they had a deal. Murdoch's power over land use brought the Disneyland dream to life. Murdoch later recalled, "After all this effort, we weren't going to let an arterial highway stand in our way."[52] The current map of Anaheim shows East and West Cerritos Avenues. Disneyland divides these two streets, neither of which runs through the park.

Disneyland was also made possible by the landowners who agreed to sell their property. Walt Disney recounted, "We had to contact 15 owners, as far away as Ohio, to buy the land."[53] SRI's C. V. Wood, who helped secure the location for Disneyland, commended these property owners for their high level of cooperation. He also acknowledged the importance of financial power when he observed that the Anaheim site for Disneyland was the "best location money can buy."[54] Walt Disney agreed: "The land cost $1,000,000 and getting that was the toughest job."[55] Yet, Disney still had a major obstacle to overcome to make Disneyland a reality.

The land that Disney purchased was not within Anaheim's boundaries; it was in county territory.[56] Anaheim needed to annex that property and 768 acres in total for Disneyland to be a part of the city. A water company from nearby Garden Grove sued to stop the annexation because it feared it would lose the rights to provide water to Disneyland.[57] The plaintiffs alleged that Santa Ana and Orange, California, needed to approve the annexation because these cities are located within three miles of the proposed land addition.[58]

The plaintiffs also claimed that the annexed land had been gerrymandered. They asserted that two properties had been "arbitrarily eliminated . . . in an attempt to circumvent and evade the intent and purpose of the statute."[59] According to one source, "The residential areas being excluded, it is claimed, would naturally be part of any city, but the city chose to annex an inhabited territory which is sparsely settled." In response to claims of gerrymandering, Murdoch argued that no evidence existed that anyone lived in the two parcels excluded from the annexation. According to a book on the history of Anaheim, written by journalist John Westcott, "City Officials carefully drew boundaries to exclude any opponents who might vote against annexation, and Disneyland was born."[60] Walt Disney was so concerned about protests, led by businesspeople from Garden Grove, that he canceled the public groundbreaking for Disneyland, scheduled for August 25, 1954.[61]

A judge allowed the annexation vote to take place, but the city could not send the results to the state capital for certification until the parties met in court or settled the issue outside of court. The vote passed 56–2. The city settled with the plaintiffs, who could continue to provide water to the parts of the annexed territory that it already serviced.[62]

## Expanding the Mickey Mouse Club

Once Walt Disney secured the support of the mayor, the chamber of commerce, and the city administrator, he dispatched C. V. Wood to broaden the Disneyland coalition to further build relational power and include the city and area's other business, civic, and political leaders. In June 1954, Wood, Winecoff, and other Disney executives, including Joe Fowler, a retired rear admiral in the Navy who was the construction administrator for Disneyland and later Walt Disney World, attended the regular meeting of the Anaheim Chamber of Commerce to discuss the history and particulars of the Disneyland project.[63] The audience members that night included Anaheim city officials, civic and business leaders, and county officials. As a follow-up event, the Disney Company hosted six hundred city and county political, civic, and business leaders and their spouses at the Little Theater in Burbank.[64] Disney arranged the program in conjunction with the Anaheim Chamber of Commerce, and the guests included members of the Orange County League of Cities, the Orange County Planning Commission, the Orange County Board of Supervisors, the chamber of commerce's board of directors, and Anaheim city officials. The night began with a buffet meal in an Anaheim park followed by a caravan of cars proceeding to Burbank. At the Little Theater, Roy O. Disney, the financial mastermind of the Disney Company, told the large audience, "Disneyland will be a park free of nuisance. It will not be a honky-tonk annoyance, but a credit to the community. . . . Its impact will not only be national, it will be international." As he did before the Anaheim Chamber of Commerce, Wood described the specifics of the park including statistics that estimated that four million guests would attend Disneyland a year, the parking lot would be able to handle nine thousand to ten thousand cars, and Disneyland could accommodate between thirty thousand and forty thousand guests at a time. Audience members were read remarks by Walt Disney, saw renderings of all phases of Disneyland, and watched parts of an unreleased Disney film, *The Vanishing Prairie*. This session represented yet another attempt by Disney to educate powerholders about the value of the theme park and, in turn, create relational power. Both strategies worked.

The city leaders' desire for industry in addition to the Disney Company's presentation and courting of political, civic, and business leaders produced a political partnership that served the Disney Company for decades to come. After the first meeting at the chamber of commerce, the *Anaheim Bulletin* noted, "City and chamber officials last night hailed the coming of Disneyland as the greatest thing that has ever happened to Anaheim and assured Wood and his aides that the city would extend its fullest cooperation to the project and work hand in hand to assure the realization of Disney's fabulous 'land of yesterday, tomorrow, and fantasy.'"[65] At the time of the announcement, even some who saw the benefits to the project understood that Disneyland could bring serious negative consequences to Anaheim as well.

Two weeks before the opening of Disneyland, *Anaheim Bulletin* publisher Howard Loudon wrote an opinion piece on the editorial page of his paper titled "Disneyland . . . Friend or Foe."[66] Loudon described the potential positive and negative effects of Disneyland on the city, its businesses, and the surrounding area. He noted, in particular, "It is natural to be concerned over a development so large, so fabulous, so new. No one can possibly know the repercussions that will develop when this new concept in entertainment opens." Loudon predicted that there "will be problems, but by study and wise decisions, these problems can be overcome to the advantage of the city of Anaheim."

Loudon called the theme park an opportunity and predicted that businesses in the area would benefit from the overflow of Disneyland visitors. While acknowledging that the communities surrounding the city "may play upon the problems of the city of Anaheim developing due to Disneyland being in Anaheim," Loudon attributed the protests and negative talk to jealousy because "not too many weeks ago every city within a day's plane ride was attempting to claim it [Disneyland.]" In his summation, he concluded that "any business established to bring happiness cannot develop into a detriment to the community in which it is situated."

Walt Disney once asserted that he had dreamed about Disneyland for more than twenty years.[67] As the calendar turned toward July 17, 1955, the opening of the park, Disneyland had become a reality. To what lengths would Anaheim go to sustain this reality or, in this case, the fantasy?

# 2

## Sky Blue Sky

C onstruction of Disneyland started on July 16, 1954. Orange groves and walnut trees occupied the land on which Disneyland now sits and the area around the theme park. Estimates suggest that Disney employees removed twelve thousand orange trees to build Disneyland. The theme park cost $17 million to build. Disney legend has it that Walt wanted to keep some orange trees but remove others. Employees put a red tag around the ones to be replaced and the trees that were to remain received a green tag. The driver of the bulldozer was color blind, however, and leveled every tree. Many people speculate that the Disney Company fabricated the story. Even though no one can verify the veracity of the tale, the Disney Company featured the story in its seventeen-minute-long film titled, *Disneyland: The First 50 Magical Years*. Comedian and actor Steve Martin, a former Disneyland cast member, tells the story of the color-blind bulldozer driver in the film.

In exchange for providing financial assistance so that Walt could build Disneyland, ABC had asked Walt Disney to produce a weekly television show, which became *Walt Disney's Disneyland*. With only three major networks broadcasting (ABC, CBS, and NBC), being on the air was a major coup, and Walt Disney used the show to tell people about the theme park. The title of the first episode, which aired on October 27, 1954, was "The Disneyland Story," during which Walt Disney showed a blueprint of the theme park and a quarter-inch scale model of Disneyland. The orange groves feature prominently in the blueprint map and in the episode. The schematics of the park from 1954 resemble much of the current theme park.

*Walt Disney's Disneyland* show featured a story each week from the theme park's four lands: Frontierland, Tomorrowland, Adventureland, and Fantasyland. The Davy Crockett television series, which swept the nation and popularized coonskin hats, was part of *Walt Disney's Disneyland*. In the sixteenth episode of *Walt Disney's Disneyland*, which aired on February 9, 1955, Walt Disney provided a progress report on the theme park. The episode featured Walt in a helicopter ride from studio headquarters in Burbank to Anaheim. The helicopter followed the freeways from Los Angeles to Anaheim. Walt said he could have driven to Disneyland because the ride from Los Angeles was a "pleasant 50-minute trip across town." This episode featured clips of the theme park's construction. According to Walt Disney, at this point, the company had moved more than three hundred cubic yards of dirt to build the park, which was to open in a little more than five months.

Park employees referred to opening day, which took place on July 17, 1955, one year and a day after construction began, as Black Sunday.[1] The blacktop on Main Street USA was poured on the morning of the opening but the asphalt didn't hold in the one-hundred-degree temperatures. Women's high-heeled shoes sank into the gooey surface and left pock marks on the theme park's thoroughfare. Disney invited about eleven thousand people to attend, but twenty-eight thousand people showed up, most of whom used counterfeit tickets to get in. Some without tickets scaled the theme park's walls. Once inside, the guests did not have the luxury of using the theme park's water fountains, which were not operational because of a plumber's strike. Walt Disney faced a choice: finish the bathrooms or the water fountains. He told Dick Nunis, a park employee and later an executive at Disneyland and Walt Disney World, "Well, you know they could drink Coke and Pepsi, but they can't pee in the streets. Finish the restrooms."[2] Less than two months after it opened, Disneyland welcomed its one millionth guest.

At every turn, city officials and the Disney Company advanced the narrative that whatever was good for the theme park also benefited the city and the area around it. One year after the opening of Disneyland, city officials touted how well Anaheim had fared since 1955, which they regarded as "Anaheim's biggest year in history."[3] According to the August–September 1956 edition of *City Scoop*, a monthly city publication for Anaheim employees and officials,

> You are now watching the miracle of change and growth in our own Anaheim community, where the walnut, truck gardens, oranges and packing houses are giving way to industry, residential districts and busy marts of trade throughout Orange County. We are undergoing a tremendous change and increase in population which staggers the imagination. "We hope it is for the best." Our prosperity here is not

founded on war-time expediency, it is based on a solid formation of industry, business, and permanent payrolls.

In his report to the citizens of Anaheim and Orange County to mark Disneyland's third anniversary, Jack Sayers, chair of the Disneyland Operations Committee, wrote, "The year by year growth and success of Disneyland has an important relationship to the overall growth and economic stability of both Anaheim and the County."[4] Sayers cited attendance figures, which indicated that more than twelve million people had visited Disneyland in the park's first three years. Park employment grew from 1,280 in 1955 to 3,450 in 1958. The annual payroll for Disneyland employees went from $6.35 million in 1955–1956 to $10 million in 1957–1958. Reports like this one served as powerful agents of social learning, which taught everyone about the collective benefits of Disneyland. Disney exercised power through this kind of social education.

Disneyland took credit for the creation of the tourist industry in Anaheim and Orange County.[5] In its newspaper advertisement titled, "The Happiness Industry," Disneyland claimed,

> The tourist and visitor business has grown and prospered in the two years that Disneyland has been a corporate citizen of Anaheim. It is now the area's fastest growing and greatest potential new industry, providing employment for thousands of people and bringing millions of dollars annually into all facets of the city's business life.[6]

By 1963, 37.5 million people had visited the park. The company claimed that its total investment in Disneyland at that time totaled $45 million.[7]

Even with this optimism about industry and this new business in the city, some signs suggested that not all this change was for the good. Traffic overwhelmed the city. On day one, the Anaheim Police Department experienced "the worst traffic mess ever seen."[8] The traffic jams were so bad that, even two months after Disneyland opened, the Automobile Club of Southern California provided alternative routes to gain access to the park.[9] The *Anaheim Gazette* published maps of these optional routes. On the first day of Disneyland, the police also had to deal with at least fifteen lost children and help guests find their cars.[10] Disneyland brought to Anaheim a "'glitter glutch' of hotels [, which] quickly sprang up around [the] park, creating a place to stay for millions of tourists but also creating a haven for prostitutes and crime."[11] Walt and his company worked for the day when they would exert complete control over the area of the city in which their park was located.

## Another World

The berm was one of the defining yet stealth features of Disneyland. This twelve-to-twenty-foot-high earthen berm rings the theme park and keeps Disneyland's guests from seeing and experiencing the outside world.[12] According to art historian and American Studies professor Karal Ann Marling, Walt Disney built Disneyland "behind a berm to protect it from the evils that daily beset humankind on all sides. It aimed to soothe and reassure. It aimed to give pleasure. Joy. A flash of sunny happiness."[13] This otherworld illusion was so important to Walt Disney that he demanded that the city's planning commission protect the park from outside intrusions in the mid-1960s.

When people look up inside Disneyland, they see nothing but Southern California sky. They don't see power lines, outside buildings, or any reminder of life outside the theme park. Walt and the company performed political magic to preserve this illusion. In 1963, Sheraton-West announced initial plans for a $15 million, twenty-two-story hotel in Anaheim.[14] The hotel's penthouse restaurant would look into Disneyland. In 1964, a local entrepreneur announced a plan for a ten-story office tower and a five-story bank to be built outside of Disneyland's gates. Later in the year, another group of developers proposed a $6 million, 750-foot tower reminiscent of Seattle's Space Needle, which would be located a few miles from Disneyland and visible from inside the park.

Any of these three projects would shatter the artifice created within the park. Walt and the Disney Company wanted the city to exercise its land-use powers and impose height limits that restricted any buildings from being visible within the park. In a June 1964 letter to the city council, Walt Disney wrote, "I don't want the public to see the world they live in while they're in the park. I want them to feel they're in another world."[15] City officials asked the Disney Company "to prepare studies showing what height buildings could be constructed without damaging the illusion."[16] In July 1964, John Wise, a Disneyland engineer, created a height limitation map that he showed to city officials. Throughout the debates on this issue, the Disney Company endorsed Wise's sliding scale concept, which allowed buildings to be taller the farther they were from Disneyland.

The *Anaheim Gazette* opposed the height restriction. It wrote that Disneyland is "a highly successful private business which is a tremendous asset to the community. It is neither a sacred shrine nor a natural resource. It is called a park in the sense of 'amusement park,' not 'national park.'"[17] The *Anaheim Gazette* argued that government should keep cement factories and slaughterhouses away from Disneyland but "telling a private developer he can build an otherwise good hotel only so high and no higher if he's within the sight of the park is not legitimate." An attorney who represented fifty property owners near Disneyland also warned that "the planning commission is here by the grace of the people, not by Mr. Disney."[18] He also claimed that the height limitations are "based solely on what is best for Disneyland."[19]

The letters to the editor of the *Santa Ana Register* about the height restrictions were voluminous and split between Disneyland supporters and opponents. While we cannot generalize from letters to the editor, these responses show that opposition existed to Disneyland. The complaints often centered on the issue of why Disneyland should receive preferential treatment over other property owners. One resident of Santa Ana asked, "Does a property owner have to be worth millions and be able to show millions of dollars in receipts in order to have property rights? Are equal rights lost sight of in these cases?"[20] At the end of his letter opposing the height restrictions, a Garden Grove resident wrote, "What has Disneyland ever GIVEN anybody? Nothing, that's what."

The height restriction debate appears to be the first time the Disney Company threatened Anaheim that it might not continue to invest in the park and the city.[21] Ed Ettinger of Walt Disney Productions, Disneyland's parent company, warned the planning commission that the company's future park investments depended on whether the city protected Disneyland's illusion.[22] Ettinger told the planning commissioners that Disney has a pot of money from which it spends on its various enterprises. Those entities that make the most money—or have the potential for the greatest profit—get the funds. If the height restrictions ended, Ettinger predicted, then Walt Disney Productions would spend its money in areas other than Disneyland.

Disney and its advocates argued that the city should protect Disneyland because the theme park served Anaheim's best interests. Story after story on the height restriction issue featured a report by Economics Research Associates President Buzz Price, who explained in detail what Disneyland meant to Anaheim's economy.[23] Price cited figures on park attendance, visitor spending, property taxes, sales tax revenues, and construction expenditures to argue that Disneyland was the engine that drove Anaheim's economy.

Local media and planning commissioners claimed that Anaheim should protect Disneyland. In his story on the planning commission's hearing about height restrictions, the *Anaheim Bulletin*'s Jerry Teague wrote, the "park is one of, if not the main industry in the city. Its importance to the local economy climbs as other industries that are dependent on defense spending wither."[24] Commissioner James L. Chavos echoed this point when he told a planning commission meeting, "It would be limited thinking on our part to neglect [Disneyland] while we search for other industry."[25] Based on the Disney Company's recommendations, the city established a commercial recreation zone, which encompassed the park, and created height restrictions according to the proximity to that area.[26] The city council voted 6–0 to approve Disney's sliding scale.

## A Government for This Other World

This kind of conflict over land use in Anaheim prompted Walt to demand the creation of an autonomous political district for Disney World in Florida. To overcome the kinds of land use problems inherent in Anaheim, Walt's brother Roy O. Disney negotiated certain concessions from the Florida state government. Walt's idea of an autonomous political district was one such request, to which the Florida governor and state legislature agreed. The Reedy Creek Improvement District provided the Disney Company with control over the land on which its business sat. Disney had never enjoyed that kind of autonomy in Anaheim. If Disney wanted to change Disneyland, it needed governmental permission. If Disney wanted to block a perceived encroachment outside the park, it needed permission from government. Disney and Anaheim needed one another for mutual success.

The height restriction issue showed that Anaheim followed a Disneyland Imperative, not an economic development one. If general development conflicted with Disney's interests, the city sided with the corporate giant. When Disney told the planning commission and city council that development didn't serve its interests, the city listened.

# 3

# Can a Golden Goose Be Milked?

## Fairytales

Walt Disney built an empire on fairytales. He communicated important messages about society and life through characters, quite often animals, who faced and solved some problem. The Disney Company has used the fairytale of the goose that laid the golden egg in *The Gingerbread Man and the Golden Goose*, a children's book, and a two-part episode of the popular kids' show *DuckTales* (1990) titled "The Golden Goose."[1] Life imitated art because Disney's supporters used the golden goose story to justify preferential treatment toward Disneyland, which they claimed represented Anaheim's Golden Goose.

### Don't Tax the Goose

As Disneyland changed the economic engine of Anaheim, some of the city's mayors, members of the city council, and residents considered imposing a tax on tickets to Disneyland and other entertainment venues in Anaheim to raise additional revenue for the city. Disneyland President Jack Lindquist was distinctly unenthusiastic: "It's not an admissions tax. Let's call it what it is. It's a Disneyland tax."[2] According to Murdoch, Walt Disney "was quite strong in his feeling about [an admissions tax.] He said, 'wait a minute, we want to pay our way and we will do so.' He was firm."[3] For the first two decades of the park's operation, no serious gate tax proposals made it onto the public agenda, but, starting in the 1970s, the idea of a gate tax became a recurring issue.

## The City Chases the Goose

In 1975, three of the city's five city council members supported a 5% admissions tax on entertainment venues in Anaheim to help pay for capital improvements around the area of Disneyland and to offset what the mayor regarded as a tough budget year.[4] Mayor William Thom thought that city government did too much to benefit Disney to the detriment of the rest of Anaheim. He once proclaimed, "I don't think the city should accommodate Disney the way that it does far and above anyone else."[5] Mayor Thom argued that the tax would be levied on tourists who used the city's streets and increased the need for services, such as police and fire protection.[6] He also stated, "It's a voluntary type of taxation. You don't have to pay it to live."[7] To provide his rationale for tax, the mayor asserted, "The bulk of capital improvements were being made in the Disneyland area, so we thought this would be a good thing to do."[8] The threat was so real to Disneyland that Lindquist, then vice president of marketing for Disneyland, collaborated with City Council Member Don R. Roth and California Angels baseball executive A. E. (Red) Patterson to create VOTE—Voters Opposed to Taxing Entertainment. When Patterson told the mayor that Angels owner Gene Autry would pull his Major League Baseball (MLB) team out of Anaheim if the council passed the tax, Thom proclaimed, "Don't let the door hit him in the ass on the way out." According to Roth, a cross section of local business interests and the Anaheim Chamber of Commerce opposed the tax as well, and Disneyland and the Angels led the opposition. These actors made up the core of Anaheim's Disneyland Political Order.

Miriam Kaywood, one of the city council members who supported the tax, "felt some of the pressure" as letters and calls came into her office. The messages, many of which came from concerned Disney employees and their family members, claimed that the tax would "kill the goose that laid the golden eggs for Anaheim." Mayor Thom responded, "What most people don't know is that golden egg is boxed up and put on an armored car every night and hauled back to Burbank," the location of Disney's corporate headquarters.

Disney applied pressure politics. Lindquist organized employees and Disney supporters, who boarded two Greyhound buses and "packed the city council chamber" to protest the imposition of a tax on theme park tickets.[9] Between 100 and 150 people, many of whom wore clothes with Disney characters on them, attended the meeting that night; that number was much higher than a usual meeting for the city council in those days.[10] Lindquist recalled,

"We had demonstrators lined up outside City Hall for blocks."[11] The tactics worked. Mayor Thom claimed he "chickened out" amid the Disney pressure and cast the deciding vote against the entertainment tax. According to Joe White, an official with the Anaheim Chamber of Commerce at the time, "Nobody could have beat Disney. They mine one hell of a lot of gold out of Anaheim."[12] He also concluded that Disney executives "are using money—a lot of money—to elected officials [who] will tell you that doesn't have any influence, but if you eat with them, play with them, and take their money, it's got to have some influence. These guys are only human." A public show of opposition and the more private use of campaign contributions ended this first serious attempt at a gate tax.

At the end of 1987, HOME (Homeowners for Maintaining their Environment), an interest group of residents in Anaheim, brought the idea of a 10% admissions tax to the council as a mechanism to close the city's $8 million budget deficit.[13] At the time, the tax was projected to generate $2.15 on a $21.50 ticket to Disneyland.[14] Mayor Ben Bay argued that "Disneyland is the catalyst that has a great deal to do with the kind of conventions and visitors we get and, in my opinion, you don't kill the goose that laid the golden egg."[15] He didn't think the admissions tax proposal should "even be given serious consideration."[16] It wasn't. A representative of the California Angels referred to the tax as "discriminatory" and claimed, "I think we pay enough taxes and also contribute through the employment that comes to the community."[17] Disneyland's manager for publicity proclaimed, "We already have an admission tax—sales tax—that's the main thing."

When he heard of the possibility of the gate tax again in 1991, Lindquist threatened to stop Disneyland's $3 billion park expansion if the city council passed such a plan (see Chapter 4 for more on that expansion).[18] Mayor Fred Hunter floated the idea of a 4% gate tax on all venues that charged admission to close a $20 million municipal budget deficit and offset the infrastructure costs associated with a Disneyland expansion.[19] Disney might have kept the gate tax at bay, but the efforts to pass such a tax came at closer and closer intervals.

At the end of 1991, Hunter dropped the idea of the admissions tax but reintroduced the possibility of the tax in 1992. He insisted that Disney should—and would—pay for the construction of a parking structure on its property. Disney, the city's other big businesses, and advocates for this large corporation claimed that federal, state, or local governments should pay for infrastructure costs, including new roadways or even parking structures. In 1992, one such Disney supporter was Tom Daly, the Anaheim city council member and future mayor, who opposed the imposition of an admissions tax. He responded, "I don't think killing the goose that lays the golden egg makes sense."[20]

Disney contended that it paid its fair share in taxes and added more than its fair share as the county's top employer.

## The Goose Escapes Taxation

At the same time the city council considered whether to impose a gate tax to offset the costs of Disneyland's expansion, people inside and outside of government began to examine the relationship between Disneyland and the city's elected and appointed officials. They questioned Disneyland's practices of distributing complimentary park tickets to city officials and hosting all-expenses paid annual fishing, golf, and drinking trips for Anaheim officials. Common participants on these trips included mayors, members of the city council, and influential people in city departments including the police chief. Members of the Anaheim Ichthyological, Sour Mash & 5-Card Draw Society, as the group that took the trip became known, would board a bus either in the city hall parking lot or at Disneyland that took them, in the early days, to Santa Catalina Island and, in later years, to San Diego.[21] During the trip, the participants wore windbreakers, backpacks, and hats that included the society's logo on them, ate deluxe dinners, played golf, drank at an open bar, and fished. Jackets and bags with the Anaheim Ichthyological, Sour Mash & 5-Card Draw Society logo sell for hundreds of dollars on eBay. Disney paid the bill for what was a male-only trip until 1974 when Council Member Kaywood became the first female to attend. At least one member of the city council stated that he never talked business with Disneyland officials while on the trip.[22] By contrast, the head of the convention center pitched the idea that the Anaheim Convention Center should host Disney's annual meeting to Disney President Card Walker at one of these sessions. Walker agreed.

Disneyland also gave hundreds of free park tickets to elected officials.[23] Mayor Hunter received 170 complimentary tickets in 1991 while one member of the city council accepted 98 and another was given 24.[24] State law prohibited elected officials from accepting more than $250 worth of gifts in a year; the park tickets cost $27.50 each.[25] The state's Fair Practices Commission investigated the issue:

> [and] banned two Anaheim city council members from voting on Disney issues for one year and also forced the two, along with City Manager [Jim] Ruth, to pay back some $6,735 in free admissions to Disneyland, which were used by family and friends. The commission found that year (collectively) city hall had been given $18,095 in free admission to the park for 658 people who were mostly out of town guests.[26]

Lindquist emphasized that the trips and tickets made "good business sense" because they built strong relations between the corporate giant and the city.[27] According to former Disney executive Jim Cora, during the trips, "We laughed, we told jokes, we drank together, we played poker until well into the night. . . . The next morning, a group of guys would go out on a fishing boat, another would go play tennis, another group would go out and play golf, and there was a group that just had bad hangovers and couldn't go anywhere. So that's what we did for a long time."[28] Cora referred to the men from Anaheim who went on these trips as "the city fathers." Ron Dominguez, a Disneyland executive whose family sold their land for the park to be built, believed that the trips and tickets facilitated governance in the city. Speaking of the trips, he claimed, "It built relationships. If you had a power outage [at Disneyland] in the middle of the night, you could get some support because you knew the individual [at the city] that had that particular function."

Council Member Irv Pickler saw the tickets and events as signs of "mutual admiration."[29] Council Member Kaywood regarded the trips as "an opportunity to chat and relax with different people." The former chief of police said, "Most of the council went. We certainly got well acquainted with officials of Disneyland. We all got along so well." Defenders of the trips and tickets argued that acceptance of these privileges didn't compel the city to support Disneyland. In 1991, Disneyland President Lindquist concluded, "In 36 years, we've never done anything we've been ashamed of. We happen to believe that any city council is made up of people with more integrity. Their votes can't be bought for a one-night trip."[30] He also asserted, "If we looked at those fishing trips as a way of buying favors from the city, it was the biggest waste of money we ever made."[31]

Other city officials who went on the trips and accepted Disneyland tickets agreed that they did nothing wrong. In 1991, Council Member Kaywood contended, "If you're looking for anything sinister in all this [trip business], you're not going to find it." City Manager Jim Ruth declared, "I don't see it as an issue. If I can be bought for $100, I don't need to be here. We've built a reputation based on integrity here. I'm comfortable with that. I've never felt the slightest amount of pressure. . . . We need to be working very closely with them. I think our department heads are encouraged to have a good relationship." The city's finance director, who accepted thirty-four free passes worth $799 so his children and grandchildren could go to Disneyland, didn't think his actions constituted a conflict of interest.[32] Of his role in the trips, Council Member Pickler argued, "It never came to my mind that I had to reciprocate. People got to know who they were working with, changes in personnel, and I think it was a plus. Everything that was done has never been a detriment to the city of Anaheim."[33] Former Mayor Jack Dutton said, "I went on a number of them [trips to San Diego]. They are a great organization. I used to say that you could eat, drink or smoke all you wanted in 48 hours and, it could never be considered a bribe."[34]

Opponents of the trips and tickets saw these benefits as a way for Disneyland to exercise its financial power and buy local officials' support. Of the trips to San Diego, former Anaheim Mayor Thom, who participated in the excursions, contended that "the tactic Disney uses is co-opting people. . . . The wining and dining, the trips to San Diego. . . . It's an obvious attempt to co-opt public officials. If you accept it and go along with it, people have every right to think you've been bought off."[35] Curtis Stricker, president of HOME, alleged, "The council has been compromised. These gifts are no different than campaign contributions. It's all done for the politicians' gain."[36] As a sign that he recognized a conflict of interest, City Manager Ruth appointed city officials to the city's negotiating team who had limited experience with Disneyland executives. He said, "Candidly, I would not have selected someone with a long history with Disney. It makes us feel that much better."[37]

Council Member Daly, who would become mayor in 1992, paid back Disneyland for the trips he took in 1989 and 1990 because he "just decided it was best in my judgment that I reimburse my expenses." At the time, California law required public officials in the state to report all gifts, so Anaheim officeholders could not participate in any Disneyland decision if they received more than $250 in gifts from the company.[38]

By the early 1990s, many people became uneasy with the free trips and park tickets. At this time, Disneyland asked the city to do more for it, and the largesse created a conflict of interest for those in authority who had to decide on Disneyland's proposals.[39] As the park considered a $3 billion expansion, it needed the city council to approve an environmental study and Disneyland wanted hundreds of millions of dollars for transportation and infrastructure improvements.[40] In one of its editorials that opposed the acceptance of free Disneyland tickets by Anaheim officials, the *Los Angeles Times* wrote, "In prior years, these ticket gifts hardly mattered because Disney needed little from the City Council. Now it's different. The proposed $3-billion expansion would require the city to make a huge investment in transportation, parking and other facilities."[41]

Looking back on the issue, Cora said, "It became . . . unfashionable to accept gifts from Disney. And the city of Anaheim didn't want to do it anymore, because it looked like they were being paid off."[42] In 1991, Disneyland's Lindquist admitted that the trips had "outlived their purpose" and became "subject to interpretation."[43] That year, Ruth prohibited Anaheim officials from taking the trips, which, from this point in time, were discontinued. In March 1992, Mayor Hunter contended that "people are fed up" with Disneyland's gifts to city staffers and elected officials.[44] Even the supporters of the free park tickets and the trips saw that these practices were no longer feasible.

According to one observer of Anaheim politics, "Disney forged really strong relationships with council members who knew that Disneyland was good for Anaheim."[45] Even though city officials no longer accepted park tickets, they continued to receive preferential treatment from Disney. Members of the city council continue to receive invitations to special events such as the opening of a new ride, an anniversary gala, or the christening of a new land. One community activist received a special red card, which allowed the bearer and three guests to enter the park with no blackout dates. According to this individual, "Disney was really good to us." Each of these tactics allowed Disney to build relational power with local public and private leaders.

### Money Protects the Goose

In place of free park tickets and trips to exotic locations for elected officials, Disney exercised financial power through campaign contributions. In 1987, Disney and its executives gave $4,250 in campaign contributions to Anaheim's officials.[46] By 1990, that amount totaled $24,250. In 1989, Mayor Hunter received $1,000 from Disney; the next year, that amount grew to $9,250. Even though he benefited from this money, Mayor Hunter referred to the effect of large campaign contributions from Disneyland and other developers to city officials as "outrageous."[47] According to a *Los Angeles Times* editorial on the subject,

> Campaign contributions made by Disney in Anaheim . . . could erode public confidence in the objectivity of elected officials. And gifts, even poinsettia plants at Christmas or Disneyland passes, obviously are intended to endear city officials to Disney. Such largesse by any company, while it may be legal, is yet another example of the need for campaign financing reform at local, state and national levels.[48]

Despite the newspaper's hopes to the contrary, Disney's campaign contributions increased over time in dollar amount and importance.

Over the decades, Disney has used various strategies to influence governmental decisions. One core strategy was to cultivate strong relationships with city council members, which the company has done through campaign contributions and inviting elected officials to movie and attraction premieres and special events and functions. According to one pro-balance actor, "Disney money interferes in elections. Disney anoints their candidates, who refer to their talking points. They seek beneficial tax treatment and subsidies for Disney." This leader referred to this treatment as crony capitalism, a term that bothers Disney's supporters. Disney has very strong surrogates and allies, such as the chamber of commerce, the hotel industry, and the convention center, but others also push and defend the Disneyland Imperative. Another pro-balance actor argued, "When Disney plays such a vital role in elections, that's where leadership is bought." The company prefers to operate behind the scenes, claimed one observer, who also stated, "Disney is not comfortable in the public eye. I was always shocked when Disney was outspoken on an issue or showed up to city council meetings."

## Power and Protecting the Goose

From February 1–4, 1992, the *Los Angeles Times* conducted a public opinion poll to get a sense of Anaheim residents' views on various topics (see Figure 3.1). The poll also asked the following question, "In your opinion, how much influence does each of the following have on Anaheim city politics?"[49] The respondents rated developers, Disneyland, homeowner and neighborhood groups, labor unions, and the Visitors and Conventions Bureau on this Likert-scale question with choices of a lot, some, little/none, and don't know (see Figure 3.2). A large number, 70% of the respondents, believed that Disneyland had a lot of influence. More than half (52%) indicated that developers had a lot of influence, and 48% believed that the Visitors and Conventions Bureau wielded a lot of influence. Only 17% thought that labor unions and homeowner/neighborhood groups had a lot of influence. By contrast, 35% of respondents believed that homeowner/neighborhood groups had little influence and 33% said the same for labor unions. Small percentages con-

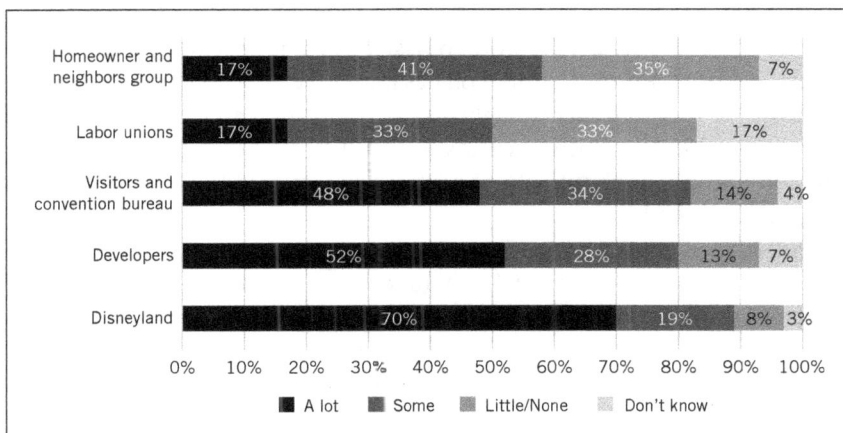

**Figure 3.1** Survey of Anaheim residents in 1992, Influence. "In your opinion, how much influence does each of the following have on Anaheim city politics?" *(Source: Kevin Johnson, "The Times Orange County Poll: Anaheim's Residents Seek Political Reform," Los Angeles Times, March 17, 1992, 1; telephone survey of six hundred Anaheim residents, conducted February 1–4, 1992. Margin of error: +/–4.)*

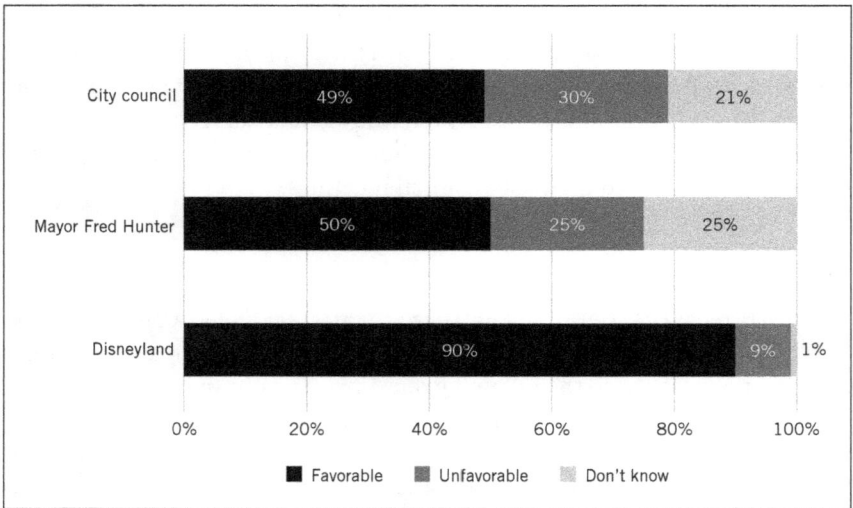

**Figure 3.2** "Do you have a favorable or unfavorable impression of these people and institutions in Anaheim?" *(Source: Kevin Johnson, "The* Times *Orange County Poll: Anaheim's Residents Seek Political Reform," Los Angeles Times, March 17, 1992, 1; telephone survey of six hundred Anaheim residents, conducted February 1–4, 1992. Margin of error: +/–4.)*

cluded that developers (13%), and the Visitors and Conventions Bureau (14%) exerted little influence. Only 8% of respondents thought that Disneyland had little or no influence, which was the lowest of the compared groups.

According to the *Los Angeles Times,* "Anaheim residents support the efforts the city is making to attract more tourists, conventions, and sports fans to the city, a *Times* Orange County Poll has found. Yet, the poll also reveals that residents are growing increasingly wary of assuming all the financial risks and want city leaders to impose a tax that would offset the mounting debt."[50] The poll found that about 54% of respondents favored the admissions tax; 42% were opposed.[51]

Ninety percent of Orange County residents held favorable views of Disneyland whether they lived in Anaheim or not, even at a time in which the tourism industry was down due to a deep economic recession (see Figure 3.2).[52] Disneyland was far more popular than the mayor or the city council (see Figure 3.2). Residents supported Disneyland because of both the park's ability to raise revenue and the fact that Disneyland was the number one employer in the county. At the time, Disneyland employed six thousand on a permanent basis and an additional four thousand in the summer. Disney's various efforts at social education had paid off because residents believed that Disneyland provided benefits shared by all of Anaheim.

In response to the prospect of an entertainment tax, the vice president of the Disney Development company asserted,

> The Anaheim taxpayers should not bear the burden of our expansion plans. That is why we are working with the city to develop a plan where a portion of the new tax revenues from the Disneyland Resort would be used to pay for much needed public infrastructure improvements. This project will not raise the taxes of Anaheim citizens. Rather, it presented an opportunity to harness the power of private economic investment to benefit the public without putting the city's general fund at risk. An additional admissions tax that primarily singles out Disneyland is unfair and would seriously undermine the fundamental economic feasibility of the Disneyland resort.[53]

At the time of the poll, the *Los Angeles Times* speculated that the enactment of an admissions tax was unlikely, in part, because of strong opposition from the business community.[54] Despite the poll's results, one member of the city council alleged, "Most people in town aren't comfortable with a new, special tax for the biggest taxpayer in town." And, indeed, the city council did not consider an admissions tax in 1992. Nevertheless, as part of the negotiations for a second park, Anaheim agreed to not impose a tax on admission at Disney parks for twenty years.[55] That deal was set to expire on June 30, 2016.

## The Latest Attempt to Protect the Goose

At the city council meeting to discuss a renewal of the entertainment tax policy and a continuation of a ban on an admissions tax in 2015, Michael Colglazier, the president of the Disneyland Resort, asserted, "What we are trying to determine right now is the scale of our next investment, as well as the viability of Anaheim for future expansion relative to other Disney parks around the world."[56] Jose Moreno, president of Los Amigos of Orange County, responded, "Please let's step back. Let's not get the same deal because we're in a different economic context. Disney doesn't pay a living wage." Former state senator Lou Correa was "dumbfounded that an issue like this could create such controversy."

At this council meeting, the groups that supported the new deal made up a majority of the attendees and included "construction trade union representatives, hotel managers, restaurant owners, police and fire union leaders, business lobby groups, chambers of commerce of various stripes, and others connected to the tourism industry . . ."[57] The opponents included several working-class Latinos and other residents who argued that the deal favored a large multinational corporation at the expense of the rank-and-file residents of Anaheim.[58] The city council agreed via a 3–2 vote to not levy an entertainment gate tax on Disney for thirty years; in exchange, Disney agreed to invest $1 billion in its Anaheim parks with work to be started no later than the end of 2017 and completed by 2024.[59] If Disney spent $1.5 billion in the parks, then the gate tax exemption would be extended for another fifteen years. If the city decided to impose an admission tax in this period, the terms of the agreement called for Anaheim to reimburse Disney for the amount of that tax.[60] When asked his views on the deal to extend a ban on an entertainment tax, Colglazier concluded, "Anaheim has been an economic success story thanks to its policies and initiatives that allow businesses to invest and thrive. We are asking city leaders to continue with a policy set two decades ago that has driven unprecedented job creation, growth and prosperity and enabled the city to invest in vital services that benefit every Anaheim resident." Of Disney's role in Anaheim's economy and the deal to extend the tax ban in exchange for park improvements, Council Member Kris Murray declared, "They already are the largest tax provider in the city. Not to tax them further in exchange for more than $1 billion in new investment is a good deal for the city."

As a member of the city council in 1996, Tom Tait supported the twenty-year ban on an admission tax. In 2015, Mayor Tait, who regarded himself as wiser than he had been nineteen years earlier, opposed the extension.[61] He asserted that the deal to extend the no admission tax policy was "the City Council binding future generations from even voting for a tax."[62] Tait also claimed, "As much as I'd like to see Disney expand, there are other ways to help them [such as] streamlining the development process and speeding up approval times. Chaining the hands of future residents on their ability to impose taxes will jeopardize the city's financial health."[63] Even though the city and Disneyland reached a formal agreement to ban the gate tax for an additional forty-five years, this issue was far from settled.[64]

## Theoretical Touchstones

Various kinds of power were on display during the first thirty-five-plus years (1954–1990) of the Disneyland-Anaheim relationship, and the Disney Company possessed or tapped into most of them. Relational power with key city officials proved crucial for the purchase and opening of the park, the imposition of height restrictions, and the avoidance of a gate tax. Disney built relational power through gifts, financial contributions, and preferential treatment to elected officials. Disney and the company cultivated relational power through the social education of the most influential people in the city and county.

The city exercised its land-use and taxation power to aid Disney and build relational power with the corporate giant. Disney also used reputational power, sometimes in the form of threats, to influence policy decisions. Its landowning power helped Disney prevail in the case of height restrictions and the gate tax ban. Disney's financial power, in effect, reinforced and further advanced the Disneyland Imperative.

The public, private, and partnership perspectives provide competing theoretical frameworks for understanding the relationship between Anaheim and Disneyland over time. Political scientist Paul Peterson, who promotes what we call the private perspective, claimed, "I find the primary interest of cities to be the maintenance and enhancement of their economic productivity. To their land area cities must attract productive labor and capital."[65] The Anaheim triumvirate of Mayor Pearson, the chamber of commerce's Moeller, and City Manager Murdoch believed that the recruitment of industry advanced the city's best interests. Anaheim's public and private leaders placed Disney's needs at the heart of city politics. They saw themselves in competition with the rest of Orange County and the region beyond. They believed that a pro-growth strategy—and its promise of tax revenues—would improve Anaheim's lot and the lives of the city's residents. These views are consistent with the private perspective, which emphasizes how city leadership responds to structural changes rather than to power and politics. Peterson argues that local governments cannot generate the property taxes necessary to provide public services unless they attract investment capital, and many leaders in Anaheim, over time, subscribed to that notion. In our view, structure affects politics, but it is not determinative.

The actors who made these decisions pursued industry and Disneyland because they thought these strategies would improve and protect the long-term economic well-being of the city. They chose to adopt this strategy. These individuals could have chosen to protect and advance the citrus industry. They could have made Anaheim a bedroom community. They could have rejected Disneyland. In fact, Mayor Pearson expressed some of the same concerns that the Burbank City Council had when it rejected Disneyland. Anaheim's leaders used their positions, power, and authority to recruit industry. They made a voluntary decision, one that came with consequences—as political scientist Brian Glenn reminds us, the temporal order of choices matters.[66]

Developmental politics aren't as consensual as Peterson argues. In terms of a tax on admission to Disneyland, plenty of actors lined up to oppose Disneyland and support a gate tax. Homeowners, mayors, members of the city council, the president of Los Amigos of Orange County, and working-class Latinos argued that the profits received by Disneyland did not extend to them. They disputed the repeated claim that what was good for Disneyland was also good for the city. Mayor Thom contended that Disneyland shipped its profits back to its headquarters in Burbank and that Anaheim residents didn't benefit. Over time, more groups joined the pro–gate tax coalition.

The public perspective argues that city leaders have agency. Cities, and the people who make decisions for them, choose actions and policies in response to the market and other structural conditions. Political scientist Clarence Stone presents the same argument in *Regime Politics* and many other places.[67] The actions of the Anaheim trio—the mayor, city administrator, and the secretary of the city's chamber of commerce—illustrate agency. These three men made choices in response to structural conditions. They went with industry. They could have followed either the agricultural path or the bedroom community route. They did not. Other communities adjacent to Los Angeles had agency as well and moved in directions that differed from the one in Anaheim. These choices show agency at work.

Despite urban agency, the public perspective acknowledges the power that corporate capital and corporations can apply in cities. Disney exercised power in Anaheim. According to one source, "Grateful for what Disneyland had meant for the city, elected officials were often willing to bend over backward for the park."[68] City leaders helped Disney secure the land, they used their authority to change local transportation, they drew favorable boundaries to facilitate the annexation of property so that Disneyland could be included inside the Anaheim city limits, and they served as project cheerleaders who defended Disneyland against the park's opponents. Even though these actors made genuine choices to support Disney, their actions show the lengths that a medium-size city would go to land what, at the time, was yet another industry partner.

The gate tax ban lends greater insight into some of the public perspective's key principles. Anaheim possessed options when it came to taxing a ticket to Disneyland. The city had the choice to impose such a tax. The idea of a tax on an entertainment ticket gained traction over time. By the early 1990s, most Anaheim residents favored such a measure. Earlier, at least one mayor and some members of the city council also thought the tax constituted good public policy and would allow the city to fix some of its financial problems. The city instead chose to continue the gate tax ban. The private perspective would argue that Anaheim saw that what was in Disneyland's best interest was also in the best interest of the city. Furthermore, competition with other cities for Disney resources compelled Anaheim to ban the gate tax. The public perspective indicates that people have power to compete against Disney, but, in each of the cases in this period, people lost every time they challenged this megabusiness.

Disney's power eclipsed the strength of those who espoused alternative plans. The city's decisions to support Disneyland did not solely center on economics because on several occasions Anaheim faced large deficits that the gate tax could help shrink. Politics and power drove these decisions. Anaheim's leaders loved the revenue generated by the corporate giant. Disney's trips, free park tickets, campaign contributions, and massive public marketing machine yielded tremendous political influence over the city of Anaheim because it drew pro-Disneyland actors even closer to the company. Some residents and homeowners screamed and shouted that what was good for Disneyland was not good for them, but elected and appointed officials chose the power of Disneyland instead. For some leaders, the need to compete against other cities was real and, therefore, Anaheim had to do whatever it could to please Disney and keep company resources in the city. In addition, local leaders succumbed to Disney's immense power and made a choice to not levy a gate tax.

The life of the gate tax ban shows how the Disneyland Imperative exerts unequal benefits and negative consequences to the city. In the late 1980s, the city faced an $8 million deficit, which ballooned to $20 million a few years later. The deficit stemmed, in part, from costs associated with Disneyland. The city's infrastructure needs, in addition to police and fire services, expanded because of Disneyland. Residents argued that they had assumed the risk for Disneyland's expenses and effects and that this wealthy entertainment company—not the taxpayers—should pay that tab. Disneyland and other large businesses thought that such a practice would be unfair to them. The city's elites agreed with the Walt Disney Company. Anaheim's developmental policies came with costs and negative effects, the likes of which the private perspective did not predict.

Members of the Anaheim city government who took Disneyland largesse claimed that democracy would win out and that they would vote on the side of their constituents on any issue that dealt with Disney. Their votes and support could not be bought. By the early 1990s, at least, Anaheim voters were not so sure. At that time, they supported governmental reforms, such as district elections, term limits, and campaign contribution limitations, which might mitigate the effect of the corporate giant on city government. Others, like former Mayor Thom, who had accepted Disney's gifts, observed that Disneyland used its resources to co-opt city officials and circumvent democracy. The public perspective argues that cities can and should pursue redistributive policies. In the pages that follow, we show how Disney wields its power in reaction to redistributive policies.

The partnership perspective emphasizes the importance of resources, coalition composition, and organizational capacity. In these areas, developmental forces in Anaheim held a significant advantage over competing interests and set the stage for building Disneyland. Business and Anaheim's public officials formed an alliance before Disneyland arrived. They brought financial and governmental resources to a partnership that facilitated the recruitment and landing of Disneyland. City government used its authority to advance industrial interests and recruit Disneyland to Anaheim. In terms of organizational capacity, the chamber of commerce provided a forum for Walt Disney and his company to sell his project to hundreds of civic, business, and political leaders. The opposition held no such advantages.

Disneyland's opposition could not match the corporate giant's power. Homeowners didn't have the same institutional capacity, economic resources, or organizational depth as Disneyland, major league sports teams, the chamber of commerce, and other business interests in Anaheim. The same can be said for neighborhoods. The 1992 poll on influence over local politics asked respondents to gauge the power of labor unions. That group, along with neighborhoods and homeowners, scored quite low on the influence scale. As we see later, however, labor unions increased their power over time and challenged Disneyland on some important issues. Despite increased power, a partnership with Disney and its allies would be out of the question at this time. In the coming chapters, we see how the partnership perspective more effectively describes the most recent period of Disneyland politics.

# Part I Conclusion

Disney's early relationship building established a political order that has lasted for decades. The Anaheim Chamber of Commerce and its membership became some of the first supporters of Disneyland, and their allegiance to the Disney Company remains and continues to be important. The California Angels MLB team, the Anaheim Convention Center, and the hotel and construction industries also supported and benefited from the Disneyland Political Order.

Before he built the park, Walt Disney used his employees and company's financial resources to convince hundreds of city and county business, civic, and political leaders that Disneyland would benefit them. The Disney Company leveraged private movie screenings, elaborate receptions, public relations campaigns, and economic projections to educate and even indoctrinate hundreds of powerful city and regional leaders about the benefits of Disneyland. These tactics provided a social education that the park would provide jobs, tax revenue, and international recognition for Anaheim and Orange County. They created social learning and helped establish a Disneyland Political Order.

The Disneys also went through social learning. Burbank and the mayor of Anaheim opposed the honky-tonk nature of amusement parks. Walt and Roy Disney taught everyone, including the mayor of Anaheim, that Disneyland was a theme park that valued cleanliness.

Industry and Disneyland came with consequences, the biggest of which was to kill Anaheim's agricultural businesses. A couple of weeks before Disneyland opened, the publisher of the *Anaheim Bulletin* informed his readers about the kinds of negative effects Disneyland might produce, raising the possibility that Disneyland could be foe, not friend, to Anaheim.

Burbank feared what Disneyland would do to its municipality. It rejected Walt Disney. The effects of that decision are seen in Burbank today. In Anaheim, the city administrator, the chamber of commerce, and, eventually, the mayor thought Disneyland would improve the city. They embraced Walt Disney. The effects of their decision are seen in Anaheim today.

Disney advanced its version of social learning at every opportunity it got in the early days of Disneyland. It reiterated to the public and government that Disneyland promoted the public good because it increased tax revenues and jobs and boosted area businesses. The narrative, or rhetoric, was clear: as Disneyland went, so went Anaheim and the region. Disney's social education had paid off because, despite the negative effects of the park and tourism, people loved Disneyland.

Disney exercised power in ways beyond its social learning efforts. The company threatened to invest in enterprises other than Disneyland and not expand the park if the city did not adopt height restrictions. It paired that threat with a massive Disney public relations campaign (or social education) that touted the incredible benefits of the park—helping convince the planning commission and the city to side with Walt Disney over other property owners and developers in Anaheim.

A Disneyland Political Order governed Anaheim. Disneyland and the city's officials, namely, the city council and planning commission, sat at the center of the city's political order. These actors represented a concentrated political arrangement that supported Disneyland. After ten years, the entertainment company's role in the city's political order had become clearer. Disneyland jumped on any issue that advanced or threatened it. The city operated under the assumption that what is good for the corporate giant is also good for it.

Proponents of the gate tax tried to educate residents that taxpayers should not pay for Disneyland expenses. This focus on the negative effects of Disneyland on taxpayers gained traction over time. A key theme that developed over the course of this issue is that the people got fed up with the largesse government officials received from Disneyland. This "we're fed up" mantra showed social learning, the kind where people began to understand that what was good for Disneyland was not good for them.

The terms of coexistence between the corporate giant and the city government skewed toward Disney from the 1950s to the early 1990s. In this first period, the city of Anaheim catered to Disney's interests to the exclusion of the interests of other actors, lacking balance between the private control of capital and the needs of the public. Anaheim's public and private leaders worked with Walt to locate the park; they even annexed property to ensure that Disneyland was located within Anaheim city limits. The city council and planning commission followed Disney's map to limit the height of buildings in the city. The attorney for property owners affected by zoning height restrictions told the planning commission that Disneyland "is here by the grace of the people, not by Mr. Disney." The planning commission sided with Mr. Disney. The city council followed Disney and banned a gate tax on entrance to the park. The gate tax issue, which extended beyond this initial period, foreshadowed that people had changed their opinions of Disneyland's role in the city.

One observer concluded that Disney had a "cozy relationship" with and influence over the city government in this era. As time progressed, however, residents grew frustrated by this influence and wary of assuming all the financial risks for Disney ventures, they became fed up with Disney's gifts to city staffers, and they warmed to the idea of a tax on park tickets.

The lack of a gate tax and the amount of money Disney spent in local elections called into question the extent to which Anaheim operated as a democracy and the efficacy of people power. Mayor Tait and some organized homeowners wanted the voters, and not three people on the city council, to decide the gate tax issue. They lost. The gate tax also showed a fundamental disconnect between what the people wanted and what the government wanted. A lack of mutual accommodation between private control of investment and representative democracy characterized this period and continued in the next era, but with greater resistance from the people.

# II

# The Luster Fades

# Part II Introduction

In the next period, which covered from the early 1990s until the early 2010s, people learned that the Disneyland Imperative came with negative consequences. The pro-balance ring of the order grew; it pushed back against the corporate giant but lacked the power necessary to stop the Disneyland Imperative. Residents, Latino leaders, unions, some members of the city council, and even the mayor sought more attention to neighborhoods, the working class, and Disneyland employees. They wanted a greater balance in priorities and policies, for example, to help all neighborhoods and provide affordable housing. The road to change began in this period with social learning and the building of relational power. Without political learning, which came later, the pro-balance actors could not defeat Disney.

While still intact, powerful, and in charge, the Disneyland Political Order lost some unity in this period. As an exercise of its reputational power, Disney threatened to leave Anaheim. Reputational and relational, in addition to financial, power might have allowed Disney to have its way in this period. The Disneyland Political Order wanted government to pay for infrastructure improvements and a new parking garage for the theme park; it asked for favorable taxing and land-use policies and greater control for Disney over the area in which its property is located. It received most of what it wanted because of its power, but the price of victory was a social learning among many residents that Disney's successes came at their expense.

# 4

# Leveraging Place

I n the summer of 1990, Disney announced it would build a second theme
park in Southern California.[1] Long Beach, California, represented one
option. Disney had purchased 443 acres on the waterfront in Long Beach
in 1989 and a year later proposed a $2.8 billion resort.[2] The new Port Disney
would include five resort hotels with thirty-nine hundred rooms and Dis-
neySea, a theme park that "would revolve around Oceana, a complex of
futuristic bubbles that depict the evolution of the seas and a working Future
Research Center, where scientists from the world's leading institutions
would gather for oceanographic studies."[3] With this announcement, Disney
created the prospect of competition among jurisdictions for further resort
and amusement park development.

## The Anaheim Theme Park That Never Happened

On May 9, 1991, Disney proposed WestCOT, a second park on the Disneyland property in Anaheim that would be a loose facsimile of Epcot Center
in Florida.[4] The $3 billion project would include three new hotels, parking
garages, and a three-hundred-foot-high golden globe called Space Station
Earth, like the silver centerpiece of Epcot. Most accounts of WestCOT compared it to a World's Fair, with attractions that highlighted the cultures of
Africa, Asia, Europe, and the Americas.[5] WestCOT would also include a five-
thousand-seat amphitheater, lakes, and a shopping district. Although the
WestCOT plans for Space Station Earth violated Disney's cherished height

restrictions ordinance, the former Mayor Bill Thom speculated, "I guess they [Disney] can visually intrude on themselves."[6]

Anaheim City Manager Jim Ruth warned that the city could not give Disney carte blanche when it came to WestCOT. In June 1991, Ruth asserted, "We've got to have a net return to the community. I don't think we're interested in breaking even."[7] Before they voted on the WestCOT project, members of the city's planning commission indicated they had not made up their minds.[8] They also claimed that they would do what was best for the public. Planning Commission Chair Robert Henninger asserted, "I think the key thing is we have to look at public interests. In my mind, the public interest is what's best for current and future residents of Anaheim and the greater Orange County area." Commissioner Phyllis Boydstun declared, "We can't make a decision until we hear both sides. I feel confident all the commissioners will go into this open-minded and make the best decision we can for the community as a whole." Of the planning commission's meeting to approve WestCOT, however, the vice president of HOME proclaimed, "As far as we're concerned, it's an all-Disney show. We don't have any illusions that it'll be an unbiased public hearing."

When Walt Disney sent Buzz Price and others to get the property for Disney World in Florida, he requested that the land overlap two counties.[9] Walt wanted his company to leverage one county against the other to get the best deal possible for Disney. In a similar fashion, during the negotiations, the Disney Company leveraged the potential park for the property in Long Beach against the one in Anaheim. If Anaheim didn't provide certain concessions, such as building two multistory garages at a cost of $500 million, the company would focus its attention on the Long Beach park.[10]

In December 1991, Disney announced it would no longer pursue the Port Disney project in Long Beach. Disney claimed that "a costly regulatory review process involving 27 federal, state and local agencies that could cost $70 million" impacted the decision.[11] As it often does with projects that do not work in one place, Disney took the DisneySea concept to another location and opened Tokyo DisneySea on September 4, 2001. Disney decided that, if it were to build a second Southern California theme park, Anaheim would be the site. It had yet to determine whether a second theme park made sense for the company's bottom line. An editorial in the *Los Angeles Times* cautioned Anaheim as it entered negotiations for a second park. It stated, "Disneyland, built in 1955, is so identified with Orange County that it is no longer possible to separate the two. However, professional distance is just what is called for in Anaheim City Hall in the months ahead."[12]

A group of two hundred business leaders formed WestCOT 2000 in the spring of 1992 to support this expansion.[13] Ed Arnold, a local sportscaster, started the organization and he enlisted Corporate Bank Chair Stan Pawlowski and Pacific Bell executive Reed Royalty to help lead the effort. According to Pawlowski, Arnold figured that some people would oppose West-COT, "but if 80% of us are behind it, we need to get together and let Disney know we want it in Orange County."[14] WestCOT 2000 kept its members informed about the progress of the project, and it created a speakers bureau that answered questions about Disney's efforts.[15] When Anaheim's planning commission received environmental regulation documentation from Disney and some resident backlash, WestCOT 2000 submitted resolutions passed by nearby city councils in support of the expansion.[16] This group served as an important support for the Disneyland Imperative. In late April 1993, WestCOT 2000 organized four thousand people to support this project. At that rally, which took place in the grand ballroom at the Disneyland Hotel, Disneyland President Jack Lindquist concluded, "This is a project that can and will transform this area and make everything that happened in the past merely a prelude to what will happen in the future. It will create a dynamic, dramatic new image that will identify Anaheim and Orange County as the number one urban destination resort n the world."[17] The executive director of the Orange County Minority Business Council attended the meeting, adding, "This project is more than just money and jobs. It's really a new spirit, the rebirth of a community."[18] WestCOT supporters claimed that the project would improve the then-recession-plagued economies in Anaheim, Orange County, and the state of California. At the time, Orange County headed toward bankruptcy.[19]

According to Disney's initial figures, the WestCOT project would add twelve million visitors per year to the city and create 17,500 jobs.[20] That job estimate grew to 28,000 over time. Disney also predicted that WestCOT would add $43 million in tax revenue to city coffers. Disney's promotion of social education also continued. More than three hundred people attended the city council meeting to approve WestCOT; most supported Disney and cited the millions in tax dollars, hundreds of millions of dollars in commerce, and thousands of jobs the project would generate for the city, region, and state.[21] Supporters of WestCOT operated with the view that what was good for Disneyland was also good for the city, the county, the region, and the state.

## Who Has Who in the Crack?

Critics asked an important but unanswered question about the Disneyland-Anaheim relationship: Which entity held leverage over the other? In April 1993, Curtis Stricker, a leader of HOME, contended, "That's what Disney does every day. They say, 'When I've got you in a crack, fella, you're gonna pay.' They think they've got us in a crack; they've got the politicians in a crack.

I say the city has got Disney in a crack."[22] Stricker claimed that Disney didn't hold the advantage over Anaheim. He believed that Disney would never leave Anaheim and the billions of dollars it invested in infrastructure, promotions, and branding in the city. Of Disney's threats to leave Anaheim and move Disneyland to another location, one pro-balance source argued, "I'll only believe that when I see the Matterhorn going down the 605 Freeway." Another asserted, "They [Disney] aren't going to pick up and leave."[23] Even Michael Eisner, the chair and CEO of the Walt Disney Company who pitted Anaheim and Long Beach against each other and remained noncommittal to WestCOT, declared in November 1994, "We're never going to let Disneyland become an aging theme park."[24]

On the night of the rally at the Disneyland Hotel, a small group of HOME members carried signs that accused Disney of corporate greed.[25] HOME argued that WestCOT and any Disneyland expansion would, at the very least, increase traffic, smog, and noise in their neighborhoods. Inside the rally, Ed Arnold, the head of WestCOT 2000, argued, "The silent majority of Orange County are sick and tired of those who don't number over a half-dozen or so making all the noise and getting all the notoriety."[26] Arnold implied that his group represented the silent majority while HOME spoke for a small minority. The head of HOME alleged that the planning commission did not listen to his group's complaints about potential negative effects.[27] He expressed hope that the city council would be more receptive, but he was disappointed again. When the city council approved the Environmental Impact Report for WestCOT, a HOME leader said, "Our representatives sold us down the river."[28]

The pro-balance ring of Anaheim's political order grew in this period. Four local school districts contended that the expansion of Disneyland, and the concomitant population explosion in the area, would overwhelm their classrooms. The Anaheim City School District sued Disney because it believed that expansion would also drain scarce educational resources in the city.[29] Disney agreed to follow Anaheim law and pay 27 cents per square foot for commercial development.[30] That amount would total around $2.5 million to schools in the area, but two school districts in Anaheim, one in Garden Grove, and the Placentia-Yorba Linda School District, wanted $220 million to cover the effects of expansion on their classrooms. In an editorial, the Orange County Register claimed that it was "nervous over the possibility that school officials might play selfish, greedy games that could scuttle the entire project." After all, the newspaper reasoned, "As much as $50 million yearly could pour into Anaheim's coffers from Disney's proposed WestCOT project, according to city officials." Opponents of WestCOT contended that most of the jobs produced by WestCOT would be of the low-wage variety. An advocate for affordable housing in the area claimed that the Disneyland expansion would exacerbate the need for affordable housing in the area, as the people who moved to the region to work in the new jobs would need places to live.[31]

The Anaheim City School District filed a lawsuit against Disney alleging that the WestCOT project would cause overcrowding in city schools.[32] The *Orange County Register* warned the Anaheim City School District that if Disney canceled WestCOT as a result of the district's lawsuit, "The school-board members and school bureaucrats at fault can look forward to being thanked individually, by name, for doing their part to sock it to the Orange County economy."[33] The school district eventually dropped the suit.[34] In response to calls by local school districts and housing advocates to contribute to their causes, Disney Vice President Kerry Hunnewell asserted, "This project cannot afford to solve all the social ills in the region. If there is extensive litigation, this project is history."[35]

The planning commission asked Disney to make more than sixty changes to the WestCOT plan to secure its approval for the development.[36] These modifications included providing five hundred affordable housing units, keeping heavy equipment at least sixty-five feet away from a local manufacturing company, establishing a childcare center, and monitoring park noise.[37] Many of the recommended changes came as the result of resident comments at public forums. Neighbors asked Disney to terrace its parking garages, add planters, redesign concrete rectangles that took up the center of the parking garage, and reconfigure street designs to "move traffic away from residential neighborhoods on Disneyland's west side."[38]

Neighbors expressed dismay and surprise at the size of the 300-foot golden globe that would be the focal point of WestCOT. In response to the proposed size of Anaheim's Space Station Earth, the vice president of HOME proclaimed, "Good God. I remember when they built the Matterhorn. That was awe-inspiring in size. Now we're talking twice that."[39] For years, the Matterhorn was the tallest structure in Orange County. At the time of WestCOT's proposal, however, the 288-foot, twenty-one-story Plaza Tower in Costa Mesa near the South Coast Plaza Mall was the tallest building in the county.[40] In response to resident feedback and backlash, Disney replaced the globe with a spire that would reach almost 300 feet.[41] Disney complied with each request submitted by the Anaheim Planning Commission. It moved its five-thousand-seat amphitheater from the park's perimeter to its interior to reduce noise.[42] Disney redesigned its parking structure and changed the Fantasmic show to cut noise.[43] Deputy City Manager Tom Wood stated these changes showed "a good faith effort" on Disney's part.[44]

Despite greater resistance to WestCOT than to Disney projects in the past, 77% of Anaheim residents supported WestCOT. They were less supportive of a people mover designed to get visitors around the Disneyland area (54%) and the construction of a parking garage (60%). Even though most residents favored Disneyland and its projects, sizable minorities opposed various attempts to expand the park or aid the company.

Disney asked all levels of government for certain concessions, and, even if those demands were met, it still needed to ensure that the deal made financial sense. As one report concluded, "Disney won't build so much as a bathroom unless there is at least a 20% profit margin."[45] Disney requested two multitiered parking garages with ramps off the Santa Ana Freeway to the new garage, and various road repairs near Disneyland.[46] Disney wanted some other entity to pay for each of these items. The four- and five-deck garages would park about twenty-eight thousand cars.[47] Disney needed the city to buy the land for the parking garages, which would serve as the east and west boundary of the new Disneyland Resort.[48] The city balked, in part, because it faced a large budget deficit at the time, and the land, which totaled seventy-seven acres, would cost around $1.6 million an acre.[49]

Euro Disney, the Disneyland of Paris, France, added to the uncertainty about economics. It lost $514.7 million for Disney in 1992 alone.[50] According to Roy E. Disney, son of Roy O. and vice-chair of the company, "Clearly, Euro Disney is making us think twice about a lot of things."[51] Euro Disney troubled Disney CEO Eisner, who concluded, "We had a very big investment in Europe and it's difficult to deal with. This [WestCOT] is an equally big investment. I don't know whether a private company can ever spend this kind of money."[52]

In July 1994, the Federal Transit Administration limited the national government's contribution to a proposed transportation center adjacent to Disneyland to $17.5 million to cover the costs toward a parking structure; pro-Disney actors had requested $131 million.[53] The federal agency concluded that the garage served Disneyland, and it calculated that only one thousand of the twelve thousand parking spaces would be available to commuters.[54] In September 1994, the House of Representatives retracted its promise of $10 million toward the garage but kept its commitment of $5 million toward the construction of freeway ramps near Disneyland.[55]

The Orange County Transportation Authority (OCTA) argued that the garage provided public benefits because the revenue from the facility would go to other transportation projects, and its transit station would service commuters.[56] The narrative that public money benefited private interests carried the day. The federal government was more willing to widen freeways and off-ramps even though these projects would benefit Disneyland, at least in part. Governor Pete Wilson committed $60 million to the parking garage and freeway ramp creation efforts. Even as Disney dragged its feet and would not commit to building WestCOT, Caltrans agreed to build off-ramps on the Santa Ana Freeway near Disneyland.[57]

On January 31, 1995, Disney announced it would not move forward with WestCOT. The project and land prices cost too much money.[58] New Disneyland President Paul Pressler assured everyone that Disney would build a second gate at Disneyland.[59] Anaheim's City Manager Jim Ruth contended, "They [Disney] are still committed to developing in Anaheim but will do so incrementally. A lot of time, effort, and energy has gone into getting us where we are, and we don't think that is lost."[60] It wasn't. The WestCOT experience led to the creation of two long-lasting aspects of Anaheim and Disneyland: the Anaheim Resort District and Disney's California Adventure.

# 5

## Expanding on Their Terms

The Disneyland experience birthed Florida's Walt Disney World. Originally named Disney World, Roy O. Disney and other company executives added the Walt moniker after the patriarch of the company died in 1966. Despite passing away five years before the Florida theme park opened, Walt Disney was the creative force behind Disney World. He wanted a park on the East Coast to capture a part of the country that seldom made it to Anaheim. In the late 1950s, market surveys informed him that 2% of Disneyland visitors traveled from east of the Mississippi River, but three-quarters of the U.S. population lived in the east.[1] The ability to attract a new audience and increase revenue appealed to Walt, but the Florida location also allowed him to fix problems that plagued Disneyland. While it may be apocryphal, legend has it that Walt, with drink in hand, would sit atop the Matterhorn ride in Disneyland after hours and bemoan what he regarded as a second-rate Las Vegas that developed outside Disneyland's doors. If he had enough money to buy more land in 1954, he would have controlled the environment for his park. Walt Disney World, with its 27,000 acres, allowed Walt to fix this problem. The entire Disneyland property was about 160 acres when the park opened, and it limited Walt's options.

In November 1965, a journalist described Walt's reaction to the area outside Disneyland in this way:

> The Disney anger flares at what has happened in Anaheim. Speculators have snatched up surrounding property and, with light regard

for justice, are cashing in on Disneyland's success. Prices are astronomical, liquor is sold to minors, in spots a honky-tonk atmosphere batters the reputation of his Magic Kingdom and no one has contributed a cent to the source of prosperity.[2]

In his 1965 speech to announce Disney World, Walt addressed the area around Disneyland. "We didn't create it," he alleged, "but we got blamed for it."[3] Disneyland has contended with, adjusted to, and attempted to change the environment outside its gates throughout its existence.

The area around Disneyland worsened over time. In 1994, the *Los Angeles Times* described it as slightly seedy with urban decay.[4] One person familiar with the area at the time put it more bluntly and concluded, "Harbor Boulevard looked like crap. The Disney area at the time was a bad place, not a great place." In exchange for a second park, Disney wanted Anaheim to pay for infrastructure changes to the area around the theme park. It also asked the city to enact zoning changes to improve standards outside its gates and address the decaying urban environment at its doorstep. Led by City Manager Ruth, Anaheim wanted to partner with Disneyland to fix the crumbling and unattractive area around the park. City leaders understood that many visiting families would not stay in Anaheim for more than a day, and inexpensive buffets represented the most prominent dining option. The city signaled a willingness to partner with Disney to make the area more attractive to longer-term visitors.

## Disneyland Becomes a Resort

In response to Disney's proposal to build a second theme park, the city council and city planning commission exercised their land-use powers to create two plans. In 1993, they adopted the 490-acre Disneyland Resort Specific Plan that covered the Disneyland property.[5] The next year, they approved the Anaheim Resort Specific Plan (ARSP), which encompassed a 550-acre area adjacent to Disneyland. The ARSP represented the city's first real attempt to create the kind of atmosphere that visitors might expect to see in proximity to a Disney property. The ARSP created special zoning to protect the area around Disneyland and provided "a unified resort identity," "improved public facilities, services, and infrastructure to accommodate projected growth," and an "improved transportation system."[6] The city spent $172 million to upgrade sewers and landscape the area, widen streets, remove neon signs in neighboring businesses, and bury cables.[7] Anaheim financed these improvements through an increase in the city's hotel tax, which rose from 13% to 15%.[8] The new rate made Anaheim's hotel tax the third highest in the country. City officials assured their constituents that they would neither raise taxes on residents nor spend general fund money to fund this resort district. The city also received another $108.9 million from the state, federal, and county governments for various transportation and utility projects.

The planning commission heard complaints that the ARSP would increase traffic, overcrowd schools, and make affordable housing scarcer.[9] Mitchell Caldwell, the lone opponent of the ARSP on the city's planning commission, wanted the city to dedicate a portion of future resort revenue to schools and low-income housing.[10] At the meeting to hear feedback on the plan, Caldwell argued, "Our neighborhoods are going to hell. We are missing an opportunity to do something about it today."[11] The Anaheim City and Anaheim Union High School Districts complained to the planning commission that the resort plan would tax their already thin resources.[12] The planning commission disagreed and passed the ARSP. Anaheim Deputy City Manager Wood claimed, "We have two very successful businesses: the convention center and Disneyland. These things need to be done to support these economic engines. The program [ARSP] is designed to do that."[13]

The standardization and beautification of the signage on the main corridor of the resort district symbolized the transformation of Disneyland's neighborhood. The city paid $5 million to replace the gaudy old neon signs on Harbor Boulevard, the main thoroughfare in the district, with uniform aluminum signs that featured the street number on the top and painted flowers on porcelain tiles on the sides.[14] Each sign cost between $18,000 and $20,000.[15] For the first two years of the program, the city replaced the signs free of charge. After that, businesses assumed the cost. Some of the more decorative signs that the city removed included the spouting whale atop the Village Inn's sign on Harbor Boulevard and the Magic Lamp Motel's benevolent genie on Katella Avenue.[16] The city celebrated the removal of the first three signs with a ceremony in August 1995. At that event, Mayor Daly asserted, "We want this area to be as visually attractive as possible. We have to keep up with the competition, and tourism is the most important industry in our city."[17] Ultimately, the city took down fifty-eight signs.[18]

## WestCOT Becomes Disney's California Adventure

In the summer of 1995, Disney CEO Eisner summoned fifty Disney employees to Aspen, Colorado, to discuss what the top company executives referred to as "the Anaheim problem."[19] At that retreat, Eisner listened to teams present ideas about theme parks based on sports, oceans, and even Route 66. After he heard Paul Pressler, the president of Disneyland, and Barry Braverman, executive producer of Walt Disney Imagineering, pitch a theme park based on the nature and culture of California, Eisner proclaimed, "California it is. That's the big idea." Eisner told Braverman, "People come to California seeking something that is more and more elusive. If we can distill it, we have an idea." Disney contacted Anaheim City Hall in December 1995 to discuss the new idea.

Disney management met with members of the Anaheim City Council to describe the company's expansion plans, which it announced to the public on July 18, 1996, the forty-first anniversary of the opening of Disneyland to the public.[20] Disney's California Adventure, the $1.4 billion, fifty-five-acre theme park that celebrated the state, would be built in Disneyland's parking lot and was scheduled to open in 2001. The plan included a 750-room hotel and a two-hundred-thousand-square-foot shopping and dining district, originally called Disneyland Center. This hotel became Disney's Grand Californian, and the district was named Downtown Disney.

In late August 1996, the planning commission unanimously approved an agreement between Disney and the city.[21] The city, state, and federal governments would pay $546 million to expand the Anaheim Convention Center, build a thirty-two-thousand-car parking garage on Disney property, relocate transmission lines at Disneyland, repave streets, upgrade storm drains, the water system, and sewers, and add new landscaping, new signage along Harbor and Katella, and new exits on the Santa Ana Freeway.[22] The resort area itself would receive $395.9 million in improvements.[23] The city would pay for its share of the projects through a combination of $395 million in bonds, a 2% increase in the hotel tax, which was approved the year before, and existing funds.[24] State, federal, and regional resources would pay for about $95 million of the costs.[25] Disney agreed to cover $200 million in bond costs if the city couldn't make its payment. Disney estimated that 8,100 of the 14,500 new jobs created by the expansion would go to people in Anaheim, the city would see $700 million in economic activity and collect $25 million in direct revenue because of the new park while the county and state would receive $10 million and $35 million, respectively.[26]

At the planning commission meeting, four people out of about 150 attendees opposed the Disneyland expansion deal.[27] Anaheim resident Tim Murphy, one of the opponents, concluded, "They pretty much get what they want, deserved or not. We are not in the city of Disney. They are in our city, and they should not dictate what they want to us."[28] The WestCOT 2000 group lobbied for the Disney's California Adventure expansion.[29] The night before the council vote on the development, WestCOT 2000 sponsored a downtown rally in favor of California Adventure, and about five hundred residents attended.[30] At the meeting at which the city council approved the plans, the cochair of WestCOT 2000 speculated, "Like love and marriage and a horse and carriage. After 41 years, you can't have one [Disneyland] without the other [Anaheim]."[31] In *Married to the Mouse*, Richard Foglesong also likened the relationship between Orlando and Walt Disney World to a marriage. He described a relationship that went through all the phases of an economic-development marriage including serendipity, seduction, secrecy, growth, and conflict.[32] At the end, he called for therapy to solve the inherent conflicts between private values and the public good.

HOME's leadership claimed that the expansion jeopardized Anaheim taxpayers. According to one member of HOME, "The general fund [of Anaheim] is at risk, and Disney will tell you that it is not. Any time you go to bonding that is what happens. The faith and credit of every property owner in the city is on the line. It certainly does impact the general fund no matter how much they deny it."[33] HOME also opposed the environmental review process through which the planning commission and city council approved the expansion.[34] The planning commission approved an addendum to the WestCOT plan, which it had accepted in 1993.[35] HOME members sought a new review. Disney claimed that the effects of the new expansion would be less than what it projected for WestCOT because it reduced the project's basic components.[36] HOME believed that the city did not address the effect of expansion on traffic, air quality, and schools in the 1993 environmental review and it called for a new report, which it did not get.[37]

Two city council members wanted to delay the vote on the agreement to build the new park. That agreement called for a moratorium on taxing Disneyland admissions or parking for at least fifteen years.[38] Bob Zemel, one of the council members who wanted to delay the vote, didn't support an admissions tax at the time but expressed concerns about "tying the hands" of future councils in regard to how to raise revenue.[39] Council Member Tom Tait supported the expansion but asked for the public to have two weeks, not one, to review the deal.[40] The council overruled them by a vote of 3–2. Mayor Daly argued, "I believe some of the motivation in the request for more time is a delaying tactic by those who oppose the project."[41] Despite these objections, the deal passed unanimously, with Zemel noting, "There is a revenue stream for the city, and it is a true partnership. This transaction is good for Anaheim taxpayers."[42]

As part of this expansion, Disney also built Downtown Disney on its property. This twenty-acre plot featured the 750-room Disney's Grand Californian Hotel, the world's second-largest Disney store, shops, restaurants, and other retailers.[43] By the year 2000, $4.2 billion worth of public and private money had been invested in the eleven-hundred-acre Anaheim Resort District.[44]

In exchange for the construction of a second Disney park, the Anaheim City Council agreed to borrow $560 million in bonds to pay for various public improvements in the Anaheim Resort.[45] In total, the city budgeted $545 million in the resort district; Disney would manage $200 million worth of these construction projects.[46] The city allocated $150 million of the $545 million to an expansion of the convention center, which represented a core feature of the Disneyland Political Order.[47] When this expansion was completed in 2000, it added 600,000 square feet to the convention center at the price of $177 million. The four previous expansions added 593,000 square feet at a cost of $75.6 million.[48]

The city committed to build a thirty-two-thousand-car parking garage on Disneyland's property for $90 million.[49] This facility became known as the Mickey and Friends Parking Structure. The city spent $108.2 million to build the garage.[50] It costs Disney $1 per year to lease the facility. When the city retires the bonds, which will include more than $1.1 billion in interest, Anaheim will transfer ownership of the garage to Disney. One pro-balance source asked in retrospect, "Who agrees to that kind of deal?" This actor also alleged, "People became enlightened as the resort built up." Another regarded the creation of the Resort District as a turning point at which Anaheim went all in on low-wage tourism. The city also moved power lines that ran through Disneyland's parking lot ($20 million), buried electric, gas, and telephone lines ($49 million), made transportation improvements ($96.8 million), converted West Street into Disneyland Drive ($24 million), modified and moved fire stations ($7.7 million), and upgraded storm drains ($31.8 million), the water system ($10.9 million), sewers ($8.7 million), and landscaping ($28.9 million).[51] These municipal contributions totaled more than $380 million and contributed to Disney's continued success.

As part of the renovations to Disneyland's neighborhood, the Anaheim City Council approved the Anaheim Resort Maintenance District.[52] Property owners within the resort district proposed the creation of a levy on businesses within the Anaheim Resort District to preserve the beautification changes that the city had made. Of property owners, 76% responded to a ballot that asked whether they approved the creation of the maintenance tax. Of those who responded, 86.1% voted for the levy. Some small businesses resented that they had to pay the tax. The owner of the Anaheim Resort Plaza, located less than a mile from Disneyland on 1770 South Harbor Boulevard, proclaimed, "If the city requires us to pay, we can pay but we're very unhappy to pay. It's unfair. There's more benefit to Disneyland, not us." An owner of a liquor store at 901 South Harbor asked, "How come the city makes us pay if they want to make the city beautiful? I'm at the end and tourists never come this side, only neighbors." In response to what he claimed were a couple of complaints, Assistant City Manager Wood speculated, "Clientele will jump significantly. You will see benefits throughout the entire resort, well beyond the resort district." He also claimed that the property values of businesses within the resort district had quadrupled since the beautification efforts had started.

As we described earlier, Anaheim had never taxed admission to Disneyland. As part of the negotiations for a second park, Anaheim agreed to not charge a tax on admission at Disney parks for twenty years.[53] That deal was set to expire on June 30, 2016.

## Changes to Disneyland's Leadership

Around the time of WestCOT, the creation of the Anaheim Resort District, and the plans for Disney's California Adventure, local leaders noticed a change in Disney's approach in Anaheim. Jack Lindquist, Walt Disney's friend, Disneyland's original advertising manager, and later the president of Disneyland from 1990 to 1993, resided in Anaheim for years.[54] Future Mayor Tom Tait lived next door to Lindquist and would go into his neighbor's yard to retrieve an errant basketball shot. Ron Dominguez, whose parents sold their property to Walt Disney in the original purchase of the land for the park, worked as a ticket taker in Disneyland's first year of operation and served as the vice president of Disneyland from 1974 to 1990. Dominguez asked Walt Disney to retain one of the palm trees on his parent's property. Walt complied and the Dominguez Tree, as it is known in Disneyland lore, stands next to the Jungle Cruise Boathouse in Adventureland.[55] With Lindquist and Dominguez in prominent positions at Disneyland, one public official concluded that "Disneyland had a more family-type feel because it was led by local Anaheim people."[56] Another prominent political actor agreed and contended that Lindquist, Dominguez, and "the first few leaders of Disneyland were different from their predecessors, who came to the park from Disney cruises or other parks."[57]

Political leaders identified Lindquist's successor, Paul Pressler, as someone who typified the new type of corporate leader at Disneyland.[58] Pressler worked for various toy companies before he became vice president of marketing and design for the Walt Disney Company in 1987. Pressler was the senior vice president for consumer products and executive vice president and general manager of Disney Stores. Pressler's successors emanated from the same Disney corporate structure, and, as such, according to one prominent individual, Disneyland "lost some of that small-town relationship" with Anaheim. Another asserted,

> Disney changed from who it was. Disney was a small business; leadership was local. As Anaheim grew, Disney became a bigger company too. As Disney developed more of a corporate structure, the city/company relationship changed. The presidency of Disneyland turned over quickly. Disney had more of a corporate culture, and quick changes in leadership changed the leadership's relationship with the city.

Pro-balance informants contend that the new corporate culture at Disney brought with it a more aggressive political style. Many used the word nasty to describe Disney's approach starting in this era. One source noted that Disney "became more and more politically active with mailers, letters to the council, and more pressure on the council. We weren't used to that." Another proclaimed, "Disney fought back nastily." In this second period, Disney's relational power, which formed a bedrock of the Disneyland Political Order, diminished, and this change helps explain why resistance to the corporate giant increased.

A community activist also recognized a change in Disneyland's approach to the city, in the 1990s, when Disneyland presidents ended the company's annual breakfast for civic leaders. This gathering of around thirty people who represented various community and nonprofit organizations communicated the interests of thousands to Disneyland's leadership. Of the company's decision to stop these meetings, this individual argued, "Disney became exclusive and they aren't talking to the community anymore. You're the kingpin company business in this city; you have to listen. . . . Disneyland lost trust as a result. Things became adversarial. If Disney ever renewed this practice, it would make a world of difference. They closed the door and became insular." This civic leader also noted that, at about the same time, Disneyland's presidents no longer met with nonprofits or provided free park tickets to hundreds of kids who participated with nonprofit groups. Over time, as the corporate giant's relationship with the city weakened, some of Disney's relational power diminished.

## Two Anaheims

In May 2000, Felix Sanchez of the *Orange County Register* wrote an article titled "Anaheim: One City, Two Faces."[59] In that story, he described two Anaheims, one that received special treatment from government and another that did not. The former part of town was a section known as Anaheim Hills. Originally known as Robber's Peak, because of its sweeping views, it was developed in the 1970s with single-family homes for the affluent, and it remains whiter and less integrated than other parts of Anaheim.[60] Residents who lived on the western side of the city claimed that the city favored the Anaheim Hills. In 1999, for example, the city opened a new community center and police substation in Anaheim Hills. Mayor Daly argued the west side of the city needed a community center, police substation, new major park, landscaping, and beautification. In the summer of 2000, Mayor Daly stated that the last "major, significant investment" in the west side had occurred in April 1978. One political actor noted that the city "allowed the flatland [the area to the west of Anaheim Hills] to deteriorate."

The creation of the Anaheim Resort District added to the Two Anaheims narrative. Those outside the district, especially residents of the western part of Anaheim, complained that the resort district received special treatment from the city in terms of tax revenues, zoning laws, and attention. Pro-Disney and pro-balance leaders disagreed over the Two Anaheim narrative. The latter are more likely to say that such a division exists. The former tend not to agree that one section of the city gets preferential treatment over the other.

Once the city created the Anaheim Resort District, Disney became even more protective of this section of the city. It fought any entity that attempted to bring about what it regarded as harm to the district. In 1998, developers wanted to build Pointe Anaheim, a high-end shopping center on the side of Melodyland, which sat close to the Disneyland property within the resort district on Freedman Way (a street that would become Disney Way as part of the Anaheim Resort District transformation). According to one report, Disney "began a quiet but intense lobbying campaign with city officials even before [Pointe Anaheim's] plans were filed."[61] It objected to the gaudy signs and traffic that it believed this development would bring and wasn't thrilled that its Downtown Disney development would have competition. Disney withdrew its opposition after the developers of Pointe Anaheim agreed to increase parking, limit signage, and alter traffic patterns.[62] The Pointe Anaheim project stalled, in part, because of the economic downturn in tourism caused by the September 11, 2001, attacks.[63] Under a new name, GardenWalk, the $130 million, twenty-acre project broke ground in 2006 and opened in June 2008.[64]

Some sources in Anaheim regarded the creation of the Anaheim Resort District as a turning point in the relationship between the city and the Walt Disney Company. More people began to question whether what was good for Disney was also good for them. Before the creation of the resort district, residents perceived the west side neighborhoods and the area around Disneyland as declining in tandem. Afterward, the resort district thrived while the neighborhoods continued to struggle. Of the Anaheim Resort District, one informant alleged, "Residents turned negative after the re-doing of signage on Harbor. They thought super-duper money came from the city for this. That wasn't the case, but the perception was that Disney doesn't pay taxes. People thought that Disney got away with murder." Some respondents argued that the change from a single theme park to a resort doubled the size of the workforce in Anaheim and many working-class Latinos filled those jobs. These low-paying jobs combined with a new revenue source for the Disneyland Political Order increased the inequality in the city in the eyes of Disney critics. In 1996, Disney paid $11 million to local coffers in the form of property, sales, and hotel taxes.[65] Was that enough?

# 6

## Living in the Shadow of the Mouse

n June 2006, the city's planning commission unanimously rejected a proposal to change the zoning ordinance to allow 1,500 homes, including 250 designated as low-cost, on a twenty-six-acre site inside the Anaheim Resort District.[1] Of the three people who attended that meeting, two represented SunCal, the real estate development company that sought the zoning change.[2] At that time, about three hundred mobile homes sat on this property, known as Satellite Mobile Home Estates, located on South Haster Street and Katella Avenue. The development of this property created a division between Disney and local affordable housing advocates. Disney wanted that property to be used for future hotel development, even if the area did not need the hotel space until 2030.[3] In late August 2006, the Anaheim City Council voted 4–1 to overturn the planning commission and allow about twenty-six acres of 225 low-income apartments and 1,275 condominiums at the edge of the Anaheim Resort District. Mayor Curt Pringle cast the dissenting vote.

Pringle believed that SunCal's project interfered with the Platinum Triangle project, a mixed-use high-density development of urban lofts, restaurants, and office and commercial space near Angel Stadium and Honda Center, about four miles from Disneyland.[4] Mayor Pringle had championed the Platinum Triangle project and made it a reality. It aimed to create a downtown that the city, and the county for that matter, lacked.[5] According to the city's planning director, "The stadium provides a reason for people to come to the area; we are hoping to provide lots of reasons to make them want to stay."[6] The Council Members Lorri Galloway and Richard Chavez expressed disappointment that the development included no affordable housing.[7] About the Platinum Triangle, Chavez said, "It's kind of heartbreaking in that we're creating a kind of segregated area."[8]

By the time of the debate over affordable housing in the Anaheim Resort District, the Platinum Triangle was already well underway with the Stadium Lofts having opened in June 2006.[9] In response to the city council's vote to allow the low-cost housing, Pringle speculated, "By approving this, we are creating a direct competitor to the units we have approved. People have spent a fortune in a district where we've said we want to maximize residential use. I hope every single one of the builders invested in the Platinum Triangle doesn't think we are running away from them."[10]

Even though the city council held ultimate authority over this issue, the planning commission needed to vote on the specific low-cost housing plan.[11] In January, it unanimously rejected the housing proposal.[12] The planning commissioners and Mayor Pringle wanted to reserve the Anaheim Resort District for commercial and tourist purposes, not residential ones.

Nevertheless, resistance to Disney was increasing. Labor unions and community groups supported the creation of low-cost housing. The president of UNITE HERE! Local 11, a union of about five thousand hotel and restaurant workers, complained, "Many of our members work full time yet cannot afford to live in Anaheim. Others have no choice but to live in overcrowded conditions just to make ends meet. . . . Although some business leaders oppose building affordable housing in the resort district, we think such opposition is short-sighted."[13] Employees believed they had a right to live where they worked. The executive director of Orange County Communities Organized for Responsible Development (OCCORD), which describes itself as a community-labor alliance, asserted, "The business community in Anaheim is saying it supports affordable housing, just not in their backyard. That's the kind of things NIMBYs in all parts of Orange County have been saying for years. I expected more leadership from Anaheim's business community."[14] One contact claimed that "working poor neighborhoods are in the shadows and neglected." This person argued that "the marginalized feel pushed out because of a lack of affordability." Each of these Disney critics cited the creation of expensive housing in the Platinum Triangle and the debate over low-cost housing in the Anaheim Resort District as examples to support feelings of marginalization and exclusion. Although the planning commission rejected the proposal, there is an appeal process allowing the issue to come before the city council, which has the authority to overturn the planning commission's decision. Utilizing this process, which requires two votes in successive meetings, the city council agreed to consider the housing plan at its February 2007 meeting.

The media recognized that the fight over affordable housing in the resort district represented a sea change in the relationship between Anaheim and Disneyland. Dave McKibben, who covered the issue for the *Los Angeles Times*, wrote the following before the second city council vote on SunCal's requested zoning changes: "A proposal to build housing near Disneyland has escalated into a battle of wills between the entertainment giant and key Anaheim officials, who once could be counted on to follow Disney's lead."[15] In the same article, he added, "The debate has left council members in an awkward position: whether to please Anaheim's biggest employer and biggest tourist draw or create housing, including low-cost residences for the resort district's workforce." One observer of local politics at the time asserted, "The housing issue riled everyone up."

Disneyland sent what it labeled as an urgent email to community leaders to defeat the housing proposal and "help save the Anaheim resort district." In another email, Disneyland spokesperson Rob Doughty wrote, "Residents and tourists have different needs that are not always compatible. Tourists like to stay up late and make noise, while residents need a quiet night sleep so they can get up to go school and work in the morning." The executive director of OCCORD responded, "This whole issue about what's compatible doesn't make sense. There're people living on that site now, and I don't think there's any glaring incompatibility with people living there and other functions that go on."

Disney worked to disqualify one of the Anaheim City Council members from voting on the zoning change discussion. On the afternoon of the meeting, Anaheim City Manager Dave Morgan asked City Council Member Lucille Kring if the wine shop she proposed to open would be within five hundred feet of the housing site.[16] If the answer was yes, the city manager informed Kring, then she would be disqualified from voting on the housing proposal because of a Fair Political Practices ruling.[17] Kring believed she would be able to vote. Minutes before the meeting was to start, Anaheim City Attorney Jack White received a letter from Disney attorneys, who told him that in 2001, a city council member in Truckee, California, was advised not to vote on a housing development that was within three miles of that council member's wine and cheese store.[18] Upon hearing this news and with the meeting about to commence, Kring abstained from the vote.

In response to the city's decision to encourage Kring to recuse herself, Council Member Bob Hernandez speculated, "If that stands, Lucille [Kring] won't be able to vote on anything to do with the resort area or anything to do with the city. I think that decision is unreasonable. That means that anybody who owns a business in the city shouldn't run for City Council."[19] In response to the intensity with which Disney and its supporters lobbied against the housing plan, Council Member Harry Sidhu concluded, "People are really rallying hard. I've never seen anything like this. The troops behind the resort district, they are woken up."[20] Disney wanted control over the resort district and seemed willing to do anything to maintain that dominance.

At the meeting itself, which lasted more than three hours, Galloway claimed, "There's no hotel crisis. There's an affordable-housing crisis."[21] Mayor Pringle stated that the resort district was "where the money to our city comes from" and that the creation of housing in the district would "kill our golden goose."[22] Pringle added, "I'm very concerned because I really feel this is a threat to reduce funding to the city of Anaheim."[23] A city-commissioned report indicated that the city could lose $4.6 million per year if houses, as opposed to hotels, were built in that space. It predicted that the area wouldn't need hotels for another twenty-four to fifty-five years but still insisted that nothing be built on the land to keep that space open for a hotel sometime in the future. Disneyland Resort's senior vice president alleged that the housing proposal "puts the entire master plan in jeopardy."

At this council meeting, Disney's supporters wore red stickers reading, "Save the Anaheim Resort District," while advocates of housing within the district sported white stickers exhorting, "Housing Here Now!"[24] Three dozen business leaders, school district officials, and community activists testified against the plan.[25] The head of a professional association that brought eighty-five thousand conventioneers to the city contended that he would need to reconsider Anaheim as a convention site because the inclusion of housing in the resort district hampered the convention center's ability to grow and accommodate them in the future.[26] About seventy-five low-income workers attended the meeting to support the low-cost housing plan. In the end, Kring's decision to recuse herself proved crucial. The city council split 2–2 on the zoning changes necessary for the housing development. As McKibben wrote in his lede for his article on the meeting, "In Anaheim, even the tie goes to Disney."[27]

Understanding that the deadlock in the city council did not mean the end of the housing issue, Disney took two further steps to kill the proposal. About two weeks after the city council meeting, Disney filed its first-ever lawsuit against Anaheim. Even though it voted against the housing development, the city's planning commission approved environmental studies necessary to build infrastructure if the housing proposal was ever approved.[28] Disney's lawsuit wanted the city to nullify that environmental analysis and conduct one of its own. Disney didn't stop at a lawsuit.

In March 2007, Disney announced it would propose a ballot initiative to require a citywide vote to approve any land-use alterations in the Anaheim Resort District.[29] Disneyland President Ed Grier called the initiative "a permanent solution to protect the resort." He also concluded, "This ballot issue ensures the resort will remain a world-class destination, and it puts residents in charge of the future." Save Our Anaheim Resort (SOAR), a Disney-funded coalition of business and community leaders, led efforts to put the resort district zoning initiative on the ballot.[30] Its members included representatives from the key players in the Disneyland Political Order, including the Anaheim Chamber of Commerce and the Anaheim/Orange County Convention and Visitors Bureau.[31] SOAR claimed that even though the Anaheim Resort District made up 5% of the city's land, it generated more than 50% of Anaheim's tax revenue.[32] The initiative "would remove authority from the Anaheim City Council to make any land-use decision within 2.5 miles of the Disneyland resort area without prior voter approval."[33]

While Disney announced its ballot initiative, California's Fair Political Practices Commission ruled that Kring was qualified to vote on any zoning changes in the district.[34] Kring responded, "I'm very frustrated by what Disney has put me, my husband, and the city through."[35] Kring's eligibility to vote on zoning changes opened the possibility that the city council would once again take up the issue of the residential complex in the resort district. Galloway, the chief proponent of affordable housing on the council, said, "I don't feel Disney is the enemy, so when they do something aggressive, I am surprised. I am always surprised when a company decides to file a lawsuit against the city and circumvent the council's authority on land-use issues."[36]

## Is Disney Responsible for Anaheim's Social Ills?

Each side had different answers to the following questions: How much responsibility does Disney have for the lack of affordable housing in Anaheim? What should the company do about this issue? Disneyland's leadership told the city that housing was Anaheim's responsibility. When Disney's California Adventure was proposed, Anaheim officials asked Disney to build five hundred affordable housing units, but the company and city council instead agreed to provide $5 million worth of bond funds for "neighborhood improvements/housing," a bulk of that money—about $4 million—went toward "neighborhood upgrades—lighting, trees, irrigation, and land acquisition."[37] A Disney spokesperson asserted that the company preferred to allocate the money because it is "not a residential builder." Of that agreement, the company spokesperson concluded that Disney "lived up to our end of the bargain." Council Member Sidhu argued, "This is not the business's problem. I truly believe in a free market. People who . . . can earn wages can stay here. If not, maybe they can move somewhere else, like Riverside, where rents are cheaper." Opponents disagreed with Disney and Sidhu. Galloway asked, "We're still begging Disney to help us with the problems they are causing. Does that make sense?"

The Anaheim City Council voted 3–2 to reconsider SunCal's housing proposal.[38] The month between that decision and the vote on the zoning changes saw heightened tensions in Anaheim. SunCal formed a group named Defend and Protect Anaheim, which sent mailers before the vote.[39] One mailer asserted that Disney is "opposing a project which will create houses where our police officers, teachers, nurses, firefighters, and resort area employees could live."[40] Another asked residents if they wanted to live in "Anaheim or Disneyheim?"[41]

Various observers noticed how the fight over low-cost housing in the district changed people's perceptions about Disney. One observer said of the debate, "Hysteria grew. People gained more perspective. The housing was a trigger point that opened people's eyes and frustration grew. . . . The frustration built. It was simmering and then it exploded. People got tired. They had enough. They got sick and tired." An interviewee claimed, "People don't like to see Disney involved in politics." According to this individual, during the low-cost housing debate, "People recognized Disney in the political division. People like Disney, but not in politics." Another leader alleged that this issue "awakened people. It definitely started with that. The light shined."

More than four hundred people attended the next city council meeting to decide whether to adopt a new zoning ordinance. Those on the side of Disney wore white stickers that read, "Save Our Anaheim Resort," while opponents handed out stickers that read, "YIMBY, Yes in Mickey's Backyard."[42] The crowd was so large that the fire department closed the council chambers. The overflow crowd sat outside the chambers or watched the proceedings on television monitors. At the conclusion of the six-hour meeting, the council voted 3–2 to allow the housing in the Anaheim Resort District. Galloway, Hernandez, and Kring voted for the measure; Pringle and Sidhu opposed.

The day after the council approved this zoning change, Disney's supporters launched a referendum drive.[43] A coalition led by Todd Ament, the president of the Anaheim Chamber of Commerce and cochair of SOAR, advocated the creation of a referendum on the council's decision to allow the fifteen hundred housing units within the Anaheim Resort District. Other antihousing and pro-Disney coalition members included state senator Lou Correa (D-Santa Ana), former Mayor Tom Daly, and current Mayor Pringle. By mid-July 2017, pro-Disney advocates collected the signatures of more than thirteen thousand registered voters in Anaheim to get the referendum on the ballot.[44] This was in addition to the ballot initiative to require citywide voter approval of any land-use changes to the Anaheim Resort District, meaning that Disney supported measures to reverse the housing decision and to limit the council's authority to make future land-use decisions without voter approval.

In response to Pringle's endorsement of the referendum, Galloway asserted, "If the mayor is going to take Disney's side, I take that very seriously. His business is to protect the city's interest, not Disney's."[45] Frank Elfend, SunCal's consultant on this project, claimed, "It is disappointing that once again the Disney Corporation is escalating Disney's war with the city of Anaheim. Disney's new referendum is just another intimidation and bullying tactic to force their will on Anaheim." Disney's reaction to housing in the Anaheim resort typified the company's nastier and more aggressive approach to city politics and policy.

Galloway wanted to strip public funding from the chamber.[46] Galloway concluded, "We're giving them up to $200,000 a year to promote and work with Anaheim businesses, not to do referendums against the city. The chamber is supposed to be promoting businesses, not pitting them against each other. Why should we give them one dime?" Council Member Sidhu supported Ament. He responded, "The chamber is doing what it's supposed to do. They are protecting the interests of the businesses in the city, so the revenue keeps coming into the city." The council continued to provide $205,000 or 9% of the chamber's budget in 2007, but the suggestion to withdraw funding revealed fissures in the partnership that had steered Anaheim government and politics since the time Disney first sought the land for its park.

As the idea of affordable housing in the resort district marched closer to reality, fights between the two sides grew more intense. According to one observer, there was no middle ground on this issue. In May 2007, Sarah Tully of the *Orange County Register* wrote, "This is the first time in at least three decades that a referendum has been launched on tossing out a City Council decision. And it's turning into the most divisive issue some long-time residents say they have ever seen."[47] Tully quoted Cynthia Ward, a long-time neighborhood advocate in Anaheim, who concluded, "I've never seen anything this explosive in our community ever. This has really got people fired up." Proponents and opponents of housing in the resort district fought each other as Disney collected signatures to get the referendum on the ballot. Three police officers responded to a call at the farmers market because SunCal petitioners blocked the Disney coalition table. Police also responded to calls at a Vons grocery store where proponents of SunCal and Disney claimed that the other obstructed their access to store customers. Of the incident, Ament stated, "I had no clue they would get that close, that physical, that boisterous." Ament claimed that he and his three daughters set up their chairs away from SunCal petitioners, who then stood in front of them and wouldn't leave. That move prompted Ament to call the police.

City council members on both sides of the issue used urgent emails to try to convince voters to support their side. In terms of spending, there was no competition. As of March 31, 2007, Disney had allocated $100,000 to

SOAR, whereas the Committee to Defend and Protect Anaheim had raised $1,165.[48] SOAR would continue to act as an important Disney surrogate that exercised financial power and funneled campaign dollars to candidates and causes that advanced the corporate giant.

In May 2007, Walt Disney Company CEO Bob Iger made his first public remarks on the housing issue in Anaheim. Speaking at a business journalism conference in Orange County, Iger contended that Disney "is probably the best neighbor that Anaheim has ever had."[49] He added:

> We believe that there should be affordable housing in this area, that it's an effort that should be a partnership between the local government and a number of businesses. Given all the employees, or cast members as we call them, that we have here, we believe that giving them affordable housing in an area that's proximate to their place of work is something that we should all work to create. But we don't believe that the property that's being talked about is property that should be developed for housing.

Advocates on both sides of the issue, in addition to the media and other experts, speculated that Disney didn't want this land to be developed for housing because it adjoined what they believed would someday be the location of a third Disney park in Anaheim.

Galloway requested that the city check SOAR's facts that the Anaheim Resort District produced 54% of the city's revenue.[50] The city's report indicated that the district accounted for 44% of the revenues, but, once Anaheim's commitments to the resort area were taken into consideration, that number fell to a net of 21%. Galloway believed that the district's contribution to city coffers fell below 21% when the calculation included costs for police, housing, and other services for the resort.

Ament concluded, "The Anaheim resort district is the largest single source of revenue to the city of Anaheim's general fund . . . regardless of how anyone slices the numbers."[51] In response to this report, Mayor Pringle argued, "We have a resort that is the economic engine of the city, without a doubt." One pro-Disney leader asserted, "The resort pays for itself." Pro-Disney forces also argued that about $14 million in sales tax revenue was not included in the city's report on the contribution of the resort to the city's coffers.

When asked to reflect on this issue, local informants saw a split between the old and the new in Anaheim. On one side of the debate was old Anaheim, anchored by residents in Anaheim Hills and the chamber of commerce, who wanted things to stay the same. On the other side of the debate, newer residents, many of whom were Latino and immigrants on the city's west side, wanted things to change. Many came to work in the expanded Disneyland

Resort. The more the demographics changed, the more the old Anaheim wanted to maintain the status quo. Until 1970, more than 98% of the population in Anaheim was white, but the population demographics changed after that. The white population dropped to 66.4% and Latinos made up 17% of the total residents in 1980. Between 1980 and 2000, the Latino population more than tripled. In 2021, Latinos made up 53% of Anaheim's population. The foreign-born population also increased during the late twentieth century. In 1960, the percentage of foreign-born residents in the city was 5.4%, but it increased to 28.4% by 1990 and 36.9% in 2010. Another observer speculated that the division between the old Anaheim and the new Anaheim characterized politics in the city starting in the 1990s. Disneyland represented the status quo, and old Anaheim wanted to preserve it as the centerpiece of the city's economy.

As the housing debate stretched to a year on the public agenda, the coalition that supported the construction of residential units expanded and provided greater power to the pro-balance forces.[52] Religious leaders joined pro-housing advocates and some labor officials in the SunCal coalition. These religious groups—including the Orange County Congregation Community Organization, a coalition of twenty churches most of which were Catholic—saw the lack of affordable housing in Anaheim as a moral issue. Five hundred members of Anaheim's religious communities attended a housing forum in July 2007. Religious leaders delivered more than two hundred letters from their parishioners to the Anaheim City Council. Those letters detailed the struggles of Roman Catholic families to get low-income housing in Anaheim.

A complication arose in late October 2007, when SunCal filed a lawsuit against the Frank Family Partnership.[53] That suit claimed that the Frank Family Partnership walked away from its $46 million deal to sell the twenty-six-acre parcel, the one at the center of the controversy over housing, to SunCal. In all this time, SunCal never owned the property. The Frank Family Partnership had retained ownership. A deal had been reached in April 2005 for SunCal to purchase the property from the Frank Family Partnership, but SunCal asserted that the Frank Family Partnership had worked in secret to sell the property to an unnamed third party.[54] A few days after it filed its lawsuit, SunCal told the city that it had dropped its request to receive a zoning amendment for the residential complex.[55] Once the deal fell through, the Anaheim City Council voted 3–2 to rescind approval of the housing project.[56] This vote made the referendum moot, but the referendum process created critical political leverage for Disney.

After the city council vote, an *Orange County Register* editorial begged for the issue to end:

The Resort—the 2.2 square-mile area around the Disney parks that provides the bulk of the city's revenue—is not something that we would have crafted, given its high level of government involvement. Nevertheless, the project has been rather successful in reviving a once-seedy area by plowing tourism-generated tax dollars back into the tourism area. . . . There is no right to a subsidized home near one's workplace. And the proposed project would only have provided a small number of below-market units. Enough is enough. Anaheim residents should be pleased to see the bulk of this problem fade away.[57]

## Disney Protects Its Land

While Disney emerged victorious in this battle, it continued to fight the larger war against any changes to the resort district. It won, in March 2008, when the city council decided that any zoning change inside the Anaheim Resort District needed voter approval.[58] Pringle, Sidhu, and Kring voted for the ordinance. Sidhu had changed his position on this matter. The month before, he stated, "I'd like to let the democratic process work rather than let the political people decide the fate of the initiative. I don't want to get in the way of the taxpayers who put this on the ballot."[59] Council Members Galloway and Hernandez wanted the city's electorate to vote to determine whether it approved this kind of authority over land-use decisions. The city council's decision nullified the need for a ballot measure on whether land-use decisions in the district required voter approval.

One predominant public narrative in the wake of the affordable housing conflict was the strength accumulated by SOAR and the pro-Disney coalition. Disney gave $2.1 million to SOAR in the organization's first year of existence.[60] SOAR used the money for political consultants, public relations, and petition collectors. Ament rejected the notion that Disney ran SOAR. He asserted, "We have 30 executive members that make decisions for what this coalition does, not Disney. . . . We have one goal, protecting the Resort District. That also happens to be Disney's goal." Former Mayor Daly claimed, "If Disney wouldn't have put the money up front, other people would have. There is fire in people's eyes. There's pride in the Resort District." Daly also marveled at what he referred to as SOAR's "deep and broad-based" coalition.[61] Daly, an original member of SOAR, alleged, "We've got neighborhood leaders from the east to the west to the Anaheim Hills, chamber of commerce members, historic district folks. . . . People are coming from everywhere to support this cause of protecting the resort."

Even though Disney won the low-income housing battle and the zoning war, for the first time since the city and chamber of commerce romanced Disney in the early 1950s, a critical mass of public and private actors opposed Disney's actions. It called out Disney on what they regarded as selfish and irresponsible actions. The pro-balance/pro-affordable housing forces persisted in a battle that lasted for more than a year, and, unlike previous issues, this one played out in public. Disney's immense financial and relational power allowed the company to prevail.

As the Disney-Anaheim relationship moved forward, several questions were unresolved. Would the company continue to enjoy the approval it had achieved within both the public and the private spheres for most of its time in Anaheim? Would resistance to Disney dissipate or strengthen as the company asked for more preferential treatment from the city? Was the push for low-income housing a limited event, or did it signal a more permanent change in the relationship?

# 7

## Outside the Gates

*Incentives to Build*

Disney opposed affordable housing, it claimed, because it preferred hotels in the Anaheim Resort District. In 2013, the city council voted 4–1 to give a tax rebate to a local developer to build a luxury hotel in Anaheim.[1] Two years later, that deal—and the tax break that came with it—became the template for any entity to build a luxury hotel in Anaheim.

### "Bonkers"

In 2015, by a vote of 3–2, the city council passed a new ordinance that allowed any developer that built a luxury hotel, defined as a four-diamond hotel by AAA, to keep 70% of their hotel bed taxes for up to twenty years.[2] Of the remainder of the taxes, 10% would go to the city, and the other 20% would pay off the bonds used for resort district improvements.[3] Mayor Tait and Council Member James Vanderbilt opposed the subsidy. Tait argued that Anaheim needed the revenue generated by the hotel taxes to pay for police, parks, road repairs, and other city services.[4] He referred to the deal as "corporate welfare" and contended, "Our tax money is to use for the neighborhoods, not to give back to the hotel developer. We have needs more than luxury hotels. It makes no sense."[5] Vanderbilt concurred, "I'd rather have economic programs that are more tangible for everyday citizens. I'd like to see those kinds of economic development first instead of what speaks to the high end, the caliber I don't necessarily represent."[6] Tait asked, "Why would other competing hotels be for a Disney hotel?" Tait was adamant in his opposition: "No reasonable person can argue for a subsidized hotel on Disney property."

Residents who spoke against the subsidy touched on two prominent themes that come up when the city has offered preferential treatment to Disney and other major corporations.[7] The first is that two Anaheims exist. Resident Yesenia Rojas asked, "You guys are talking about hotels, corporations, blah blah blah, but what happened to the neighborhoods?" The second theme is that the resort district does not provide collective benefits for the entire city, at least not commensurate with its ability to contribute. Resident Richard Ward commented, "[The argument] that the other residents and non-resort businesses who make up the general fund somehow stand to benefit from giving to rich hoteliers—to what, build luxury hotels and pamper the wealthiest guests of our cities? We've already been giving up too much for too long."

One pro-Disney source, who claimed that the "city is better off with four-diamond hotels than without," claimed that "all hell broke loose" when people learned of the tax rebate. This individual said that people accused the city of "crony capitalism." A Disney advocate identified this issue as a "turning point" in the relationship between residents and the city. This actor concluded the "wheels came off" after this deal, and people continued to regard the rebate as a "taxpayer giveaway." A person involved with Anaheim politics argued that Disney has "mega bucks, they don't need a tax incentive. The tax idea split the city. It was ugly around here. Residents got upset." Another informant called the people's reaction to the tax incentive "bonkers."

City staff and business leaders in the resort district argued that the subsidy would triple Anaheim's hotel tax revenue and increase sales and property taxes in the district.[8] Trade union leaders believed the subsidy would boost construction. Anaheim's community development director contended, "The resort, I cannot overstate it enough, this is the most significant economic engine for the city. . . . We've been trying to establish this (luxury) market for 15 years in Anaheim. We thought we could do it with a smaller incentive package, but we have not been able to do so."[9] He used a study from Visit Anaheim to make the following claims: "Each year, we are losing more than 100,000 visitors. Many of them are the high-end clientele and conventioneers. We're losing them to the coast and the danger is we're also losing them to Los Angeles. L.A. has a nice four-diamond market built around the Staples Center and their convention center." Mayor Tait responded, "If there was a market for luxury hotels here, they'd already be here."

In early 2016, Mayor Tait proposed the Let the People Vote Amendment, a change to the city charter that would mandate voter approval for alterations to occupancy taxes as economic assistance for hotel developments. If Tait's amendment passed, developers could only receive the 70% rebate on hotel bed taxes with voter approval. Tait speculated, "This will be a check written out of our general fund to each of these hoteliers. The developer can make the case to the voters. The voters are smart. If they want it, they will do it, but my guess is that they won't."[10] The city council voted 4–1 against this measure.

At a July 2016 meeting, the council voted 3–1 to award subsidies to two developers to build three luxury hotels.[11] Disney received one of them. It proposed a 700-room luxury hotel and parking structure at 1401 Disneyland Drive, which is located at the north end of Downtown Disney.[12] Disney planned to break ground on the property in 2018 and open in 2021.[13] At the time, the Disneyland Hotel and Disney's Grand Californian, which runs adjacent to Downtown Disney, were Anaheim's only four-diamond hotels. Mary Niven, senior vice president of Disneyland, claimed that Disney would not have built a new luxury hotel without the tax incentives. She also argued that the new hotels would provide "a new and direct revenue stream for the city to help pay for essential city services for its residents for decades to come." The Wincome Group received tax subsidies on a $208 million, 580-room hotel at 1700 S. Harbor Boulevard and a $225 million, 700-room hotel near the convention center.[14] Council Member Vanderbilt cast the lone dissenting vote. Mayor Tait would have voted no, but he left the meeting to take a flight to Washington, DC, to meet with President Barack Obama and other mayors and police chiefs about police-community relations. Tait wanted the vote postponed until he returned, but a majority of the council disagreed.

## Theoretical Touchstones

Intercity competition serves as Paul Peterson's central thesis.[15] The private perspective argues that cities compete against each other for mobile capital. During its negotiations with Anaheim, Disney emphasized the importance of its mobile capital and competition. It pitted Anaheim and Long Beach against each other to be the site of a second Disney park in Southern California. However, federal, state, and local regulations made it next to impossible for Disney to build a waterpark in Long Beach. Even though Long Beach was no longer in the picture, Disney continued to emphasize the importance of its mobile capital and reputational power. It communicated to Anaheim that unless the city gave the company what it wanted, Disney would allocate its resources to other parks and enterprises. Disney exercised reputational and financial power when it threatened to spend money in Long Beach or on other ventures. The company added a second city into the discussion of a new park to get Anaheim to meet its demands. Anaheim gave Disney what the company wanted in exchange for the construction of a second park. Advocates of the luxury hotel tax subsidy articulated points that conformed to the private perspective propositions. They contended that Anaheim competed against Los Angeles and other cities for conventioneers, and, without luxury hotels, the city lost one hundred thousand visitors to cities that had these kinds of accommodations. Proponents also seemed to suggest that the city had no alternative other than to concentrate on its main industry, tourism.

The private perspective emphasizes that urban economic development projects are not the source of contentious politics but instead produce collective goods for the community. In fact, many opposed Disney's development projects during this era. HOME and four local school districts opposed Disney's plans to expand because of the negative effects a second park would have on them. Proponents and opponents of affordable housing and the resort district fought each other to the point that the police had to be called. Some residents and members of the city council opposed the luxury tax subsidy and asked Anaheim to concentrate on neighborhoods, city services, and their interests. HOME believed that WestCOT would increase traffic, smog, and noise. The local schools argued that expansion would overwhelm them because employees at the new park would move to the area with their children and fill classrooms beyond capacity. Each of these complaints was familiar. Residents noted the negative effects of Disneyland on their quality of life. They also concluded that Disneyland increased demands on city services, which the company didn't subsidize with its taxes.

The private perspective claims that the economic environment, rather than politics, shapes urban public policy. The affordable housing and hotel tax subsidy issues suggest otherwise. Disney exercised relational, financial, and reputational power to win. Its political strength enabled Disney not only to limit development within the Anaheim resort to the kind that it endorsed but also to collect substantial land-use and tax benefits from the government. At the same time, the size and political capacity of supporters of more balance were growing. The power of pro-balance advocates did not match Disney's institutional capacity, but those with an alternative agenda challenged the corporate giant in unprecedented ways.

Inequality became a prominent theme in this era, and it drove change. Favoritism toward Disneyland and Anaheim Hills had produced two Anaheims. Disneyland and Anaheim Hills received special governmental attention. Areas with large percentages of Latinos suffered and lacked governmental resources. A member of the planning commission alleged that the city had neglected neighborhoods, schools, and housing while it paid too much attention to Disneyland. He claimed that "our neighborhoods are going to hell," while the city promulgated pro-Disney policies. The collective benefits that the private perspective argues extend from developmental policies, in this case, pro-Disneyland policies, did not materialize. Instead, the haves benefited and the have-nots suffered.

The evidence from the Anaheim Resort District suggests that developmental policies further the interests of Disneyland but do not promote the collective good. The advancement of the Two Anaheims thesis supports the idea that some parts of the city benefited from pro-Disney policies whereas others did not. Some voices in the city at this time pointed out the discrepancy and opposed deals for Disneyland, but they lacked power. They offered choices to the city, but Anaheim's leaders took the Disneyland route.

The public perspective questions the extent to which modern urban politics follows democratic theory. In Anaheim, HOME expressed similar reservations. The president of that homeowners group argued that the city's planning commission showed bias toward Disney. He believed that public hearings were a show, an illusion meant to suggest democracy, even though the pro-Disney results had been determined in advance. HOME asserted that the planning commission ignored resident complaints about the negative effects of Disneyland expansion on the city. The president of HOME concluded that the city council sold the voters down the river when that body approved the environmental study for WestCOT.

The public perspective argues that corporations threaten democracy because they play a dominant role in urban politics. Evidence of that threat can be seen in the case of the subsidies for luxury hotels. Disney and its allies won with three votes on the city council. On two occasions, opponents of the subsidy attempted to use democratic channels to have the electorate decide the fate of this issue and, both times, they failed. Disney prefers to operate within strictly defined arenas, and, in this case, the city council carried the corporate giant's policy preferences to victory.

Disneyland and its allies do not tend to use democracy as a primary political strategy. Instead, they try to limit public involvement and get things passed with as few people voting on an issue as possible. As a case in point, two members of the city council asked their colleagues to press pause and take an extra week to consider whether they wanted to prevent the people from deciding whether to tax a Disneyland ticket for decades. The three-person majority on the council disagreed and passed the gate tax ban, which would serve Disney's interests and limit public input. By contrast, Disney and its allies used democracy only when other channels did not work for them.

The public perspective finds that development policies produce unequal benefits. In Anaheim, opponents of the Disneyland expansion argued that many residents would suffer as Disney thrived. The school district's attorney claimed that economic growth benefited private industry while public education suffered. Homeowners near the park felt the negative effects of traffic, air quality, overcrowding, poor water quality, and the presence of mammoth parking garages in their neighborhoods. Small business owners also said that they suffered as Disneyland thrived. They complained that they had to pay additional taxes as part of the Anaheim Resort Maintenance District, even though it benefited Disneyland much more than their businesses. By contrast, the convention center and hotel industries constituted major winners from the building of a second Disney park. Government allocated $177 million to expand the convention center as part of its overall plan to improve the Anaheim Resort District and prepare for Disney's California Adventure.

As the public perspective argues, cities have choices. During the West-COT negotiations, Anaheim city officials showed the kind of agency that the public perspective argued municipal leaders possessed. Even city officials who supported Disneyland balked at giving in to Disney's demands. The city asked Disneyland to make more than sixty concessions in its designs. The pushback was real this time, and the city did not cave, even though it approved parts of the project. The city council also chose to oppose Disney and support low-cost housing in the Anaheim Resort District. In the end, Disney power prevailed, but officeholders in Anaheim made genuine choices to go in a direction opposite of the one favored by the entertainment power.

The fight for low-income housing in the resort district supports the public perspective's point that cities can be the locus of political activity. The pro-Disney side understood that only the local level could meet its desires, which is why it promoted two ballot measures, sued the city, and flooded city council meetings with its supporters. The pro-low-income housing coalition also sought to exercise influence through city politics. Its members packed city council meetings, protested, and led drives to inform people of the consequences of Disney's ballot measures. This kind of struggle exemplifies the public perspective's stance that the new urban politics is one in which various actors fight over who wins and loses as the backdrop to development policies.

Law professor Richard Schragger misses a couple of points about the new urban politics. First, this politics is not new. Political scientists Clarence Stone and Heywood Sanders and other commentators on urban politics have reported on anti-growth coalitions spanning the past half century.[16] In 1987, the Stone and Sanders case studies illustrated that development politics was far from unified. In Kalamazoo, Michigan, for example, empowered by a referendum and fearful of increased taxes, the electorate defeated the construction of a new mall in their city.[17] Homeowners believed that this construction would disrupt their quality of life and used the ballot to slow growth. Second, Anaheim struggled to enact redistributive policies because the forces in favor of such strategies lacked power. With its massive financial, reputational, relational, and landowning power, Disney navigated policy toward the resort district, in favor of its interests and away from redistribution. Disney exercised power to push back against and defeat its opponents. Cities cannot prioritize the public good unless the public possesses power.

People power proved insufficient in this era. Schragger does not show what happens when opponents of development attempt to set the agenda.

The partnership perspective draws intellectual attention to the importance of coalitions and relational power. HOME and local school districts opposed WestCOT. They complained that WestCOT would produce effects that city services couldn't handle. Disneyland maintained financial power because of its resources and organizational capacity. In the WestCOT case, city government did not give in to Disney's demands and instead used its land-use power to push back against Disneyland. Without government on its side, Disneyland was not as powerful as it had been in the founding of the park, promoting height restrictions, and blocking gate tax proposals. This case shows the power of city government. When the city of Anaheim exercised agency and asked Disney for certain concessions and rejected Disney's demands, the corporate giant wasn't as powerful.

In the case of the Anaheim Resort District and the creation of Disney's California Adventure, Disney's relational power consisted of Disney (obviously), the tourism industry, professional sports teams, and hoteliers, in addition to public actors, including the mayor, the deputy city manager, and most of the city council. The antiexpansion coalition didn't have the same kind of financial resources or relational power that Disney's alliance wielded. The opponents included some homeowners, a member of the planning commission, and the school district. The silent partners in this opposing coalition were both poorer residential neighborhoods and Latinos. Other potential allies in the anticoalition included the homeless and poor families. In his study of Los Angeles, sociologist Leland Saito finds that unions and faith-based groups, in addition to other community actors, low-income residents, and neighborhoods, counter the pro-growth coalition led by corporations and developers. Some of these actors had yet to engage the scene in Anaheim, by the early 2010s, but their might was on the way.

The pro-Disneyland coalition wielded resources, was bolstered by organizational capacity, and had many powerful partners. The pro-balance coalition included fewer players and controlled fewer resources than its Disneyland counterpart. But, from the 1990s to the early 2010s, the pro-balance forces broadened their coalition and became better organized. These strengths allowed them to fight Disney, although, ultimately, they suffered defeat. Disney skeptics, particularly service unions, had learned about the theme park's negative effects on their lives. To defeat this economic powerhouse, they would need to cultivate and exercise greater power more effectively.

While the partnership perspective presages the decline of Disney's power over time, it does not fully explain politics in this medium-size city. Disney still maintained the preponderance of political influence, and it was unwilling to collaborate with community groups during this period. For its part, the resistance to the Disneyland Imperative did not possess the resources necessary to compete against Disney at this point. The question became, Would they ever have enough resources to challenge Disney? Could they marshal enough power to become governing partners with Disney?

# Part II Conclusion

Social learning changed in Anaheim as people recognized that Disneyland produced negative consequences for them and the city. The time when nearly everyone accepted the argument that Disneyland provided for the collective good had passed. Even government actors argued that the city needed professional distance from the Disney Company.

Disney's power explains why the city sided with the company. Disney exercised relational, financial, and reputational power to set the agenda, but change characterized the Disneyland-Anaheim relationship from the 1990s to the early 2010s. As inequality increased, opposition to the Disneyland Imperative intensified, even though the city continued to promulgate pro-Disney policies. As time progressed, more people in Anaheim pushed back against preferential deals for Disneyland.

The city's relationship with Disneyland changed from the 1990s to the early 2010s. The city council opposed Disney on the issue of affordable housing, and this kind of conflict between these two entities hadn't occurred in the history of Disneyland. Pushback against Disney had reached new levels during this debate, which also featured a battle of ideas. Disney rejected the idea that it maintained responsibility for the creation or alleviation of the affordable housing shortage. Opponents believed that Disney had a social responsibility to its workers and the people in its home city to fix the problems caused and exacerbated by the theme park. The quiet partnership that Disney established with Anaheim at the inception of Disneyland was a thing of the past. The Disneyland Imperative maintained strength in Anaheim, but, by 2007, relational, financial, reputational, and landowning power facilitated it more than did an overarching belief that Disney saved the city. Raw power had replaced social learning.

Opponents of Disneyland continued their social and political learning after the debate over low-cost housing in the Anaheim Resort District. They labeled tax subsidies for luxury hotels as a corporate giveaway. The pro-balance coalition continued to believe that benefits for Disneyland did not enhance the collective good. In this second era, opponents regarded these measures as giveaways and corporate welfare. They also operated on the idea that they needed to take Anaheim back from Disneyland. These ideas served as the foundation for a new, counter-Disney social education and learning, which emphasized the effects of Disneyland on Anaheim and the city's neglect of issues that affected residents.

The pro-balance actors determined that they needed more power to defeat the economic behemoth. Disney and its allies had the capacity to place two initiatives on the ballot. By contrast, the pro-balance advocates could not get the requisite signatures to place the issue of tax subsidies for luxury hotels on the ballot. Their defeats within the city council highlighted the need for greater relational, financial, voting, and people power.

# III

# There, and Back Again

# Part III Introduction

A new politics emerged in Anaheim from the 2010s to the present. Through political learning, social education, and greater relational power, the pro-balance part of Anaheim's political order scored some significant policy victories. It used government to reject forms of preferential treatment for Disney. This empowered part of the political order also advanced governmental reform and paid more attention to how public policies affected marginalized communities, including Latinos, the working class, Disneyland employees, and the city's neighborhoods. Anaheim's city government showed it possessed the agency to choose a path that did not give undue advantage to Disney.

This new politics changed the terms of coexistence. It removed from the table tax breaks and government subsidies for Disney and its allies. It demanded that public and private actors explain how their actions advanced neighborhood interests. Disney learned that it could not ask government for as much as it was used to getting.

The People's Council, as the new city council came to be called, did not prioritize Disneyland in the same manner as its predecessors. Its reign did not last long because pro-Disney forces recaptured a majority of the city council seats in the next election. However, the People's Council established some boundaries for future city councils. Tax incentives and rebates were now the third rail of Anaheim politics. Touch these two topics and suffer grave consequences.

In the post–People's Council era, Disney narrowed its public wish list to zoning changes, which it received. Its allies received favored treatment as well, in part, because the pro-balance coalition could not match corporate power. Favorable treatment included generous government expenditures toward the chamber of commerce and the agreement to sell the baseball stadium and surrounding land to the Angels for what many considered to be below market price. An FBI investigation brought to light the preferential treatment received by Disney and the company's allies, and it toppled a mayoral administration and killed the proposed Angels Stadium.

# 8

# "Forgotten by the City"

*The Emergence of Latino Power*

On July 31, 1988, the headline in the *Orange County Register* read "Anaheim Hispanics growing in number, not political power."[1] Reporter Barbara Serrano described Anaheim's Latino community as "largely invisible to Anaheim's white power structure." She also characterized Latinos in Anaheim as "noticeably quiet, stymied by a lack of political organization and a city government that has not helped open the doors to citizen participation." Latinos in Anaheim lacked both descriptive and substantive representation. Across Anaheim's history, more members of the KKK (4) had served on the city council than had Latinos (3).[2] At the time of Serrano's story, no Latinos served on either the city council or the planning commission; Latinos represented 3 of the 129 people on Anaheim's boards and commissions. Only 1 had been appointed in the previous five years. During this period, Latinos made up about one-third of the city population and had increased from 17% of the population to 30.5% from 1980 to 1990.[3]

Advocates of greater Latino representation wanted to switch from at-large to district city council elections in the same manner that the civil rights movement of the 1960s called for an end to at-large elections. It was thought that Latinos would make up a majority in at least one of the city's voting districts. Serrano wrote that Latinos lacked voting power, in part, because they were young and recent immigrants. Less than half of the city's Latino population of twenty-two thousand were eligible to vote. Linda Ureno, a longtime resident and activist in Latino organizations, said of city government, "They totally disregard the Latino community. I don't think they view us as a viable group with any political impact, so consequently, we are to be ignored." Nonetheless, Council Member Miriam Kaywood expressed a different view: "I think (the community) has been quiet because needs have been met."

When asked about the lack of representation of Latinos on city boards and commissions, Council Member Kaywood contended, "To me, people are people." She blamed cultural differences for the reduced participation of Latinos in Anaheim politics. Kaywood claimed, "To get parents out to a meeting is almost an impossibility. The culture is different, and the women particularly don't do anything without the father's or husband's permission." She referred to Latino leaders who bring community issues to the city council as "a small group of confrontationalists who want to be fighting (with the city) all the time." Kaywood argued that Amin David, a local activist and the head of Los Amigos, "doesn't ask; he demands."

According to Serrano, "The City Council, Hispanic leaders say, is not doing enough to accommodate a more ethnically diverse community and address issues that will become increasingly crucial to residents: education, housing, jobs, childcare and gang violence." Serrano added, "Hispanics say they want a voice in directing the city's future. Yet no organized effort is under way to help them get a foot in the door." She concluded that "Hispanic community leaders blame themselves for not being more aggressive and better organized. But they also view city leaders as insensitive and politically repressive toward Hispanics."

## Flashpoints in the Relationship between Latinos and Police in Anaheim

When asked about divisions that exist in Anaheim a generation later, in 2020, one local source asserted that the largest division existed "between the minorities and city hall with law enforcement. We [the city] haven't been good." Several flashpoints provide historical context for this contentious relationship.[4] During what was known as the Little People's Park Riot of 1978, police who came to investigate gunshots by rival gangs at Little People's Park became aggressive with Latino youths, who were innocent bystanders. About thirty officers took on thirty-five to forty Latino youths.[5] In total, fifty people were injured, and twelve were arrested.[6] Among those who claimed police brutality was Alfred Acosta, who was dragged one hundred feet by the police.[7] The Orange County District Attorney's Office did not prosecute the police because, it claimed, the reaction by the officers was "necessary to meet force directed toward them." Subsequently, a federal jury awarded $60,500 in damages to Acosta, who had asked for $15 million. On appeal, a federal judge threw out the verdict. Regarding the general police response, a grand jury found "no clear evidence of indictable offenses." It also described "a clear-cut case of bad communication between citizens and those persons hired to protect and serve. The grand jury reminded the Anaheim Police Department that [its] allegiance is owed to every member of the public, regardless of socioeconomic status."

The city council held a meeting to discuss the riot and heard story after story of police abuse of Latinos.[8] At that hearing, Council Member William Kott proclaimed, "I'm appalled and can't help but wonder if this is America. We have heard enough evidence here, and something should be done." Anaheim Mayor John Seymour asserted, "I think the first steps that we have to take forward is one to admit that this great city of Anaheim has . . . a problem. Don't sweep it under the rug; don't look the other way. Admit that we have a problem." On August 23, 1978, in response to an invitation from the community, the city council held a meeting at Little People's Park. At the conclusion of that gathering, Seymour told the attendees to "stay organized and keep prodding." According to journalist Gustavo Arellano, "as with most political promises, little eventually happened."

Some changes did occur. Josie Montoya, a legendary local activist, organized protests after the riot at Little People's Park. In response to Montoya's activities, the police agreed to number their squad cars, have police officers hand out business cards upon request, and require officers to wear name badges.[9] Lieutenant Joe Vargas said, "Josie Montoya was a fitting example of grassroots activism. She was passionate about her causes."[10] According to Montoya, in response to her protests after the violence, "My name became a sore subject to people in Anaheim. I was labeled a rabble-rouser and a communist."[11] Another change in response to the civil disobedience was the creation of the Latino civil rights organization Los Amigos of Orange County.[12] Chicano artist Emigdio Vasquez painted a mural on the wall of a market that faces Little People's Park to commemorate the protests during the violence.[13]

For its part, the Anaheim Police Department claimed it did nothing wrong.[14] In February 1979, the police department released a report on its investigation of the Little People's Park Riot, and the new police chief claimed, "I believe that appropriate police policies and procedures were followed by our officers during the course of the riotous condition in which they found themselves. It is my strong recommendation that the incident now be considered closed by the Anaheim Police Department." Mayor Seymour followed suit and asserted that the police report "removes the cloud hanging over it." A U.S. Department of Justice report concluded that the Anaheim Police Department followed all laws. In the wake of the Little People's Park Riot, Mayor

Seymour removed Latino advocate Amin David from the city's planning commission, contending that David "politicized the Chicano community at every opportunity" and had a "negative rather than positive approach."

Another flashpoint came in the early 1990s when Officer Steve Nolan reported instances of police brutality against Latinos in Anaheim. He was fired. Nolan claimed that the department got rid of him because he broke the so-called code of silence.[15] The Department of Justice asserted that it lacked sufficient evidence to substantiate Nolan's claims about police abuse of Latinos.[16] An internal police review found that the police department did nothing wrong.[17] A Santa Ana jury did award $340,000 to Nolan because it found that the police had fired him because he reported abuse.[18] According to the *Los Angeles Times*, "The verdict galvanized a group of Latinos in the city who believe the reported incidents prove a pattern of racism and abuse by Anaheim police."[19]

In the mid-1990s, Anaheim was the first city in California and one of the first in the country to participate in a sixty-day pilot program through which two Immigration and Naturalization Service (INS) officers embedded in the local jail to check on the immigration status of those arrested.[20] During this period, 24% of those arrested in Anaheim were undocumented.[21] Council Member Zemel contended, "The Police Department is bringing the criminals to the INS' doorstep. To say that's not a good system flies in the face of what their mission is. We can make a difference here."[22] Council Member Tait argued that the presence of INS agents in the jails helped decrease crime. He proclaimed, "The program has been working. If it didn't, I wouldn't be for it. Everybody goes through it. It's not based on race or ethnicity."[23] He also claimed, "It's an effective criminal-identification measure, and anything that helps reduce crime in Anaheim, I am for it." Tait, who partnered with Zemel to bring the INS program to Anaheim, thought it "would be crazy" to end the program after sixty days.[24] The program did end at that point. Tait cited the city's 40% drop in crime since 1994 as evidence that this program disrupted criminal activity, even though crime had decreased across the country at the same time.[25] The backdrop to this controversy and Latino-city relations at this time was a gang membership that had increased in Anaheim since 1993 and was estimated at more than five thousand in 1996.[26]

Latinos and the police expressed radically different views of police tactics to control crime and gangs in the city. A year after the INS program ended, an Anaheim police lieutenant contended, "What keeps gang crime from getting out of control again are exactly the firm tactics we've been using. And yes, it's probably going to irritate the gang members a little bit, and it's probably going to irritate their family members and their friends. But I think our actions speak for themselves. We don't trample all over civil rights."[27] The approach, popularized by the zero-tolerance tactics of the New York Police

Department under William Bratton, blurred the lines between public safety and the protection of civil rights.

In the mid-1990s, Montoya said of Latinos' views of the police in Anaheim, "There is a growing anger, a frustration, it's close to the point of explosion. I pray every day that some changes are made before an officer or a youngster is seriously hurt." Speaking on relations between Latinos and police in Anaheim at the same time, the director of the Orange County Human Relations Council claimed, "The gulf between them is pretty large. It's a problem of a tough history to overcome, and a problem of the balancing act between how the police can be tough on crime while changing their ways of dealing with people to account for the changing city." As seen across America, middle-class residents typically supported the police chief's firm tactics to control crime. The divisions over policing and Latino civil liberties presaged the Two Anaheims. Montoya was right about the anger, frustration, and an explosion, but the boiling point was still close to fifteen years away.

In 1999, former Anaheim police officer Harald Martin, who at the time was a member of the Anaheim Union High School District Board, proposed that the district bill Mexico $50 million to educate the students who were undocumented.[28] By a count of 4–1, the board passed a measure that would bill a foreign nation if the school district educated an undocumented student from that country of origin. The Department of Justice concluded that the school board lacked the legal standing to carry out this policy, and the issue died. Two years later, Martin, still a board member, introduced a measure to require the district's students to prove they were American citizens. The school board voted 4–1, with Martin as the lone dissent, to drop the issue when corporation counsel advised it that this action was illegal.[29]

A year later, then City Manager Jim Ruth asked Police Chief Roger Baker to prepare a dossier on some of the city's Latino leaders.[30] The chief conducted a link analysis that attempted to connect Latino leaders, including Amin David, to suspected criminals.[31] Richard Chavez, a firefighter and labor activist, was also a subject of the link analysis, in part, because he had a contentious relationship with Ruth.[32] Lorri Galloway, the director of Eli Home, a service-providing organization for abused and at-risk children and their families, was investigated because of her strong connection with Chavez.[33] Chavez won a city council seat in 2002, and Galloway joined him on the council two years later.[34] The city council reviewed the thirty-six-page Baker report behind closed doors.[35] The report was reminiscent of McCarthyism or the old days of FBI dossiers. When the state's attorney general's office investigated the link analysis, it concluded, "Even if these assumptions are made in Chief Baker's favor, he still demonstrated extremely poor judgment in using a link chart." According to Adam Elmahrek of the *Voice of OC*, "The existence of the dossier became symbolic of the Anaheim Latino community's plight. It was clear evidence, said David and other activists, of an orchestrated plan by the city government to stifle dissent."

## Displacement of Latinos in Anaheim

Redevelopment projects had also exerted negative effects on Anaheim's Latino community. Anaheim redeveloped the Chevy Chase neighborhood and, as a result, dislocated two hundred families.[36] Estimates indicated that Latinos made up about 90% of the families in Chevy Chase. Amin David referred to this redevelopment plan as the "Chevy Chase Dislocation Program," and he wrote that "Los Amigos of Orange County and its many friends will resist and make every effort to defeat [it]."[37] Of the redevelopment of Chevy Chase, David also concluded, "It's part of an overall plan to gentrify the . . . area. To get rid of the minorities, have the place redone under the auspices of beautification and raise rents. That's where it's going. . . . This is the undercurrent. We're petrified at the thought this is the way they're going to do it. They are going to get rid of the people."[38] Nativo Lopez, an activist, asserted, "These people (the city) are trying to stop the inevitable. They are trying to stop the concentration of immigrant families in the county." He also explained, "Anyone just has to go take a ride around Disneyland to find Disneyland is living in a sea of immigrants."[39]

In 2000, Anaheim redeveloped the Jeffrey-Lynne neighborhood, located just west of Disneyland, into Hermosa Village.[40] Jeffrey-Lynne was more than 90% Latino and low-income; it was also the site of heavy gang activity and high crime. While the Anaheim Redevelopment Agency claimed that the purpose of this redevelopment was to provide for safer and more sanitary conditions for residents, but, in fact, the city displaced hundreds of Latino residents and up to 40% of the neighborhood to make this project a reality. *OC Weekly* referred to this project as "ethnic cleansing."[41] According to one source, "The result of the renovation was an affordable gated community that looked nothing like the old, rundown Jeffrey-Lynne neighborhood."[42] While calls for police services decreased in the rebranded Hermosa Village, fear of redevelopment and displacement increased among local Latinos.

Another critical event occurred in 2001, when Anaheim's planning commission rejected Gigante grocery store's application for a liquor license in Anaheim Plaza.[43] Lisa Stipkovich, the executive director of the city's redevelopment agency, told both Gigante and Anaheim Plaza management, "Our research has confirmed that Gigante is a more specialized supermarket that does not cater to the public at large." Stipkovich wrote that Gigante's "product selection catered primarily to the Hispanic market." According to urban planning scholar Stacy Anne Harwood, "Though the question of whether

Gigante should receive a liquor license was procedurally appropriate, the denial represented a rejection of the legitimacy of Latinos as members of the public at large. In the context of Anaheim's history of anti-immigrant and anti-Mexican attitudes, to the supporters of Gigante, the planners and the planning commission looked guilty of discrimination."[44] Communication professors Tracey Quigley Holden and Sandra L. French concluded, "Rejection of Gigante as an anchor store in Anaheim Plaza as 'too Spanish' mirrors the rejection of the Hispanic culture and identity demanded of the area's Hispanic residents."[45] Mayoral candidate Curt Pringle supported the liquor license for Gigante.

## Demonstrations in 2012

The relationship between Latinos and the police seemed to improve under Police Chief John Welter, who took over in 2004.[46] The new chief adopted some elements of the community-policing model, including substations and officers on bikes, and used regular meetings with Latino leaders to build trust between the department and Latinos. In 2005, Amin David said, "I truly believe there's a renaissance going on in the Anaheim Police Department with Chief Welter coming in."[47] However, tensions increased following an uptick of police shootings of Latinos. Latino leaders made regular visits to the city council to complain about the shootings, and six Latino families started weekly protests in front of police headquarters in 2010.[48] These flashpoints helped convince Latinos and others that police and overall governance needed to change in Anaheim. They all led to 2012.

In June 2012, the ACLU of Southern California sued Anaheim because it claimed that the city's system of at-large elections discriminated against Latinos and violated the state's Voting Rights Act.[49] Jose Moreno, Amin David, and Consuelo Garcia were the three plaintiffs. Four of the five members of the city council at the time lived in Anaheim Hills.[50] The ACLU stated in the lawsuit that in the history of Anaheim, only three Latinos had ever been elected to the city council (even though Anaheim was then 53% Latino).[51] Historically, at-large elections favor whites over traditionally excluded groups.[52] One pro-balance source argued that "racial discrimination is inherent in at-large elections." The ACLU contended that reform would produce at least one majority Latino district.[53]

One Latino leader concluded, "It's hard to run citywide; you can't cover the city with volunteers. With at-large elections, you need special interests to put you in office. Districts shrink the area so you can go door-to-door." Another Latino leader claimed that districts allow us to "stand up to corporate candidates who get thousands of dollars from Disney in independent expenditures. We can't take that on." When asked whether there was a time that everyone got together behind an issue, a local Latino leader responded, "district elections."

A month after the filing of the voting rights lawsuit, Anaheim police shot and killed two Latinos on consecutive days.[54] The first fatality occurred on Anna Drive in Anaheim's predominantly Latino east side when Anaheim Police Department fired on unarmed Manuel Angel Diaz, who was running away from the police at the time.[55] The police union claimed that Diaz was shot because he reached for something in his waistband.[56] The police never found a weapon.[57] According to one report, "Diaz was stopped and chased by police for unknown reasons, was reportedly shot in the leg and back of the head, then handcuffed and left lying on the lawn of a residential apartment building while officers searched for evidence. He later died at the hospital and many residents insist valuable time in trying to save his life was lost."[58] Protests began immediately along Anna Drive as people threw bottles at the police. Officers shot beanbag rounds, used to stun and stop their targets, into the crowd, and a "police dog broke free and attacked protesters."[59]

The day after Diaz's death, police shot and killed Joel Mathew Acevedo after Acevedo had fired at an Anaheim police officer.[60] Two days after the Acevedo shooting, a thousand protesters demonstrated in two locations—close to city hall and about a mile away from city hall.[61] They threw rocks, bricks, bottles, shoes, and traffic cones at police, started fires in dumpsters, smashed storefront windows, and looted the Anaheim Towne Center mall.[62] After the police declared an unlawful assembly and told the crowd to disperse, they fired nonlethal projectiles into the crowd as people ran down the street.[63] On July 29, 2012, approximately fifty people protested the shootings outside of Disneyland's main entrance.[64] On the same day, about four hundred protesters marched in front of the police department and city hall; nine were arrested.[65] The protests lasted more than a week and resulted in dozens of arrests.[66]

On August 10, 2012, the Anaheim Police Department conducted Operation Halo, a sweep for gangs that occurred mainly in Latino neighborhoods.[67] The action resulted in thirty-three arrests and the confiscation of forty guns and close to twelve pounds of crystal methamphetamine. Latino leaders believed that the police used this sweep to reassert the department's force over Latinos in the city. One Latino activist asserted, "I think they're doing a payback to the community. They're trying to tell us that they're the ones that control Anaheim. They want us to be afraid." In response, the police claimed that they needed to act when they did. According to Police Chief Welter, "We decided we couldn't put this off any longer. We can't wait until another person gets shot."

In the aftermath of the demonstrations, people tried to understand what happened. Decades of mistreatment and abuse at the hands of the police tell part of the story. One Latino-based news organization described the Anaheim Police Department as a "trigger-happy police force."[68] Statistics supported its claims. The number of times that the Anaheim police had opened fire on civilians and the number of civilian deaths because of the police had increased over time.[69] At the time of the Diaz and Acevedo shootings in late July 2012, the police had fired in the line of duty a total of eight times in that year alone.[70] The police shot four times in 2011 and once in 2010. After the two deaths in July, the number of people killed by police in Anaheim had risen to five that year.

Police brutality was one of many reasons for the demonstrations of 2012.[71] Latinos also continued to face extreme underrepresentation in all aspects of city government, including on the police force, city council, boards, and commissions. Latinos believed that the political system had failed them. According to one Latino resident, "We have been forgotten by the city. We're put into a system that is doomed to fail us."

Inequality also explained the protests. Latinos and others in the city disliked how Anaheim city government and the police department focused public resources and attention on Disneyland and the Anaheim Resort District. One Latino leader said that Latinos "live in the shadows in working poverty neighborhoods" in Anaheim. According to Alejandro Moreno of Los Amigos of Orange County, "There are more police dedicated to making sure that those resort areas are crime free rather than the rest of the Latino communities in Orange County. These people want to create 'the happiest place on earth' and have Latinos come and help and clean up, but they don't want them living there because they say they don't look good, and don't take care of their homes."[72] The attorney for the Diaz family claimed that the police and the government treated people differently based on race, ethnicity, and class. She argued, "Police don't roust white kids in affluent neighborhoods who are just having a conversation. And those kids have no reason to fear police. But young men with brown skin in poor neighborhoods do."[73]

The protests were also a comment on power. As one journalist wrote, Latinos were "at best marginalized and at worst oppressed in their own neighborhoods."[74] A number of Latino leaders in Anaheim asserted that resort workers and Latinos, who, in many instances, were one and the same, were marginalized in the city. Despite all the promises of what Disneyland and development could do for the residents of Anaheim, Latinos in the city did not have representation, and the resort district did not serve their needs. The city chose to focus on where Latinos worked as opposed to where Latinos lived. The protests served as another sign that Latinos knew that the government's focus on Disneyland, the Anaheim Resort District, and Anaheim Hills did not work for them. According to Alejandro Moreno of Los Amigos of Orange County, "The people here who hold the power, don't want to let it go, and Latinos have finally had it."[75] Latinos and advocates for district elections used the shootings and protests to organize and place these issues on the public agenda.

## UNITE HERE! Local 11

A major change occurred because of mistreatment over the years and the latest tension with the police. UNITE HERE! Local 11, a service union representing many resort workers, got involved in Anaheim politics and empowered groups marginalized by the Disneyland Political Order. According to Jose Moreno, this union "realized that workers deserve a voice in their neighborhood, not just the workplace." Moreno contended that, on their own, Latinos and residents in neighborhoods "can't get it done," but the financial and people power of unions in combination with demographic power locally can bring about change. UNITE HERE! became more involved after the police shootings, and it helped to switch local elections from at-large to district, oppose a tax subsidy for luxury hotels, and pass a living wage ordinance. UNITE HERE! helped found and finance OCCORD, which also provided organizational capacity for Anaheim residents excluded by the Disneyland Imperative.

In August 2012, Mayor Tait proposed that the city council approve a measure to allow voters to decide whether the city should switch to district elections.[76] At a population of about 336,000, Anaheim was California's largest city to employ at-large elections.[77] Former Mayor Pringle and the chamber of commerce opposed district elections. They were core members of the Disneyland Political Order. In their official statement against the switch to district elections, Pringle, Chamber of Commerce President and CEO Todd Ament, and others wrote, "Currently, all Anaheim citizens vote for all council seats. If Measure L passes, you'll have one city council representative, not four. It's a system designed by politicians, for politicians. Maybe that's why no actual neighborhood group leader signed their ballot argument? Measure L carves up a great city. It pits Anaheim against itself instead of uniting us."[78]

Disneyland supported this change. Before the city council voted on the matter, Resort President George Kalogridis wrote a letter to city officials in which he stated the following: "We believe that city leadership should reflect the diversity of its entire population. We support a City Council elected from districts and encourage the city of Anaheim to move from at-large elections to district voting. This shift will allow each valued neighborhood to be represented by a local member of their choosing."[79] Disney's supporters emphasize that the company contributed $50,000 in support of the passage of the district measure. Disney's critics argue that the company remained quiet about the switch to district elections for most of the time and made its feelings known and the contribution at the end of the debate when the outcome became clear. According to one pro-balance leader, "When we were pushing for district elections, Disney was very quiet. They were not involved until the very end when they said they were in support of district elections." Another added, "Disney put out a letter saying it supported district elections. District elections were heavily favored by a lot of unions, so Disney realized they'd be stepping into a battle with their own cast members." In terms of the resources that Disney can and has provided, $50,000 is not a huge commitment. Despite Disneyland's public position, the city council voted 3–2 against the proposal.[80]

The civilian shootings and district election issues reinforced the idea that there were Two Anaheims. In an interview with Reuters, Mayor Tait concluded, "I think there's a feeling of many people that there's not one Anaheim, and maybe a sense of not belonging and feeling that they don't own their government, and none of that's good."[81] Census data and survey statistics supported Tait's assertion about Two Anaheims.[82] An OCCORD study found that approximately 60% of households in the predominantly Latino areas of west and central Anaheim earned less than $50,000 a year. By contrast, 75% of households in Anaheim Hills made $50,000 or more annually. OCCORD also reported that West Anaheim had less than five parks per fifty thousand whereas Anaheim Hills was home to eleven parks per fifty thousand.[83]

In July 2013, the ACLU and citizens' suit against Anaheim received a court date for March 17, 2014.[84] Faced with a legal bill of $1.45 million and rising, in January 2014, the city council decided to settle with the ACLU.[85] The plaintiffs agreed to drop their lawsuit against the city, and, in exchange, the city council voted to allow the city's electorate to determine if it preferred district elections. The electorate would also consider whether to expand the number of members of the city council to six.

In November 2014, the district elections issue passed with 68.3% of the vote, while the measure to increase the city council to six garnered 53.1%.[86] Jose Moreno, one of the three plaintiffs in the voting rights case and president of the Anaheim City School District, referred to the outcome as "an overwhelming display by the voters that it was time to modernize our electoral system and provide a voice for residents who have felt neglected, ignored, and disrespected by the current system."[87]

In February 2016, the city council accepted a committee's recommended district map, which Latino advocacy groups and unions referred to as the People's Map.[88] Latinos did not make up a majority in any of the six districts but constituted a plurality in half of the districts. Mayor Tait claimed, "This map is not perfect for any one group . . . but these are all estimates with a margin of error of 3 or 4 percent." For the November 2016 city council election, voters in the three plurality-Latino districts and a district on Anaheim's western edge would elect their members of the city council. Elections for the mayor and the other two seats would be held in November 2018. Of the switch to district elections, one prominent pro-balance leader asserted, "At least our side now has a chance to win." Disney's opponents assumed that the change to district elections would allow their grassroots allies to compete with the hundreds of thousands of dollars that Disney could spend on campaigns.

## 2016 Election

Heading into the November 2016 city council election, candidates backed by Disney held a 3–2 advantage on the council.[89] Disney contributed $1.22 million to PACs involved in the 2016 Anaheim City Council election.[90] Disney-backed candidates outspent their opponents by wide margins. In District 1, Steve Chavez Lodge outspent Denise Barnes, $281,430 to $59,852. In the District 3 race, incumbent Jordan Brandman received $330,358 in campaign contributions as compared to Jose F. Moreno's $85,363. Incumbent Lucille Kring outspent her opponent Arturo Ferreras, $271,792 to $63,334, in District 4. In the open seat race in District 5, Stephen Faessel outspent Mark Lopez, $293,093 to $52,793. Disney-supported candidates won two of the four council seats but lost their majority on the council. Barnes and Moreno joined Tait and Vanderbilt to form what some residents and the media began to call, "The People's Council."[91] Many saw Moreno's victory as a sign of the importance of district elections to Latino political power. One source acknowledged, "Latinos had little role in Anaheim politics before district [elections]. They couldn't beat back all that Disney money or special interests, like police and fire."[92] Another concluded that the wins by Moreno and Barnes showed "the promise of district elections."[93]

The question that emerged during and after the campaign was whether the council would support Disney or the neighborhoods and the people who lived in them.[94] After the election, Mayor Tait, who now led a majority on the council for the first time, claimed, "It's the City Council's job to prioritize how we spend. When you give away taxpayer money to hotel developers, we're not spending it in the community." Council Member Kris Murray believed that pro-Disney policies advanced the collective good. She contended, "Anaheim has been successful because of the economic programs that have been set in place. The Anaheim way has always been to partner with the business industry to grow the local economy. Not only does the city benefit, but other surrounding cities and the county." Tait responded, "We want to be very business friendly. We don't want to be just about giving to Disney or big businesses in the resort. We want to equally support small businesses and make it easier for them to grow, expand and create jobs." The neighborhoods versus the corporate giant narrative began before this election and would continue well afterward.

## Anaheim's New Politics

A new politics had emerged in so many ways during this period in Anaheim's history. Decades of mistreatment and neglect led to the political awakening of Latinos. Organizations like Los Amigos of Orange County, OCCORD, and leaders and workers within those entities mobilized and educated Latinos and others in Anaheim. Latinos claimed that the Disneyland Imperative failed to serve them; they helped make district elections a reality to make way for a new governing arrangement and, thereby, change the city's political order. Change it, they did. In the first election by districts, Disney lost its ironclad grip on the city council majority. Could the new council change the city's focus from Disneyland to those discordant interests excluded by the Disneyland Political Order? Disney's entrenched interests in Anaheim remained. Would the corporate giant accede to the new political landscape, change how it exercised power, or revert to old patterns? The next several years provided many opportunities for Disney to show how it would react to the new politics.

# 9

## The People's Council

P ublic policy and rhetoric changed under the new city council, which many referred to as the People's Council. In its first meeting, the new council ended subsidies to developers who planned to build four-diamond hotels in the future, but the preexisting hotel subsidies stayed in place.[1] The council also ended a proposed streetcar project that would have shuttled people from the Anaheim Regional Transportation Intermodal Center (ARTIC) to Disneyland and the convention center. In January 2017, by a vote of 6–1, the new council passed a resolution "expressing opposition to a streetcar system in Anaheim."[2] The previous council supported the streetcar by a margin of 3–2.[3] New Council Member Denise Barnes referred to the streetcar project as a "$300-million boondoggle." At her swearing-in ceremony, she proclaimed, "This is an opportunity for a new City Council to come together and put the good of Anaheim residents first ahead of special interest or political agendas."[4] The new council canceled the city's $67,000 per year contract with the chamber of commerce.[5] Council Member Kris Murray responded, "This is being hostile to the business community. There's a number of programs that they've helped."

Prior to the election of the new city council, Disneyland announced plans for an eastern gateway, which would include a new seven-story parking structure with sixty-nine parking spaces, a security checkpoint, and a pedestrian bridge over Harbor Boulevard.[6] Disneyland proposed the twenty-three-acre development as part of its $1 billion commitment to the city in exchange for the continuation of no gate tax. Disney had purchased the Carousel Inn and

Suites on Harbor Boulevard and additional land for more than $100 million to construct this new gateway.[7]

Businesses on Harbor Boulevard believed the bridge would allow park visitors to go from their cars to the park without walking past their premises.[8] At the time of the proposal, thousands of people walked past restaurants, hotels, shops, and convenience stores on their way to the park. Disneyland needed a myriad of approvals from Anaheim public entities, but the city council maintained the ultimate authority over the project.[9] One political actor speculated of Disney and the eastern gateway, "I guess they would have gotten approval before" the new council. Under the People's Council, however, the passage of plans to support Disneyland at the expense of local businesses, many of them small businesses, was much less certain. The Merchants Coalition estimated that this development would have affected more than twenty-five businesses and about ten thousand hotel guests per day.

Less than a year after the voters of Anaheim elected a new city council, Disneyland canceled its plans to build a new eastern gateway.[10] Disney shifted its focus to the western end of the resort, where it built the sixty-five-hundred-space Pixar Pals Parking Structure adjacent to the Mickey and Friends Parking Structure. The individuals who had served as the city attorney, city manager, and planning commissioners when Disneyland proposed the eastern gateway no longer held those positions. Anaheim's political order had changed, and this transformation had consequences for the Walt Disney Company.

Mayor Tait claimed he aimed to help Disney but did not want the company to have undue influence. For example, he favored the swift approval of code changes that allowed Disney to expand and sought to eliminate codes that were a needless impediment to Disney's progress because he believed that the company's success served the city's interest. However, he also argued that the relationship between the corporate giant and the city had gotten out of balance in recent years. Tait supported the new parking structure but drew the line at subsidies. He didn't want to give anything to Disney at the expense of the people, and he decided that subsidies like those granted to Disney by the previous council were now off the table. When asked whether he thought balance between Disneyland and neighborhoods was possible, Mayor Tait responded, "Yes. I thought we did it."

Another major change in policy came when the new council asked for and received the resignation of City Manager Paul Emery.[11] The council vote split 4–3 along pro-balance and pro-Disney lines. Tait's coalition carried the day. Three weeks after Emery's resignation, Tait acknowledged, "We [the new council] were looking for a change in direction. This [decision] is a strong pivot toward the neighborhoods." During the previous city council term, Tait had opposed Emery's focus on the Anaheim Resort District but couldn't enact change because he was in the minority on that body.[12] Emery had recommended the deal that banned a gate tax for up to forty-five years.

Not everyone agreed with the new narrative that the city's long-standing focus on Disneyland produced negative consequences for the city.[13] One pro-Disney leader concluded, "Politics is more complex than Disney versus the neighborhoods. Resort success doesn't take away from neighborhoods, as Tom Tait and Jose Moreno contend. The resort pays for neighborhood amenities. Every city in Orange County has raised sales tax by ballot measure, not Anaheim." Another pro-Disney source concurred, "Tait and Moreno somehow convinced people that resort success takes away from neighborhoods." Many pro-Disney people emphasize how Disneyland has allowed Anaheim to not increase the local sales tax, whereas the city's neighbors have raised their sales taxes. A Disney-financed report by economists at Cal State Fullerton's Woods Center for Economic Analysis and Forecasting estimated that the Disneyland Resort produced an $8.5 billion economic impact and generated 78,299 jobs in Southern California.[14] It concluded that Anaheim spent more per resident than Santa Ana without raising additional taxes.

When asked about the Disney versus neighborhood tension, another leader asserted, "That's blatantly false. On every metric—gangs, criminal activity, graffiti, human trafficking—the neighborhoods have improved because of the resort district." One pro-Disney leader declared, "Disney is the largest tax contributor. We have low-income residents, immigrants, and undocumented people who need city services and don't have to pay out of pocket because of the resort district. Disneyland is a sexy target, but when you dig in, it's misinformation." Pro-Disney actors continued to believe and advocate that what was good for the park and resort district was good for the rest of the city. The majority on the council now advanced an alternative narrative.

The removal of City Manager Paul Emery and Mayor Tom Tait's vow to pay attention to neighborhoods began a contentious discourse in the *Orange County Register* among those who saw pro-Disney policies as beneficial for the city and Tait, who did not. On July 30, 2017, Lucy Dunn, president and CEO of the Orange County Business Council, wrote an opinion piece in the *Orange County Register*, the title of which was "Anaheim: Instability Breeds Instability."[15] Dunn described Anaheim's economic picture in the following way: "By any reasonable measure, Anaheim is thriving with a recent infusion of $6 billion in private investment. Tax revenues are way up, despite not having a local utility users' tax and no sales tax increases as recently passed by four other local cities. Tourism is strong as are other industry sectors." Dunn concluded that Anaheim had "an embarrassment of riches" because "the creation of thoughtful planning and the wisdom of previous elected leaders and city managers, generates a net positive cash flow to Anaheim of over $80 million per year." If the revenue from the Resort District disappeared, Dunn argued, then the city would have "fewer police officers, closed parks and libraries, less community outreach." Pro-Disney actors now emphasized how the Disneyland Imperative promoted the collective good and facilitated and improved city services.

Yet, many residents and leaders ask a question like this one, "If Disney is an economic engine, why can't I get my sidewalk fixed." One popular answer to the sidewalk question was that the city did not effectively use the resources it already had in hand. One longtime observer of Disney politics asked, "Why is it Disney's fault that the city hasn't prioritized?" One political actor claimed that Anaheim should have gold-plated fire hydrants because of the resources that Disney provided. Another asked, "Why aren't we the best place without an ocean to live in Orange County?"

Mayor Tait offered his response to Dunn in a column titled, "Anaheim: Change for Good."[16] He claimed, "elections matter," and voters sent a clear message in November: "Pay attention to neighborhoods, not just lobbyists and well-connected businesses." He called for a change in culture and practice. "For many years," Tait wrote, "the city has paid too much attention to special interests in the Anaheim Resort District at the expense of our neighborhoods." Tait acknowledged that the city needed to support the Resort District, and he claimed that it did. "What's been missing is balance," he wrote. "The November election was about restoring focus on our neighborhoods and ending deals that benefit just those that employ particular lobbyists." As examples of imbalance, Tait listed the luxury hotel tax rebate and the deal to exempt "the Disneyland Resort from paying taxes on admission or parking for up to 45 years." Tait wrote, "Strong neighborhoods attract business and investment, as companies locate where their employees want to live. There are many obvious examples throughout Southern California." He concluded with this statement: "After decades of investing in the Anaheim Resort, it is time to also invest in the 360,000 residents of Anaheim, who look to the council to protect their best interests."

A week after Tait's opinion piece, Council Member Murray followed with one titled, "Focused on Taxpayers and Neighborhoods."[17] After Murray trumpeted that Anaheim hadn't imposed new taxes or fees to maintain services since the Great Recession of 2008, she claimed that "Anaheim's economic model has worked for decades." She referred to the choice between investment in either neighborhoods or the Anaheim Resort as a false narrative. She wrote, "The city can expand dedicated services to our neighborhoods because we have a thriving tourism industry. The added benefit is that Anaheim taxpayers pay less out of pocket for these services."

Murray concluded that the Anaheim Resort, the convention center, Angel Stadium, and Honda Center "serve our residents by providing funding for the services they expect and deserve without adding to the local expense of Anaheim taxpayers." This three-piece op-ed exchange illustrated how actors on both sides of the Disneyland divide attempted to socially educate the citizenry on the value of their policy approach. Tait's version of reality won out in 2016, but the former leaders of the Disneyland Political Order aimed to regain the narrative upper hand and reassert their control of city government.

For Mayor Tait and the new majority on the city council, the 2016 election signaled a sea change in Anaheim politics. Voters had grown tired of giveaways to Disneyland and wanted the city to focus on its neighborhoods. This narrative established that investments in Disneyland benefited Disney and not residents in the neighborhoods. Representatives of big business and members of the new minority on the city council argued that Disneyland and the Resort District provided collective benefits. Unions, nonprofits like OCCORD, community groups such as Los Amigos of Orange County, and individuals including Amin David also served as agents of social learning, and they possessed a new form of relational power.

The 2016 election and the conflict over its meanings revealed that the various rungs of the Disneyland Political Order were in conflict and flux. The Business Council, SOAR, the Anaheim Police Association, the building trades, Visit Anaheim, hoteliers, the Anaheim Chamber of Commerce, and conservative Republican members of the city council supported the Disneyland Imperative. A new mayor, progressives, service unions, the school board, Latinos, and residents in most neighborhoods sought greater balance and a new agenda. When asked to describe the divisions in Anaheim, one respondent asserted, "It's all communities versus large industry." Another contended, "It's business versus those screwed by business." One prominent actor claimed that the divisions were "special interests versus diffuse interests of the common good." A prominent pro-Disney leader concluded, "Anaheim got where it did because of the relationship between the city and entrepreneurs. The city embraced and joined entrepreneurs for the better of the community." These varying opinions now clashed in ways that they had not previously because the pro-balance ring of the political order now held power commensurate with its agenda.

## The Anaheim News Desert

Many leaders, regardless of whether they supported Disney, recognized that Anaheim had become a news desert, a place where people struggled to get information about the city.[18] Anaheim lacks a television station and most residents rely on news outlets based in Los Angeles. "We don't have our own news," acknowledged one local contact. The number of papers that cover

Anaheim has declined over time, and even the *Orange County Register* pro-vides less coverage than in the past. The trend of dwindling news coverage has impacted the ability of the citizenry to follow local issues.[19] According to one interviewee, "Even the city council meetings don't have reporters at them all the time." This individual bemoaned the loss of papers like the *Anaheim Bulletin*, the *Anaheim Gazette*, and the *Santa Ana Register*, which either went out of business or were purchased by larger news companies. Another leader noted that the *Los Angeles Times* no longer has an Orange County bureau and barely covers Anaheim and Santa Ana. This person ar-gued that "Disney propaganda has increased and reliable information has decreased" over time. When asked how people learn about Anaheim, one source claimed, "Getting information to the people in Anaheim is hard. We don't have our own television station, our paper [*Orange County Register*] has shrunk to nothing. It's hard to communicate with the people and hard to extract information from them." According to one pro-balance leader, "Less press isn't best, unless you benefit, like Disney."

Others complained about the close relationship between Disney and the *Orange County Register*. One contended that "the *Orange County Register* is pro-Disney and pro-business. They don't provide critical coverage of gov-ernment and the business community." Another leader proclaimed, "There's no strong independent media who would question these deals. When the city decided not to tax the gate at Disneyland because of Star Wars Land, you should have seen the headline in the *Orange County Register*. It was big-ger than the headline announcing the end of World War II." Another long-time observer of city affairs alleged, "The *Orange County Register* is pro-Disney and pro-business. Its coverage of Star Wars Land was uncritical." This individual continued, "There's no critical coverage of local government and the business community." These views align with the work of journalist and media expert Robert E. Gutsche, who has concluded that local newspa-pers practice a form of civic boosterism that excludes any negative discus-sion of the dominant social mores of a place.[20]

Pro-balance leaders often mentioned that the *Voice of OC*, a nonprofit news source, provided critical coverage of Anaheim government, politics, and business. One applauded the work of *Voice of OC*'s Nick Gerda and col-leagues on the ways in which Disney funneled money through various PACs to support their candidates and defeat pro-balance actors. This individual was amused by the *Voice of OC*'s use of a graphic that featured Mickey Mouse, complete in his sorcerer's outfit, pushing money into a funnel of PACs. On the other side of Mickey stood the candidates who received Disney PAC money and those who were the objects of attack ads financed by it.[21]

In the absence of significant media coverage, local leaders maintained the importance of direct communication, such as campaign mailers, to enhance the social learning of Anaheim residents. The glossy cards provide a direct voice for campaigns, interest groups, political parties, PACs, and other entities to be dropped in voters' mailboxes around election time. Disney helps finance many mailers and their content. One source concluded, "The biggest barrier to having a minority voice in the city is the thousands of dollars Disney spends on glossy mailers. They have infinite cash. It's truly disgusting." Both sides relied on direct communication with voters, but, given the Disney resources, Disney's allies were better able to educate and mobilize via mailers.

Both before the People's Council took power, in 2017, and in the era of this council, Mayor Tom Tait would educate the public about the dangers that a Disneyland deal posed for the city. The mayor talked at length to reporters and editors about the negative effects that preferential tax deals for Disneyland exerted on Anaheim. Disney's advertising dollars fuel the local media, so the mayor believed he fought an uphill battle in that regard. Tait wrote editorials as soon as an issue surfaced. According to one interviewee, "Tait used the bully pulpit to get his message across" and utilized official press releases to communicate with the public. Tait's efforts worked, as more residents came to conclude that the city's business dealings with Disney were out of balance. One informant alleged, "Because of Tait, resident views changed. A huge section of the populace became discontented." Tait said, "My strategy was to go straight to the people and state the case and bring those [pro-Disney] deals to light. Sunlight is the best disinfectant."[22]

Unions, such as UNITE HERE! Local 11 and the county employees union, and Council Member Jose Moreno highlighted to the residents that the Disney/Anaheim relationship was out of balance and needed to change. Many credit Moreno for organizing Latinos and bringing UNITE HERE! Local 11 to Anaheim; they regard these moves as essential to winning the change to district elections, the election of the People's Council, and the passage of the living wage ordinance (see Chapter 10 for more on this issue). When asked about district elections, one prominent actor credited Moreno with changing the method of election in Anaheim. He said, "Jose did that."

Moreno has more than his fair share of critics. One pro-Disney leader proclaimed that Moreno doesn't support capitalism or free enterprise and has a "socialist bent." Another criticized Moreno for seeking publicity by getting arrested in the streets of Anaheim to support wage increases for hotel workers at the Sheraton Hotel/Anaheim Hilton Park in January 2019.[23] Moreno was arrested along with about twenty others, including UNITE HERE! Local 11 copresident Ada Briceño, for sitting in the middle of the street (in front of the convention center, which was soon to host the National Association of Music Merchants). Hundreds of workers from UNITE HERE! Local 11 in addition to clergy and union leaders joined Moreno in the demonstrations.

Actors across the ideological spectrum regard Moreno as an agent of social learning. Some applaud Moreno for this role; others do not. The old regime often attacks new actors who enter the political arena and promote ideas that are antithetical to it. Of course, the public debates over particular issues, such as the creation of the Anaheim Resort District, the affordable housing conflict and the Anaheim Resort District, and the tax rebates on luxury hotels, in themselves taught many people that what was good for Disney was not good for them.

## The People's Council Agenda

In the next several paragraphs, we describe the People's Council agenda. The People's Council addressed parks, government reform, homelessness, the city's professional sports teams, and neighborhood improvements to areas that hadn't received significant public attention in decades. The new council signaled its commitment to the second Anaheim as it turned its attention to city parks.[24] The city council unanimously passed a budget allocating $6.9 million to complete and staff the new Ponderosa Community Center and provided $13 million in new capital spending for parks.[25]

In a move to reform the city government, the new council passed the Sunshine Ordinance, which barred council members from hiring policy aides who also work at local firms that lobby city government, instituted a fee to register as a lobbyist with the city, and required lobbyists to disclose the projects upon which they were working.[26] The new law required lobbyists to register and file quarterly reports and banned elected officials and city employees from lobbying Anaheim government for two years after they left their positions.[27] The ordinance represented a distinct move away from the cozy government-industry relationship that had existed in Anaheim since the start of the postwar period.

In addition to the neighborhood versus Disney debates, homelessness was perhaps the biggest and most contentious issue in Anaheim confronting the People's Council. In early May 2017, nine hundred homeless people lived in Anaheim and more than four hundred homeless people had created a six-mile-long encampment along the riverbed of the Santa Ana River, not far from Angel Stadium. By the fall of that year more than eleven thousand citizens had signed a petition that demanded the city take back the recreation area along the riverbed.[28]

Anaheim ran into two problems regarding homelessness. First, the demand for shelters dwarfed the supply. Second, U.S. District Court Judge David Carter advised the county that it could not remove homeless people unless they offered shelter for those so displaced.[29] Carter oversaw a civil rights case filed against the county, Anaheim, and the neighboring towns of

Orange and Tustin by seven homeless people and the nonprofit Orange County Catholic Worker.[30]

The *PBS NewsHour* dedicated a segment to the housing crisis in Anaheim.[31] It used the struggle for a living wage in Anaheim to ask how Disney affected the homeless problem in the city (for more details on the living wage issue, see Chapter 10). Mayor Tait asserted, "It's bigger than one company." Defenders of Disney often used this kind of response to suggest that Disney bore neither full nor even partial responsibility for Anaheim's problems.

The *Voice of OC*'s Gerda had speculated that Disney played a role in clearing out a homeless encampment in the summer of 2016.[32] Orange County Supervisor Shawn Nelson requested that the encampment be cleared, and the county claimed that this action took place to facilitate flood control. Homeless activist Lou Noble asserted that the clear out occurred because the Disneyland Half-Marathon was two weeks away, and runners along the route would see the homeless encampments. The county maintained that it swept homeless camps on the west side of the river the day prior to the event in order "to maintain the channel and protect the community in the event of a flood."

The city received considerable media attention in July 2017 after it removed twenty benches at bus stops near Disneyland in the Anaheim Resort District, where homeless persons would sleep at night and encamp during the day.[33] According to the *Los Angeles Times*, "Callers alerted City Hall to reports of vagrants drinking, defecating or smoking pot in the neighborhood near the amusement park's entrance." A city spokesperson said, "We're not taking this action because of tourism. We never had a request from Disney. But we did hear from small shop owners and motel owners about the safety issues so we stepped up." The spokesperson also contended, "It breaks our heart to have to remove those benches. But their purpose is to provide seating for someone waiting for a bus." The *Los Angeles Times* story indicated that homeless people fought each other for spaces on the sidewalk near Disneyland after the removal of the benches.

After the county moved homeless people into motels, opened temporary and emergency shelters, and announced the construction of a more permanent facility with between four hundred and six hundred beds, Judge Carter settled the case against Anaheim and ruled that the city could enforce its anticamping ordinances once the facilities came online.[34] In the words of one Anaheim leader, "The city had to be sued" to deal with housing. The owner of the industrial building that housed the emergency homeless shelter leased the property at no charge to Visit Anaheim, the new name of the Anaheim/Orange County Visitor & Convention Bureau. In turn, the city reimbursed $600,000 to Visit Anaheim to convert the building into the shelter. A group called The Illumination Foundation received $805,000 to operate the shelter. Disneyland, the Anaheim Ducks, and the Angels baseball team, among other organizations, donated approximately $300,000 for the effort.

Mayor Tait and the People's Council reached a new deal with the Anaheim Ducks, in late November 2018, that would keep the NHL team in Anaheim through at least 2048.[35] Under the agreement, the arena management bought city-owned parking lots around the arena for $10.1 million. It planned to develop most of that land into homes, offices, and retail shops but agreed to keep the space for at least thirty-nine hundred cars. Anaheim Arena Management, which owns the arena and the team, also agreed to run the Anaheim Regional Transportation Intermodal Center (ARTIC). This move would save the city about $2.5 million per year. The city also ensured that the team would remain the Anaheim Ducks, as opposed to the baseball team, which changed its name from the Anaheim Angels to the Los Angeles Angels of Anaheim in 2005. By 2018, most major news sources no longer used Anaheim in the name of the baseball team. Mayor Tait emphasized that the agreement served the interests of the city and did not provide undue benefits for the Ducks.[36] All the same, both the Angels and the Ducks benefited from and supported the Disneyland Political Order.

One longtime resident of west Anaheim referred to the area around Beach Boulevard as "the black sheep in the city."[37] She had said, "We've been crying for something to be done for 20 years. West Anaheim is a gold mine. We need something better than what we have." In early 2018, the chair of the West Anaheim Neighborhood District concluded, "We have no shopping here. We have no economic base. When businesses left, there was nothing to replace them. The city, instead, put in high-density apartments and low-income homes. There's no place to shop and children here have no place to play. We've been deprived." According to the *Orange County Register*, "Residents have often complained of blight, prostitution activity and other quality-of-life issues." The new council set out to revitalize Beach Boulevard and west Anaheim. In late 2016, the city sold a vacant 25-acre capped landfill near the old Tower Records to a developer that planned a shopping and retail center.[38] Beach Boulevard, which extends beyond Anaheim, is dotted by cheap motels, which have been the center of illicit activity.[39] Caltrans provided the area with grants to improve its walkability.[40] At the end of 2017, the city council agreed to spend $14 million to purchase 3.6 acres of land, which included the Americana Motel, Beach-Lin Car Wash, and a Shell gas station, along Beach Boulevard.[41] A new car wash located at the site of the old Lyndy's Motel filled the need for the Beach-Lin Car Wash.[42] In the statement to announce this deal, Anaheim's spokesperson proclaimed, "Unfortunately, Beach is not seeing the amount of development we would have liked over the years."[43] When asked about the city's historical attitude toward Beach Boulevard, Mayor Tait responded, "No one's ever really worked together and thought about

Beach Boulevard as an entity that we could create value around."[44] In another development that started with the People's Council, the next city council struck a deal with a developer to build a high-end grocery store, at least sixty-five townhomes, and later a hotel on the site of what was known as "Stinkin Lincoln" and "Sinkin' Lincoln," a 25-acre former landfill characterized by unstable soil and a smell.[45]

## Does Disney Pay Its Fair Share?

If the world did not know about the Disney-Anaheim friction, a two-article series from the *Los Angeles Times* revealed it in September 2017.[46] In the first article, titled "Is Disney Paying Its Fair Share in Anaheim," reporter Daniel Miller considered whether Disneyland advanced the collective good or provided selective benefits. He summarized some of the deals that Anaheim had given Disney over the years. Included in that list were the $108.2 million Mickey & Friends Parking Structure, the $1 per year lease for use of that facility, the $510 million in bonds and close to $1.1 billion in interest on those forty-year bonds to pay for various infrastructure upgrades, the extension of the ban on a gate tax for forty-five years, and the luxury hotel tax rebate.

The article listed many benefits that Disneyland brought to Anaheim.[47] Disney employed 30,600 workers in Anaheim that accounted for 19% of the total employment in the city. The Anaheim Resort District paid $171 million in tax revenue, which made up 43% of the general fund in the 2015–2016 fiscal year. Miller described how Disney claimed that it paid $125 million in taxes, bonds, levies, fees, and contracts to the city in 2016. Disney paid $10 million per year to the city for police, fire, and paramedic services in the resort property. Miller cited Disney's contributions of more than $20 million to nonprofits located in Orange County and another $4 million to those in Anaheim. Daniel Miller's second article, "How One Election Changed Disneyland's Relationship with Its Hometown," focused on Disney's financial power, the significance of the 2016 election, and racial and ethnic politics in the city.

The relationship between Disney and the city of Anaheim had changed. For most of the sixty-plus years that Disneyland called the city home, the company had what Miller described as "chummy relationships" with the city council.[48] He wrote about how members of the city council had received silver passes to Disneyland and the company took government officials on fishing excursions and golf trips to places like Coronado on the San Diego Bay and Santa Catalina Islands. Though no longer offering these junket incentives, Disney continued to enjoy a close relationship with the city council. For example, Carrie Nocella, Disneyland Resort's director of government relations and minority business development, attended a 2016 meeting on the tax rebate with Council Member Jordan Brandman, who had asked

Workers United Local 50 if he could bring a Disney representative with him. In response, Christopher Duarte, president of Workers United Local 50, asserted, "I don't believe that government and big business should be that close together—in tandem." Jose Moreno described Nocella as Disney's "political gatekeeper" and claimed that she determined Disney's political strategies and which PACs would receive the company's financial support.

This criticism of Nocella had earlier roots. *Los Angeles Times* reporter Daniel Miller and others wrote that Nocella's relationship with Anaheim government came under scrutiny after she and Council Member Murray were part of a group that vacationed together in Europe after the 2014 municipal election.[49] According to the *Voice of OC*, Murray, Nocella, and other friends whose children attended the same school visited Europe in November 2014. A Disney spokesperson said that Murray paid for the trip and never discussed business with Nocella. The *Voice of OC*'s story on the trip featured a picture of Murray and Nocella smiling as their cheeks were pressed together. It questioned whether Murray had crossed ethical boundaries. The article stated that "the trip rankles some city hall watchers, especially in the light of the controversial deal with Disneyland the Council approved last month in a 3–2 vote." In a statement printed, in part, by the *Voice of OC*, Murray argued, "As an elected official, I independently evaluate all issues that come before the City Council on the sole basis of whether they are in the best interest of Anaheim. When I travel on personal time, I do so at my own expense and comply with regulations and policies governing public officials." Murray stated that her friendship with Nocella predated her professional relationship with Disney. She also alleged, "We all are capable and equipped to distinguish the difference between our personal relationships and our work to represent the residents of Anaheim, and I have certainly been able to do that during my tenure." Miller wrote that Murray voted for Disney-related deals, including the ban on the Disneyland gate tax, after she took this trip with Nocella.

Dunn told Miller that she was "sort of baffled" that the Anaheim City Council wanted a new relationship with Disneyland. She claimed, "They are investing $1.5 billion in that town. It's odd to me that there isn't a better working relationship between leadership at the city and Disney." In a statement to Miller, Disney characterized its relationship with the city in the following way: "While there are some differences in opinion between Disney and several Anaheim officials regarding policy issues and how best to secure Anaheim's economic future, our relationship with the city, its administration and the majority of its political and community leaders remains strong."

Miller expounded on the idea of Two Anaheims. He wrote that Jose Moreno ran on the platform that special giveaways created the Two Anaheims, one that reaped the benefits from the subsidies and one that suffered from homelessness, poverty, and high crime.[50] Moreno proclaimed, "We've invested billions, really, in the children of tourists. We'd now like to really turn our investments toward making sure we take care of the children of Anaheim so that they can have that magical life that I think we all want for our kids and families." This comment bothered pro-Disney actors, one of whom argued, "It's not true that the city subsidizes the children of tourists; it's tourists who subsidize the city." In the 2016 election, the voters disagreed. Disney denied that it contributed to Anaheim's problems and insisted that Anaheim suffered from problems common to cities across the country.

Miller also tackled the underrepresentation over time of Latinos on the Anaheim City Council and the ACLU lawsuit. He highlighted that three of the four candidates that Disney supported in the 2016 election were white "while three of the four candidates who were targeted with negative campaigning by PACs with direct or indirect financial connections to Disney were Latino." Moreno believed that Disney endorsed candidates based on "its bottom-line" and not race. Disney agreed. It stated, "Our support of candidates is not based on ethnicity; it is based on candidates who support business growth and the continued development of the resort district, both of which help ensure a strong local economy and vibrant community." One observer claimed of Disney's politics, "Disney isn't for Democrats. They aren't for Republicans. They're for Disney."

A pro-Disney coalition member concluded, "Disney isn't partisan. They are supportive of economic development in the city; they support both parties." This leader contended that Disney "was hardly involved in the last mayoral election. . . . The company isn't conservative at all. Disney doesn't negatively advertise. PACs send the negative mail. Disney is sensitive about its brand." Pro-balance actors see the massive influx of Disney money as a way for company allies to attack their opponents while the corporate giant focuses on positive messages. For them, Disney dollars facilitate negative campaigning. Another informant asserted that Anaheim politics does not pit Democrats against Republicans and said that the city is "not very partisan."

Those perceptions to the contrary, partisanship is relevant in Anaheim. The core supporters of the Disneyland Imperative are conservative and Republican. They include the chamber of commerce, the Business Council, the Anaheim Police Alliance, the Taxpayers Association, the Visitors Bureau, the Firefighters PAC, and building trade unions. The pro-balance coalition of Latinos, labor, and the school board are much more likely to support the Democratic Party.

Evidence suggests that Walt Disney and his company were far from social progressives. A Black person did not hold a guest-facing job in Disneyland until 1968, almost two years after Walt's death.[51] Before 1968, Black people worked only backstage or as performers.[52] Disney ended its twenty-eight-year ban on same-sex dancing in the park in 1985.[53] Walt Disney "strongly identified himself with the countersubversive tradition of 1950s America and built Disneyland as a reinstatement of traditional social values that seemed threatened by the hegemony of the New Deal and its brand of liberal modernism."[54] Disneyland had also employed rigorous dress codes for its employees and guests, although the company has greatly relaxed these standards in recent times.

In response to this two-part series, the Walt Disney Company stated that the *Los Angeles Times* "showed a complete disregard for basic journalistic standards."[55] It called the series "biased and inaccurate" and claimed that the reporter, several editors, and the publisher ignored "numerous indisputable facts" that Disney shared with them. Disney asserted that the series was "driven by a political agenda," and it cited an *Orange County Register* editorial, which regarded the articles as a "hit piece" with a "seemingly predetermined narrative." The response was in character. Anaheim's leaders stressed how much Disney cares about the company's image. The Walt Disney Company has a family-oriented and wholesome image, and it is resolute in protecting that brand.

After Miller's series, the *Orange County Register* responded in an editorial, "Yes, Disneyland Pays Its Fair Share to the City—if Not More."[56] It cited jobs and taxes as two main reasons for its conclusion. The editorial stated the city's problems, such as unfunded pension liabilities, high poverty rates, and the poor condition of city streets are the responsibility of the city council, not Disney. The paper claimed these problems are "hardly unique to Anaheim" and they are "not one company's burden to fix—that's the City Council's job." The *Orange County Register* wrote, "It's reasonable to criticize Anaheim's willingness to offer costly incentives to select businesses. But putting blame for any significant portion of the city's problems on Disneyland is utter nonsense." It regarded Disney's continued investments in the city as "a net benefit." The editorial concluded with the following advice: "Moving forward, Anaheim officials should focus more on making the city a better place to do business and make better decisions about how finite resources are used instead of casting blame where it doesn't belong."[57]

Disney retaliated against the *Los Angeles Times* by denying media credentials to that paper's movie critic for its film, *Thor: Ragnarok*. In its public remarks on the matter, the *Times* wrote, "This year, Walt Disney Co. studios declined to offer *The Times* advance screenings, citing what it called unfair coverage of its business ties with Anaheim. *The Times* will continue to review and cover Disney movies and programs when they are available to the public."[58] The New York Film Critics Circle, the Los Angeles Critics Association, the Boston Film Critics Association, and the National Society of Film Critics announced that they would exclude Disney films for their awards until the company lifted what they regarded as an action that was "anti-thetical to the principles of a free press."[59] Several news sources and movie critics also boycotted Disney's advanced screenings. Four days after it began, the Disney ban of the *Los Angeles Times* movie critics at company screenings ended. In a statement, Disney wrote, "We've had productive discussions with the newly installed leadership at the *Los Angeles Times* regarding our specific concerns, and as a result, we've agreed to restore access to advance screenings for their film critics."[60] The *New York Times* speculated that fierce backlash from movie associations, media outlets, and actors who were set to star in Disney movies led to the cancellation of the boycott.

## The Legacy of the People's Council

The People's Council changed the terms of coexistence between Disneyland and the city of Anaheim. This council was not as favorable to the corporate giant as were its predecessors. It took hotel subsidies off the table, would not allow Disney to move a proposed hotel location, and approved a ballot measure to force Disney to pay a living wage. The People's Council and its supporters offset the corporate narrative. They concluded that what was good for Disney was not good for the city, and the people listened and believed. When asked about the era of the People's Council, one interviewee remarked, "It was different." Another asked, "What got better?" One pro-Disney leader said of the People's Council and its tenure, it was "miserable, horrible, lose your mind. They tried to undo everything the previous council had done."

Opinions vary about this council. Pro-balance actors believed that the People's Council incorporated neighborhoods in ways that previous councils had not. One pro-Disney leader called this notion "hogwash," and another claimed that the narrative that the city didn't pay attention to neighborhoods before 2016 didn't match the facts. The latter individual alleged both that the neighborhoods versus Disney narrative was not that simple and that no dichotomy of this sort existed.

One pro-Disney actor referred to the People's Council as "a fluke" and speculated, "If Anaheim fought Disney and Gene Autry [former owner of the Angels] since 1960, we wouldn't be here." This individual argued that the city's adversarial stance against Disney only spanned the short period in which city affairs were driven by the People's Council. "It was a one moment battle. It's not a common thread." This person characterized the relationship as "symbiotic." Another pro-Disney leader asserted that the relationship between Disney and the city was "historically, very strong. There have been bumps over politics, policy, and approach, but historically, overwhelmingly strong." One observer noted that there have been "tides" in a relationship that "depends on the political winds." Another stated, "We hate Disney sometimes."

While change occurred during the 2016–2018 city council term, the question became, Would it last? Was the People's Council a fluke or would it have lasting effects? One source remarked that the People's Council "didn't have enough time" and that this council operated in a "short window." Despite the short window, the People's Council played a vital role in making companies pay a living wage to their employees.

# 10

## The Haves and the Have Nots

I n early 2018, an online survey of approximately five thousand Disneyland resort employees indicated that three-quarters of the respondents
claimed they did not earn enough to pay basic expenses such as rent,
food, and gas.[1] Of the respondents, 11% were either homeless or had no place
of their own over the past two years. These hardships occurred even though
Disney reported a 78% increase in quarterly profits as compared to the previous year and raised ticket prices by 18% in February 2018. The Economic
Roundtable, a nonprofit research organization in Los Angeles, and the Urban & Environmental Policy Institute at Occidental College conducted the
survey, which was "underwritten by a coalition of nine labor groups that
represent workers at the two parks. Three of those unions are now negotiating contracts with Disney and other unions are scheduled to begin talks in
the next few months."[2] The executive summary of the report highlighted the
economic struggles faced by Disneyland Resort employees. It included the
following points:[3]

- Despite steep increases in the cost of housing and other necessi-
  ties, Disneyland workers have suffered steady pay cuts and continue
  to struggle to make ends meet.
- Disneyland employees worry about keeping a roof over their heads.
- Many Disneyland workers do not have reliable access to affordable
  and nutritious food.
- Disneyland employees often struggle with erratic work schedules.

- Disneyland parents are among the most negatively affected by the resort's policies.
- Many Disneyland workers can't afford health care or dental coverage.
- Most Disneyland workers are mature adults, and the job is their career and livelihood.
- Many Disneyland workers live in outlying communities in order to find housing they can afford.
- Raising the wages of Disneyland workers will be a powerful regional economic stimulus.
- Declining wages for Disneyland workers have weakened the regional economy.
- An extraordinary pay gap exists between the Walt Disney Company CEO and the frontline workers at Disneyland.
- Disneyland produces large profits and can afford to pay workers a living wage.

Disneyland spokesperson Suzi Brown responded, "This inaccurate and unscientific survey was paid for by politically motivated labor unions and its results are deliberately distorted and do not reflect how the overwhelming majority of our 30,000 cast members feel about the company."[4] The survey report indicated that the average annual wage for Disneyland employees, when adjusted for inflation, decreased by 15% from 2000 to 2017.[5] Disney claimed that the average annual salary for hourly employees was $37,000, which worked out to $17.80 per hour.

After it released the survey results, the coalition of unions behind the survey held a town hall meeting in Anaheim to discuss the findings.[6] At that session, the coalition announced it would propose a ballot initiative that would mandate a minimum wage for any company that receives city subsidies.[7] The coalition possessed people power and financial power. Service unions provided the money, political capacity, and people power necessary to compete against the Disney giant. One prominent community advocate argued, "As a community, we don't have the kind of money that labor has. . . . On our own, we can't get it done. Labor is essential." The coalition of unions filed a petition for the initiative with the city clerk's office one day after the meeting. It needed about twenty-one thousand signatures from registered voters in Anaheim to qualify for the ballot. Christopher Duarte, the president and chief executive of Disneyland's union, claimed, "We are not attacking Disney. But if taxpayers are going to subsidize a large corporation, then that corporation should pay a living wage and not contribute to poverty."[8]

One week after the coalition released its results and filed the petition, it organized a group of Disneyland Resort employees, who demonstrated at the Walt Disney Company's annual shareholder meeting in Houston.[9] They held signs that read, "#stopdisneypoverty." CEO Bob Iger didn't take any questions about the living wage issue, but he announced that Disney had committed $50 million to an education initiative that will cover tuition costs for its hourly employees.

The Anaheim City Council discussed the survey and the living wage ordinance at its monthly meeting.[10] Council Member Murray argued that the report singled out Disney even though the problems laid out in the study plagued workers across Southern California.[11] Todd Ament, the CEO of the Anaheim Chamber of Commerce, speculated that the measure would result in the cancellation of luxury hotels that received tax subsidies. The chamber, Council Member Murray, the Orange County Hispanic Chamber of Commerce, the Orange County chapter of the California Restaurant Association, and other members of the Disneyland Political Order formed a group named "No on the Anaheim Job-Killer" coalition.[12]

## Pro-balance Power

The pro-balance coalition grew during this period. The Orange County Labor Federation hosted a May Day March & Rally to recognize International Workers' Day. That event focused attention on the living wage ordinance.[13] A common refrain from those who marched was "This is how democracy works."[14] Mayor Pro Tem Moreno spoke to the crowd of marchers that gathered at Saint Boniface Church.[15] The Korean Resource Center participated in the march as well. When asked how Anaheim residents responded to the petition to sign the living wage ordinance initiative, the copresident of Local 11 concluded that Anaheim residents "reacted positively. . . . They realize the city has given tremendous subsidies to these large companies, some of which should come back to the workers."[16]

Ament and Murray expressed different reactions than the leader of Local 11. Ament claimed, "It is vital that local officials work to find real solutions for Anaheim's high cost of living, like more affordable housing. Gouging businesses will not solve this problem; it will make it worse." Murray asserted, "Less than two percent of Anaheim residents work at the resort. The proposed measure would reduce job opportunities and increase the cost of services for all residents."

A small group of Disneyland workers went to the company headquarters in Burbank to deliver a petition, with more than 120,000 signatories, that asked for a living wage.[17] The petition read, "Disney's profits do not magically appear—they're gained by the employees who work hard to ensure that visitors have a joyful experience. And these profits should be shared with the people who make them happen." Disneyland described the petition as a "blatant stunt" and "political grandstanding" and wrote that the living wage ordinance would come with "severe, unintended negative consequences."

During a heated meeting, the city council voted 4–3 to place the measure on the November 6, 2018, ballot. The four members of the People's Council supported the ordinance. Council Members Murray, Kring, and Faessel voted no, arguing that the proposal should be subject to a preliminary economic analysis.[18]

As the living wage ordinance campaign moved forward, Disney negotiated a new deal with ninety-seven hundred of its thirty thousand employees.[19] The two sides reached an agreement that workers would receive an automatic increase from $11 an hour to $13.25 an hour and $15 an hour starting in January 2019. In 2020, covered workers would receive a 3% raise that would take their hourly wages to $15.45 an hour. Disneyland President Josh D'Amaro wrote, "The cost of living in Orange County is incredibly high. There are broad societal issues that communities are grappling with and no one company or entity alone can solve them. But we want to do our part." The secretary-treasurer of the United Food and Commercial Workers Local 324, who also served as a lead negotiator for this deal said, "We are pleased this is a step in the right direction. . . . Disney is a very wealthy company that had not been paying a fair wage for a long time. And Disney's profits come from the image that these hardworking employees portray day in and day out. You still can't live comfortably in Los Angeles or Orange County on $15 an hour." The deal only covered one-third of Disneyland's workers, so the campaign to pass a living wage ordinance continued. The living wage ordinance would supersede this or any other agreement.

The Disney Company and its employees had been in a tenuous relationship since the days Walt Disney ran the company. Disney animators went on strike in 1941 to challenge inequality in pay and treatment.[20] Walt contended that communists had organized the action. Tensions were so high that the only way the company could settle the strike was for Walt to leave the country. The two sides reconciled while Walt was on a goodwill tour for the U.S. government to combat Nazism in South America.[21] Close to two thousand Disneyland workers from five different unions, which represented employees in attractions, food, merchandise, and custodial, conducted a twenty-two-day strike in 1984 to protest a pay freeze, safeguard the employee health plan for part-time workers, and stop outsourcing.[22] Disney instituted the pay freeze but continuing employees who worked a minimum of sixteen hours per week maintained their company-sponsored health benefits, and Disney limited outsourcing. New hires would need to work a minimum of twenty-five hours per week to secure these benefits. In March 2018, the OC Weekly's Gabriel San Roman observed that the situation faced by Disneyland employees had changed since 1984.[23] In the mid-1980s, Disneyland wages allowed people to stay in the middle class and send their kids to college. "The 1984 strike was not about starvation wages," he concluded. By the 2010s, however, Disneyland wages didn't allow employees to cover basic living expenses. For San Roman, Latinos suffered the brunt of these inadequate wages as they took on more jobs with the company because of the creation of the Disneyland Resort in 1996. One source referred to this as "the Browning of the resort." The person who made this remark asserted that the living wage issue "became much more pronounced after Disneyland became a resort." The corporate giant needed more workers, and Latinos filled that labor gap.

## Change of Plans

Disney wanted to move its proposed luxury hotel about fifteen hundred feet from its original location on 1401 Disneyland Drive to the Downtown Disney area on 1601 Disneyland Drive.[24] The city informed Disney that the move of the hotel location constituted a substantive change and that its pending tax break applied only to the original location. In a letter to the city of Anaheim on August 15, 2018, Disney announced it had suspended its hotel project, which was scheduled to begin after a city planning meeting on August 20, 2018.[25] David Ontko, chief counsel for Disneyland Resorts, wrote, "Given the city's position that our project does not comply with the requirements of the Agreement, you have given us no other choice than to put construction of the hotel on indefinite hold as the resort reevaluates the economic viability of future hotel development in Anaheim."[26]

Less than a week after this decision, D'Amaro wrote the following to the mayor and city council:

> Since Disneyland opened its gates for the first time in 1955, our mission has been to create a special place dedicated to our Cast, our Guests and the city we call home. One of the keys to our success throughout the past 63 years has been our healthy relationship with the residents and leaders of the city of Anaheim. Over recent months however, it has become apparent that certain policies that were adopted to enhance the Anaheim Resort District and benefit the City, including the Entertainment Tax policy [ban on gate tax] that was originally adopted in 1996, have instead created an adversarial climate where there should be cooperation and goodwill.[27]

D'Amaro then took aim at the issue of the luxury hotel subsidy:

> We believe the practice of utilizing tax incentives to encourage business investment was, and continues to be, an effective approach and

sound public policy to create jobs, increase economic activity, and generate significant taxes and other fiscal benefits to the community. In fact, cities around the nation have implemented similar incentive policies with great success. However, unfortunately in Anaheim these policies have become divisive, leading to an unstable business climate and a difficult working relationship with the City.

D'Amaro asked the mayor and city council for a favor:

Good friends will not always agree; however, the current level of animus is unprecedented and counterproductive. In light of this, we've come to believe that the Agreement Concerning Entertainment Tax Reimbursement [gate tax ban] and the Operating Covenant Agreement [luxury hotel tax rebate] which Disneyland previously entered into with the City no longer serve the purpose for which they were intended and, in fact, have become a flashpoint for controversy and dissension in our community. Consequently, we are asking the City to join us in terminating both agreements.

Mayor Tait was "very surprised" by Disneyland's request, which he referred to as a "bold move," but he added, "Disney did the right thing. These agreements had become toxic. I'm very pro-business, but I'm also fiscally responsible with the people's money."[28] A week after Disneyland asked for the end to its incentives, the city council voted unanimously to end the two subsidies.

Disney's actions suggest that the company did not want to pay the wages that would be mandated by Measure L, also known as the living wage ordinance. Disneyland representatives told the media and others that its recent agreement with four of its largest unions to raise hourly pay, by 20% in some cases, with another 13% boost at the start of 2019, showed the company's commitment to a living wage.[29] The cancellation of the deals and the agreement with some of the unions did not stop living wage advocates. After Disney asked to terminate its deals with Anaheim, a representative of UNITE HERE! Local 11 proclaimed, "We are still calling on Disney to do what we think is right and lift those people out of poverty."

The decision to repeal the pro-Disney policies inflamed controversy. One individual speculated that Disney calculated that the financial benefits of not paying Measure L exceeded those offered by a tax rebate and no admissions tax. One Disney critic contended that the cancellation of these agreements was "genius maneuvering by Disney and its high-powered lawyers." According to this leader, "By tearing up [these agreements,] they get out of paying a living wage." Once the city nullified the hotel tax subsidy and ended the gate tax ban, the question became, If passed, would Measure L apply to Disneyland? In response to the city council meeting that ended Disney's benefits, *Los Angeles Times*'s Hugo Martin wrote, "Disney critics say they believe the resort has ulterior motives: By eliminating certain tax agreements, Disney may be ensuring that it isn't affected by a Nov. 6 ballot measure that, if passed, would require the resort to pay all its workers a living wage."[30]

The debate then centered on whether the city's bond payments for the Mickey and Friends Parking Structure and the $35 million Disneyland gets from parking fees constitute subsidies. The traditional factions in Anaheim took their respective sides on the issue. Organized labor argued that Measure L still applied to Disneyland. Richard McCracken, a lawyer who helped write Measure L for the union, concluded, "This bond financing [for the parking structure] was arranged to help Disney and all of the taxes used to pay for the bonds will be going to benefit Disney."[31] Council Member Faessel predicted that "this will likely see the inside of a courtroom."[32]

Shortly after a city council meeting on whether the Mickey and Friends Parking Structure was a subsidy, Disneyland canceled its plans to build a fourth hotel. A spokesperson for the company concluded, "While this is disappointing for many, the conditions and agreements that stimulated this investment in Anaheim no longer exist and we must therefore adjust our long-term investment strategy."[33] This decision, and the debate over tax breaks and incentives for Disneyland, called into question the relationship between the theme park and its home city. According to Dunn, "This unfortunate outcome underscores just how important it is for the business community to have good city partners who understand economic development and the consequences of bad public policy." Council Member Murray said, "We need to figure out a way to have a constructive partnership." Mayor Pro Tem Moreno offered a different perspective on the city's shifting relationship with Disneyland: "When people say we have changed our posture, we have. We are now saying, 'What about our kids?'"

Even though Disneyland and its allies argued that Measure L did not apply to it, the company spent large amounts of money to try to defeat the referendum. By early November, unions had outspent Disney by a total of $1.9 million to $1.6 million.[34] Most of labor's money went toward passing Measure L.[35] When asked about union spending, Briceño responded that the 2018 ballot measure was "a complete referendum on the way the city has done business by taking care of billion-dollar companies and leaving workers behind."[36] It was all about Disneyland.

Disney and its advocates wanted the living wage issue to be decided in the board room, not via a popular vote. According to Disneyland's Brown, "We believe issues like these should be solved at the bargaining table rather than the ballot box."[37] Measure L passed by a margin of 54.20% (45,237) to

45.80% (38,229). The city's attorney continued to argue that Measure L applied only to two luxury hotels under construction and a shopping district.[38] Briceño believed that the issue of the applicability of Measure L would head to court, and she claimed, "We have plaintiffs ready to go and we have attorneys ready to litigate."[39] She was correct.

The workers and others had enough of the tax breaks for Disney while the company paid meager wages to its employees. With the help of unions and an empowered electorate, they now possessed the political capacity to advance their agenda. The new politics in Anaheim included tactics such as initiatives and referenda, demonstrations, rallies, and in-person addresses by a popular presidential candidate. Bolstered by the financial and people power possessed by service unions, the pro-balance ring of the political order challenged Disney's power. The content of a new social education was clear: if Disney continues to get public largesse, the company needs to pay a living wage. Faced with new politics, Disney responded with a surprising maneuver. It asked the city to cancel pro-Disney policies, including the hotel tax rebate and the gate tax ban to reset the now strained relationship with the city.

The passage of Measure L and the end of the hotel tax rebate show how Anaheim continued to inch away from an exclusive focus on the Disneyland Imperative. The nature of political interaction had changed in the city. Led by Mayor Tait, the Anaheim government rejected Disney's request to keep the rebate when the company proposed to relocate its hotel. That kind of rejection was atypical in Anaheim's history. The new city council also placed Measure L on the ballot. Previous city councils were reluctant to favor pro-balance interests in such an obvious way. As one political actor speculated, "Without the four votes [of the People's Council], Measure L might not have been on the ballot even though it had the signatures." Victories for pro-balance actors and defeat for those who favored the corporate giant illustrated the new politics in Anaheim. Unions helped secure the victories. Their financial power and people power facilitated a change in electoral and policy outcomes. The passage of Measure L marked the new leadership's attempt to reduce the amount of exclusion that this group faced. The 2018 mayoral and city council elections in addition to the subsequent city council session would determine whether the People's Council would stay in power and further its agenda.

# 11

## Biding Their Time

In 2018, Anaheim voters chose a new mayor for the first time in eight years. The top two candidates were Ashleigh Aitken, a consumer protection attorney, and Harry Sidhu, a licensed mechanical engineer, owner of fast-food restaurants, and former member of the city council. Sidhu received endorsements from the Anaheim police and fire unions, the Orange County Business Council, hotel developers, and Disneyland.[1]

In their messages to voters, candidates attempted to balance the needs of Disneyland and the Anaheim Resort District with those of people in the neighborhoods. Aitken told the *Wall Street Journal*, "Like most Anaheim residents, I love Disneyland. And I, like most of Anaheim, got fed up being taken for a ride outside the park."[2] She also asserted, "Taxpayers should not be on the hook to fund development projects for extremely profitable corporations. As mayor, I'll insist any future proposals be fair and equitable, with a strong community benefit and taxpayers in mind."[3] Pro-Disney businessperson Sidhu claimed, "Disney and the city both agreed to end the tax incentive program for Disney's proposed hotel. Ending this program has removed one of the major sources, if not the biggest source, of contention between the city and Disney. We need to be able to work together as partners to provide benefits that all Anaheim neighborhoods and families deserve."[4] Sidhu got the message that any benefit for Disney needed to be couched in terms of how that advantage would aid neighborhoods. Like previous pro-Disney mayors, Sidhu referred to Disneyland as the city's "golden goose."[5]

At a candidate forum in late October 2018, Aitken took a hard line against Disney's campaign spending. She argued, "When we read in our newspapers that some of the richest corporations spent over a million-and-a-half dollars to take out community leaders and certain candidates, we need to stand together to make sure that this type of tactic and dark money is not acceptable."[6] At this forum, which Sidhu did not attend, Aitken criticized Sidhu for accepting $2,000 from Disney.

Sidhu won the election with 26,422 votes and 32.5% of the vote. Aitken finished second with 31.9% and 25,944 votes. Lorri Galloway, a former city council member, took home 15.2% of the vote (12,367 votes), and Cynthia Ward, a community activist, garnered 8.7% of the vote with 7,121. No other candidate received more than 4% of the vote. In reaction to his victory and Disney's hand in it, Sidhu responded:

> I was elected by the voters, and no one else, because they knew I was the only candidate who could bring this city together, end the divisiveness and improve the quality of life for every resident. The best way we can do that is to make sure we take the huge tax revenue generated from our Resort District and spend it in the neighborhoods.[7]

Disneyland and its advocates exercised financial power to defeat members of the People's Council and elect pro-Disney city councillors. Disney contributed $1,235,000 to the SOAR PAC.[8] That PAC gave $635,000 to a slate of pro-Disney candidates.[9] The amount of money spent in the Anaheim elections eclipsed the record set in 2016.[10] When he analyzed the amount of money Disney and the SOAR PAC donated in the municipal election, Mayor Tom Tait claimed, "It certainly looks like they expect something, and I think that perception creates distrust in government."[11]

In the District 2 campaign, the city council candidates disagreed about how Anaheim should treat Disney. Challenger Jordan Brandman wrote, "District 2 residents deserve a council member who will work with Disney to ensure their private investment is providing the greatest possible community benefit—as well as hold them accountable so the city's largest employer is doing right by all residents. You can count on me to be the neighborhood's champion."[12] His opponent, Council Member Vanderbilt, acknowledged that "Disney is the most important job creator in Anaheim" and that he supported the park's expansion plans.[13] Unlike Brandman, Vanderbilt continued to oppose tax subsidies.[14]

In his statement of qualifications to the voters, District 3 incumbent Moreno wrote, "We have begun a new era in our city. For too many years, our political system favored crony corporate interests over the needs of our neighborhoods. I was elected in 2016 to bring balance to our city."[15] He also acknowledged, "We all want a prosperous Disney. Anaheim has invested over $1 billion in the development of the resort district. It's time to invest in our children. As one of the most profitable corporations in the world, Disney does not need precious local tax dollars that we need to fund fire, police, and parks. To improve the relationship with Anaheim, Disney should avoid massive funding campaigns to influence local elections in its favor."[16] Even Disney's fiercest critics want the theme park to succeed. The people are not enemies of Disneyland, but they do oppose imbalance. They want Disney to do well but they also don't want to give too much to the Walt Disney Company. Where is the line? How does a city not give too much to a corporate giant? The Anaheim experience suggests that the power imbalance led to the policy imbalance. Pro-balance actors like Moreno tried to marshal enough power to create more balance between the city and the giant.

The top two District 6 candidates clashed over how government should treat Disneyland. Trevor O'Neil, the president and owner of Colonial Home Care Services, wrote, "I will work to improve relations between Disney and Anaheim through policies that encourage investment and streamline development. Tax incentives should only be used if they are open to all comers and bring new incremental revenue to Anaheim above the incentive's cost."[17] Patty Gaby, a retired teacher and city commissioner, wrote, "The Disney Corp. does not need our tax dollars for their projects."[18] Gaby supported Mayor Tait and his stance against tax subsidies for Disneyland and the Angels MLB team.[19]

On election night, the pro-Disney slate prevailed as Sidhu, O'Neil, and Brandman won. They joined Lucille Kring, who had two years left in her term, to form a pro-Disney majority on the city council.[20] In District 2, Brandman captured 39.4% of the vote to 29.9% for Vanderbilt. O'Neil won the District 6 race with 45% of the vote. Moreno won reelection with 54% of the vote.

## The 2018–2020 City Council

The new city council tackled two major issues, both of which revolved around either Disneyland or the theme park's interests. The first issue was how to proceed with the Angels. With the ball club's lease about to expire, the city council needed to negotiate with the Angels about a stadium. Disney's main interest focused on a future project, titled DisneylandForward. For both issues, the Angels and Disney made sure not to ask for subsidies or tax breaks of any kind. The People's Council had left its mark. We discuss these issues in the next couple of sections.

## The Angel Stadium Deal

Mayor Sidhu's priority was a new Angel Stadium deal. In mid-January 2019, the city council approved a fourteen-month extension of the ball club's stadium lease.[21] Sidhu wanted to keep the Angels in Anaheim because of "thousands of jobs, millions of dollars in annual revenue, global exposure for Anaheim, and a decades-long partnership."[22] Previous mayors used the same kinds of justifications to explain favorable deals toward Disneyland. Unlike most of his predecessors, however, Mayor Sidhu demanded that the Angel Stadium deal include community benefits, such as affordable housing, parks, and open space. In the post-Disneyland-subsidies period, the mayor appealed to prodevelopment and proneighborhood interests.

The Anaheim City Council voted 5–2 to sell Angel Stadium and 150 acres around it to SRB, an entity created by Angels owner Arte Moreno to purchase the property.[23] In exchange, the Arte Moreno–led management group would pay $150 million to the city for the stadium and property, build 466 affordable housing units as part of this development, and create a seven-acre park on this property. The city reduced the price of the purchase by $123 million for the inclusion of affordable housing and by $46 million for the construction of the park. City officials referred to these features of the deal as "community benefits credits." The original price of the property had dropped from $325 million to $320 million because the city retained about two acres for an existing water well and a future fire station.

The total development called for 5,175 apartments and condominiums; of those, 259 would be reserved for households that made less than 50% of Orange County's median household income; households that made 80% of the county's median household income would occupy another 207.[24] The property was designed to include 2.7 million square feet of office space, 1.75 million square feet for commercial purposes, including retail and restaurants, and 943 hotel rooms. SRB management paid $5 million to the city in December 2019 and was due to pay $45 million in October 2020 after the council approved the deal. From that point forward, SRB would pay the rest of the $100 million in equal annual installments over a multiyear period.

Council Members Moreno and Barnes voted against the agreement.[25] Moreno argued that the amount of affordable housing dedicated to the development fell below the need. He also opposed the deal because the project never went out for bid, and, instead, the city offered the land and stadium to one person, Arte Moreno, the owner of the team. Of the agreement, Council Member Barnes characterized it as "a gift, not a sale." Like Jose Moreno, she wanted an in-person meeting on the deal and more time to deliberate the substance of the agreement. The council voted 4–2 against the motion to allow for an in-person public workshop on the deal. Former Mayors Tait and Daly believed that the city should have gotten much more for the property than $150 million in cash.[26] Mayor Sidhu claimed that opponents of the agreement overestimated the value of the land around the stadium.[27]

The stadium deal also brought to the forefront how Mayor Sidhu initiated rules changes that limited dissenting voices on the council.[28] For example, any agenda item needed a second and a third. One pro-balance leader referred to the new internal rules as "problematic" and contended that they "gagged the voices of the minority" and "silenced and disenfranchised people of color communities." One Latino leader concluded that Sidhu "put a strain on access to residents. He cut public time for comments." Sidhu also changed city council rules to reduce the time council members could speak on an agenda item to two five-minute rounds.[29]

### Disneyland

During Sidhu's first term, Disney tried to show Anaheim that it was committed to its employees and the city. Through its ASPIRE program, Disney provided free tuition so that ninety thousand of its eligible hourly employees and cast members at the company's parks across the United States could pursue a high school diploma, various college degrees, and trade skills.[30] Mayor Sidhu used his state of the city address to commend ASPIRE and Disneyland Resort's $5 million donation to the Orange County Housing Trust.[31] In announcing Disneyland's contribution to the Orange County Housing Trust, the President of Disneyland Resort Josh D'Amaro asserted, "I feel we do have a responsibility. I think about Anaheim not just as where we do business, but this is our home."[32] Another pro-Disney leader complimented the annual CHOC (Children's Hospital of Orange County) Walk at Disneyland, through which the corporate giant has raised millions of dollars for Southern California children's health care programs, education, and research over a three-decade span.[33] Another pro-Disney informant claimed that Disney doesn't publicize some of its charitable acts, such as its efforts to help build KaBOOM! playgrounds in Anaheim. Disney works with KaBOOM! a national nonprofit, to build playgrounds in city parks.[34] As of September 2019, Disney and KaBOOM! had built eighty playgrounds nationwide, including twelve in Anaheim. The Disney Company was clearly intent on rehabilitating its local reputation as a heartless corporate behemoth.

In the aftermath of the People's Council and the subsidies and deals gone wrong, Disneyland didn't ask the city for much.[35] In the postsubsidy period, one local informant observed that Disney "is quiet now" and a second acknowledged, "We're in a quiet period." Another said, "Disney waits for a friendlier environment and then they'll do something." This hesitancy indicated that the nature of political interaction between the Disney Company and the city had changed. When Disney made a request in this new era, it let everyone know that its actions had nothing to do with previous deals or future subsidies. For instance, Disney applied to the city to conduct a conceptual development review of a 350-room tower it would construct next to the Disneyland Hotel. Disney's timeshare, the Disney Vacation Club, wanted to provide lodgings for its members to stay at Disneyland. Disney and the Disney Vacation Club insisted that this development was not a hotel and that the company would not ask the city for a tax incentive. Disney also touted the number of jobs and amount of revenue this development would create. In July 2020, the city's planning commission unanimously approved a conditional-use permit for the tower.

Disney's employees persisted in wanting the company to adhere to Measure L and pay them a living wage.[36] In December 2019, five resort workers accused Disneyland and two of its subcontractors and lessees of not following the terms of Measure L, which passed in the 2018 municipal election. The suit claimed that the law obligated Disney to pay a living wage because Anaheim uses bonds to pay for the Mickey and Friends Parking Structure.[37] In November 2021, an Orange County Superior Court Judge ruled in favor of Disney when he concluded that the company may have benefited from its agreement with the city, but the deal did not constitute a public subsidy.[38] In the summer of 2023, however, California's Fourth District Court ruled that Measure L applied to Disneyland and ordered the company to raise wages and provide back pay to its employees.[39] Disney appealed to the California Supreme Court, which decided not to hear the case, subsequently solidifying Measure L's applicability to the theme park.

Disneyland closed for 412 days because of COVID-19. Pro-Disney and pro-balance leaders had different perceptions of COVID-19 and the park closure. One informant summarized the pro-Disney side by saying, "The city has financial problems because the resort isn't open. With COVID-19, Anaheim is not the happiest place on earth." Others acknowledged that the "city suffers without bed tax," the resort's closure is "killing us financially," and "this can't go on forever. It hurts." Pro-balance leaders recognized the importance of the resort to Anaheim and the surrounding area, but they saw the park's closure from a different point of view. One asserted, "COVID is a wake-up call. We can't put all our financial eggs in one basket." On April 30, 2021, Disneyland resumed its operations at 25% capacity with enhanced safety measures, such as temperature taking, mask requirements, and social distancing. The parks reopened without fireworks, parades, fast passes, character meet and greets, and indoor lines.

## *DisneylandForward*

On March 25, 2021, Disney announced DisneylandForward, "a multi-year public planning effort with the city of Anaheim to update development approvals that meet the current and future demand in entertainment."[40] While its plans lacked specifics at that time, Disney set the stage to ask the city to change city zoning regulations, which Disneyland characterized as "inflexible."[41] According to Jeanette Lomboy, an executive at Walt Disney Imagineering, "We've had a long history of being bold in Anaheim, and we want to continue to be bold. But we do have constraints here in Anaheim. For our Imagineers, there is no shortage of good ideas, content and stories to tell. Unfortunately, if we can't bring these ideas to Anaheim based on the current limitations, then Disney's investment goes elsewhere to other parks."

DisneylandForward teased the idea of integrating hotels and theme park experiences and creating shops and places to buy merchandise at the Toy Story Parking lot. Current rules, most of which are laid out in the Disneyland Resort Specific Plan, mandate that only theme park attractions can be built in the theme park district, only hotels can be constructed in the hotel zone, and parking is relegated to the parking zone. Disneyland wanted the flexibility to create an integrated experience, one in which people could eat, drink, and go on theme park attractions in the Downtown Disney District or near the Paradise Pier and Disneyland Hotels on company property. Disney representatives noted that the city had previously amended the Disneyland Resort Specific Plan more than a dozen times.

Disney also claimed this new project will "create thousands of new jobs" and threatened to spend money on other parks unless Anaheim made zoning changes. The company was, in effect, adhering to the new terms of coexistence. Disney acknowledged that the project would benefit neighborhoods. It alleged that the development and expansion would "help support Anaheim's funding for important services such as fire, police and public schools."[42]

Under new terms of coexistence, Disney had to identify how its plans would benefit neighborhoods. Disney also stated, "It is important to know that Disneyland Resort is not seeking any public funding in this effort and is not seeking to develop any additional square footage or hotel rooms beyond what is already allowed. We will be working with the city and community to update existing approvals to allow for future integrated immersive experiences to be appropriately placed and built throughout Disney properties."[43] The company sought neither tax breaks nor a government subsidy. It did want the kind of internal control over zoning that Walt Disney craved but lacked when the park opened.

Even though Disney did not ask the city for much during Sidhu's first two years as mayor, Anaheim and its elected officials nevertheless promoted the corporate giant's interests in several ways. The city provided favorable treatment toward Disney allies like the Angels, Visit Anaheim, and the Anaheim Chamber of Commerce. The Angels deal can serve as a template for future Disney deals and Visit Anaheim and the chamber of commerce work to promote Disneyland's interests. With Sidhu in the lead, the council also provided a $6.5 million economic development recovery package to Visit Anaheim to promote tourism and make certain that business at the convention center would return to normal as soon as possible. Sidhu also partnered with the chamber of commerce and Visit Anaheim in the process through which neighborhoods will propose the improvements they wish to see from government.

The People's Council and the forces that made it a reality changed the terms of coexistence between the Disney Company and the city of Anaheim. Subsidies and tax breaks came off the table, and greater attention to neighborhood concerns went on the table. In terms of holding seats on the city council, the tenure of the People's Council was temporary as pro-Disney candidates took over the majority on the city council after only two years. However, the terms of coexistence have not reverted to pre–People's Council days. If Disney advocates want to change the terms of coexistence back to favoring subsidies and tax breaks for the entertainment company, then they would need to marshal the power to do it. Likewise, the pro-balance actors would need power requisite to keeping the terms as they are now.

After the People's Council, the city returned to some old patterns not because of the prevailing political environment but because of an election. Anaheim voters picked a slate of candidates and a mayor who championed developmental policies. Power determined the policy outputs in the city. Disneyland and its allies spent millions to elect a mayor and city council majority that espoused its interests. As a result of the 2018 municipal election, Anaheim city government went from pulling public funds from the Anaheim Chamber of Commerce to awarding a $425,000 no-bid contract to that entity.

The People's Council showed that city government—even in a place with a corporate giant—does not have to single-mindedly pursue developmental policies. Public policy is a choice. The city council under Mayor Sidhu promulgated developmental policies because its side won an election. It prevailed in a political fight that it lost two years before. The new council and mayor argued that they concentrated on tourism, development, and the Anaheim Resort District because these policies and entities produce collective benefits. They reempowered prodevelopment interests like the chamber of commerce, which allocated significant resources to ensure that pro-Disney actors got elected. To the victors went the spoils.

## 2020 City Council Election

In their preview of the 2020 city council election, the *Voice of OC*'s Spencer Custodio and Brandon Pho wrote, "The Anaheim City Council races are a battle between Disneyland resort-backed candidates against underfunded, anti-resort subsidy candidates in an election year that could see the current resort-friendly council majority swing the other way."[44] Disney-backed candidates outspent their opponents by wide margins and won every city council race in 2020.

Disney learned how to use its financial power to win district elections. Through the SOAR PAC, Disney spent $1.5 million to get its candidates elected in 2018. Disney contributed another $1.5 million in 2020, and, because of these two elections, five of the six city council members and the mayor favored Disney and the resort district. Before the 2020 election, one pro-balance respondent was asked whether the city was better off with district elections. This person responded, "Yes and no. Yes because residents have access to specific elected officials, who advocate for their districts. No because there's still huge competition from large entities like the police, Disney, Angels, and the Ducks." Before the 2020 city council election, another pro-balance advocate acknowledged, "The jury is still out on district elections, politically. Right now, the council is majority-white and majority-Disney." District elections did not diminish the role that money plays in elections.

COVID-19 presented greater challenges to the pro-balance candidates in 2020. The pandemic made it difficult to campaign at the grassroots level, the core strategy for these underfunded candidates. One pro-balance leader concluded, "There's no headspace to organize politically during the pandemic. . . . It's hard to organize when everyone is home." Public health risks especially limited door-to-door campaigning.

UNITE HERE! Local 11 was notably absent in the 2020 Anaheim municipal election. In the past, union members campaigned door-to-door in Anaheim's neighborhoods. The union believed that its grassroots activities, particularly in Latino neighborhoods, were crucial in earning the support of Latino residents. According to one union representative, "They know our red shirts. They trust us." The union admitted that there was only so much it could do in Anaheim. One interviewee said, "Disney casts a political shadow over Anaheim." Another asserted, "Disney is still heavily involved in politics and the majority is stacked in its favor." UNITE HERE! Local 11 made the decision to concentrate on the municipal election in nearby Santa Ana and not Anaheim in 2020. The same union members who knocked on doors and walked the streets of Anaheim in the past focused their efforts on Santa Ana in 2020. With the support of the union and the Orange County Democratic Party, which was also led by Briceño, a Democrat won the mayor's race and union-backed candidates became the majority on the Santa Ana City Council. After the 2020 election, Briceño speculated, "We have to see where the future of Anaheim lies for us [the union]. We've made gains in other places." As one prominent pro-balance actor acknowledged, "going to city hall" to press your claims and grassroots organizing "is hard to sustain. The coalition starts to eat itself. Leadership changes. Most folks are gone or retired. People burn out."

The post–People's Council period illustrated how hard it is to compete against Disney's power. Before the 2020 municipal election, former Mayor Tait argued that it is "super difficult" to compete against Disney. He added, "It is hard to find viable candidates. [When you run against Disney,] you get the snot beat out of you." Tait continued, "You need your own money and courage. It must be grassroots. It's very difficult to go against Disney. It would be impossible without districts." Tait also contended, "It's hard to find people with courage" to run against Disney.

Disney's power over Anaheim started long before the post–People's Council era and the *Citizens United* decision, which allowed corporations to spend unlimited amounts on campaign messages.[45] One longtime pro-balance leader described city politics in this way: "Anaheim, California is a medium-size city run by a city council overawed by Disneyland, which gets undue respect." This person also said that the "city's elected officials kowtow to Disneyland on a regular basis. Anything Disney wants, Disney gets." This individual also said the following about the relationship between city government and the entertainment company: "We're overmatched: the city attorney vs. Disney; that's not close to fair." One Disney advocate asked, "Do you want to take on Disney lawyers?" Disney deploys multiple forms of power, and, when it exerts its power, it tends to win. After it lost in 2016, the corporate giant and its allies regrouped and helped elect a probusiness mayor and city council that favored the Anaheim Resort District and big businesses like the Angels baseball team. The city did not have to support Disney and these interests, but the corporate giant used its resources and power to elect and support elected officials who would promulgate pro-Disney policies.

The 2020 municipal election provided a clear picture of the composition and strength of the Disneyland Political Order. Disney constituted the center of the order. It received support from the SOAR PAC, the Anaheim Chamber of Commerce, Visit Anaheim, hoteliers, the Angels and Ducks sports franchises, police unions, and what one source called, "behind the scenes actors," who included realtors, housing developers, and the construction trades. In the fall of 2020, one local actor claimed, "The business class runs everything" in Anaheim. The 2018 and 2020 election results showed the strength of this order, which captured most races with relative ease.

By 2020, pro-balance actors had lost strength. Pro-Disney and pro-balance actors agreed that "anti-police activists and the left," Latinos, the working class, Democrats, labor organizations, and nonprofits made up the core of the pro-balance coalition. Many also noted that members of this coalition were among Anaheim's most marginalized. Service workers, Disneyland Resort employees, and the working poor in the neighborhoods made up a large share of the pro-balance voting base. The results of the 2018 and 2020 elections showed a weakened pro-balance coalition. Labor helped pass Measure L in 2018 but the pro-Disney city council and mayoral candidates otherwise took firm control of the city's executive and legislative branches. Then, seemingly "out of the blue," FBI investigations emerged to challenge the strength of that reacquired control.

## The FBI Intervention

In the middle of May 2021, the FBI released affidavits that alleged criminal activities by the leader of the chamber of commerce, a prominent political consultant, and Mayor Sidhu. These affidavits, and the investigations and wiretaps that produced them, provided a behind the scenes look at politics, power, and agenda setting in Anaheim. According to the FBI, Chamber President Todd Ament and the political consultant, identified in popular media as Jeff Flint of FSB Core Strategies, conspired to defraud their client (a cannabis business), embezzled money from the chamber, committed mortgage fraud, laundered money, or actively worked against their clients' interests.[46]

The affidavit contained details about how a self-described cabal wielded power in Anaheim. The FBI Special Agent Brian Adkins, who led this investigation, wrote extensively about "AMENT's and Political Consultant 1's Influence over the City of Anaheim."[47] In particular, Adkins noted, "Based on their use of the terms 'family members' and 'cabal' coupled with their primary metric of trust to determine which individuals they felt comfortable inviting into the group, I believe that Political Consultant 1 and AMENT had defined a specific, covert group of individuals that wielded significant influence over the inner workings of Anaheim's government."[48] Flint and Ament were accused of holding what they referred to as retreats with a small group of elected officials, city employees, and private actors to set Anaheim's policy agenda. In Ament's words this group was a "cabal" and "family." He classified the retreats as family meetings and offered invitations "to family members only." Adkins concluded that Ament and Flint were "the ringleaders" of the family.[49] He also noted that an employee of Company A was a subordinate ringleader.[50] The *Los Angeles Times* identified Company A as Disney and the employee as Carrie Nocella.

According to the affidavit, "AMENT, Political Consultant 1, and Company A Employee scripted statements made by Elected Official 1 at an Anaheim City Council meeting."[51] The media identified Elected Official 1 as

Mayor Sidhu. Intercepted phone calls and text messages indicated that Flint wrote Sidhu's speech for the meeting and that he shared several drafts of the speech with Ament and Nocella. Sidhu's assistant asked Flint if the script needed to be changed and Flint replied that Nocella wanted any references to the Disneyland parking lot stricken from the text. The mayor made the requested changes. The FBI concluded that Flint and Nocella shared the following exchange via text as they watched the city council meeting in question: "Company A Employee's text read, '[Elected Official 1] reads your script so poorly.' Political Consultant 1 replied, 'Lol,' followed by, 'He doesn't practice.'"[52]

In a second affidavit, Adkins accused Mayor Sidhu of committing major acts of corruption.[53] The FBI alleged that Sidhu used a false Arizona residence on an aircraft registration to avoid paying more than $15,000 in California taxes. The FBI used Ament as a cooperating witness to record conversations with Sidhu, who allegedly leaked confidential information about the pending stadium sale to the Angels, destroyed evidence on his cell phone that would show his wrongdoing related to the stadium land sale, lied to the grand jury, and encouraged Ament to do the same. The affidavit maintained that Sidhu insisted on being part of the negotiating team for the Angel Stadium deal to help the Angels and increase his campaign war chest. In a recorded conversation with Ament, Sidhu explained how he sought to increase the amount of money he wanted the Angels to donate to his campaign from $500,000 to $1 million after the completion of the stadium sale. Like the affidavit he filed the day before, Adkins used this document to discuss the nature of power and politics in Anaheim. He wrote, "The FBI learned that the city of Anaheim was tightly controlled by a small cadre of individuals, to include SIDHU, a particular member of the Anaheim Chamber of Commerce ('the Chamber'), and others." He reiterated his position that Ament, Flint, and Sidhu "wielded influence over the Anaheim City Council majority at this time."

After the allegations surfaced against Sidhu but before the mayor resigned, the Angels sent a letter to the city and asked Anaheim to approve the stadium deal in less than a month. In that letter, the Angels wrote that the city should finalize the deal, which "was the result of an honest arms-length negotiations with city staff and its advisors and has been thoroughly analyzed and debated."[54] The city council disagreed with the Angels and unanimously canceled the Angel Stadium deal on May 24. The Angels decided not to contest the decision. With the stadium deal now dead, in August 2022, team owner Arte Moreno announced that he was exploring options to sell the Angels.

The news of corruption in Anaheim encouraged Council Member Jose Moreno to step up his advocacy for reform in the city. After Sidhu announced his resignation on May 23, 2022, Moreno tweeted, "The resignation of Ana-heim Mayor Harry Sidhu is a necessary, but not sufficient step. The corrosive effects of money in elections pervades our city. Bring out the 'Fabuloso' and let's clean this up Anaheim."[55] With Sidhu out of the picture, the council changed its policy that required a second and a third to put an item on the agenda. Instead, one member could now place topics on the agenda.[56] Two pro-Disney members of the council opposed this change.

Moreno also championed a gate tax and campaign finance reform, both of which failed. Moreno wanted voters to decide whether to impose a 2% gate tax on venues such as Disneyland, but the council rejected the idea.[57] After the council opposed Moreno's proposal, audience members chanted, "Let the People Decide." The mayor pro tem told the crowd, "The voters can hold us accountable at the next election as to whether we've adequately rep-resented them." Council members who opposed the ballot measure on the gate tax argued that taxes were already too high. Moreno countered, "The reality is, colleagues, that Disneyland, the Ducks, the Angels are raising pric-es regardless."

In advocating campaign finance reform, Moreno proclaimed, "The pow-er of money in politics is so seductive. We lose ourselves."[58] He went on to say, "Let's get rid of the conditions that create that seduction." Moreno's plan called for recusals from voting on topics related to campaign donors, fund-raising in election years only, and a seventy-two-hour reporting window after receiving a contribution.[59] The council deadlocked 3–3 on these mea-sures. Pro-Disney city council members opposed the reforms. One of them, Council Member Gloria Ma'ae, a former member of the SOAR advisory board, expressed concerns that the new ordinance would place undue bur-dens on city staff and that state law already prevented pay-for-play schemes. Ma'ae also speculated that the city council had no control over independent expenditures.

Despite calls for campaign finance reform, Disney and its allies contin-ued to use their financial power in Anaheim. Disney transferred $1.3 million to SOAR ahead of the 2022 municipal election.[60] SOAR spent $50,000 on mailers that it distributed in late spring and early summer of 2022.[61] In a July 2022 article in which he detailed Disney's financial power via campaign contributions, the *Voice of OC*'s Nick Gerda wrote, "Disney is by far the largest spender on Anaheim's elections, putting over $1 million into SOAR in each of the last two elections, which SOAR spent on campaign ads for candidates backed by Disney and other resort-area businesses, public cam-paign disclosures show."[62]

In the aftermath of these allegations and Sidhu's resignation, about six-ty residents attended a city council meeting to continue to complain that city government had excluded them while it advanced other interests.[63] They focused on the favorable and clandestine deal that the city council gave to the Angels. They used words like corruption and lack of transparency to characterize the workings of the city council and city government. They also contended that the chamber of commerce ran the city. One of their policy priorities this evening was to have the city council void the Angel Stadium deal. The executive director of OCCORD told the city council,

> At this moment the residents of Anaheim do not have an inclusive democracy in the city of Anaheim. A pillar of this type of democracy is an economic democracy; which is shifting the decision-making power from corporate managers and corporate shell shareholders to a large group of public stakeholders, including workers and residents. The sale of the Angel Stadium is highlighting the corruption, lack of transparency and lack of public input regarding the land that belongs not to a single politician, but to all taxpayers of Anaheim. We call on the city council to halt the sale of . . . the stadium and negotiate with real transparency and public input.

Residents also complained about how Disney and other large-scale corporations benefited at the expense of citizens. Marisol Ramirez, OCCORD's director of programs and development and an Anaheim resident, told the city council,

> In the midst of the pandemic and moments when residents in Anaheim were dying due to complications of COVID and struggling to pay for food and rent, our mayor and the majority council were negotiating deals and accepting campaign contributions with no benefit and transparency to the public. As residents we all have eyes on the corruption that is taking place inside the walls of city hall. Our city includes major businesses and corporations such as Disneyland, Angel Stadium and home to major entertainment, our convention center and Honda Center . . . what role have all these entities played in influencing contracts and city elections with little to no community benefit? Everyone is watching.

## Post–FBI Investigation Reforms

In the wake of the revelations of the FBI investigation and the release of information about the self-proclaimed cabal, corruption and reform took over the Anaheim public agenda. Ashleigh Aitken, who narrowly lost to Sidhu four years earlier, won the mayoral election in 2024 and promised governmental reform. SOAR backed two of the three winners for the city council.

The city council paid $1.5 million to the JL Group to investigate city governance and make recommendations to reform government.[64] The JL Group interviewed 150 people and reviewed more than fifty thousand documents to make the following overall recommendations: "Review the applicability of local ordinances, policies, or procedures. Make appropriate recommendations relative to improving the transparency, ethical conduct and interactions of Anaheim public officials, City staff, and those doing business with the City." The report recommended an ethics officer, a recommitment to the council-manager form of government, lobbying activity reform, and reconsideration of the relationship between the city and the Chamber of Commerce and Visit Anaheim. The investigation concluded that Visit Anaheim secretly diverted $1.5 million of its $6.5 million COVID-19 grant to the Chamber of Commerce. The JL Group asserted that this payment was "inappropriate and likely illegal."[65]

Based on these recommendations, the 2023–2024 city council expanded the definition of lobbyist. The new definition required outside lobbyists and those employed directly by companies to register with the city. Under previous law, in-house workers were not considered lobbyists. Consequently, Disneyland's Carrie Nocella was not considered a lobbyist under the old law, but under the new ordinance, she had to register with the city as a lobbyist. In 2022, the Anaheim city council also had made it a criminal penalty to break local voting rules.

Other reforms enacted by the city council included requiring city council members to retain their emails for twenty-four months instead of ninety days, post the names of those with whom they are meeting, and conduct city business on government-issued phones and emails as opposed to personal phones and email addresses. The council also created an ethics officer position. According to the city, the city council made two changes to local campaign finance ordinances. "The first reform places a $100,000 limit on the amount candidates can lend their campaigns. The second reform requires candidates to pay off campaign debt within 12 months of an election."[66]

In her 2024 state of the city address, Mayor Aitken said, "We are on the cutting edge of having the most transparent government in Orange County."[67] Moreno asserted, "They didn't really touch the most important element of corruption, and that's the influence of campaign money on local decision making." At least one pro-balance actor claimed, "And despite minor, cosmetic 'reforms,' very little has changed." In the post–FBI era in Anaheim, UNITE HERE! Local 11 supported a referendum to increase the local minimum wage for hotels to $25 an hour. It also was behind an effort to recall Natalie Rubalcava, the pro-Disney city council member in District 3. Both measures failed at the ballot box. In September 2023, former Mayor Sidhu pleaded guilty to obstructing justice, committing wire fraud, and lying to the FBI.

The city council unanimously approved DisneylandForward in 2024.[68] Disneyland received the right to build theme park attractions alongside its hotels. It promised between $1.9 billion and $2.5 billion in park investments. Disney paid $39.6 million to the city of Anaheim to buy some streets near the theme park. It also agreed to allocate $30 million for affordable housing, $8 million for parks, and $45 million for infrastructure improvements.

From the late 2010s until the present, real and meaningful competition over power and decision-making had emerged, and Disney responded. Disney at least partially reestablished its governing power, but at a time when the company was subject to much greater scrutiny. As corruption erupted on the political landscape, and the reputations of elected officials were tarnished, the public voiced concern and dismay. Nonetheless, Disney sustained its political power in the face of these disclosures by carefully managing its influence over local politics.

## Theoretical Touchstones

The private perspective argues that cities must concentrate on developmental policies, which are consensual and benefit everyone. The public perspective contends that cities have choices and do not have to pursue the economic development imperative. It questions the extent to which economic development policies further the collective good. The evidence in this era supports the public perspective to a point. The service workers union at Disneyland and their allies provided data that large subsidies to the corporate giant did not help their cause. They listed many of Disneyland's negative consequences, such as lack of affordable housing, the wage gap between top executives and line workers, inadequate health care coverage, and an inability to pay for food.

The People's Council provided the clearest example that the city of Anaheim possesses agency. Leaders in the city with a corporate giant can pursue an agenda that does not promote that company's imperative. However, they need power to set and sustain the agenda. Helped by unions, people power, and an institutional change that gave it the majority on the city council, the People's Council chose neighborhood improvement and government reform over policies that favored Disneyland. It increased public participation over government decisions and eschewed corporate giveaways and policies viewed by its members as boondoggles. The People's Council showed that city councils had choices beyond the Disneyland Imperative. In Anaheim, the pro-balance coalition begged the city council to do something other than promote Disneyland. With few exceptions, the council chose the option favored by the Walt Disney Company. From 2016 to 2018, the city council recognized that it had options and, for the most part, made choices that neighborhoods, taxpayers, and Latinos wanted and declined those preferred by the Anaheim Resort District and Disneyland. Agency and the ability to pursue policies opposed by a corporate giant also support the public perspective.

The politics of Disneyland tells a story about democracy. The Disney Company preferred politics with little citizen participation. It won because a handful of people with authority supported Disney. Initially, the change to district rather than at-large elections of city council members provided more representation for rank-and-file residents of Anaheim. In the first election with this new electoral system, Disney lost its majority on the city council. Voter mobilization for reform candidates led to Disney's defeat and changes to the local government's relationship with the company. The new council promulgated policies that increased citizen feedback and favored additional governmental reforms. Mayor Tait and Council Member Moreno touted the Sunshine Ordinance as a policy that would increase governmental accountability and transparency.

Law professor Richard Schragger and the public perspective highlight how corporations can threaten democracy by allowing markets, rather than voters, to make local decisions. The unions and their allies used democratic methods and instruments to cope with the corporate giant. They launched a ballot initiative to demand a living wage from companies that received government subsidies. Workers who marched the streets in favor of this initiative proclaimed, "This is how democracy works." As it had in the past, Disneyland wanted less public participation and as little government regulation as possible. Its spokespeople argued that the living wage issue should be decided at the negotiating table rather than at the polls.

The public perspective cautions that large-scale capital can threaten democracy. Jose Moreno, Tait, and mayoral candidates in 2018 complained about the ways in which Disney used massive campaign spending to influence local elections. The *Orange County Register* inferred that the chamber of commerce received a quid pro quo no-bid contract from the city in exchange for donating to then candidate Sidhu's campaign. Federal allegations in 2022 supported this claim.

Financial power helped determine the direction of Anaheim's policies. Supported by millions of Disney dollars, prodevelopment candidates won elected office in 2018. They took the rubber match in 2020 as well. The new mayor and council chose to redirect city policies toward Disneyland, the Anaheim Resort District, the Anaheim Chamber of Commerce, Visit Anaheim, developers, and others. The previous council chose to rescind the chamber's contract, reject government subsidies and tax breaks to Disneyland, and pursue governmental reform. Paul Peterson and the private perspective downplay the importance of power, politics, and political choices. In Anaheim, various kinds of power shaped policy, and elected officials made genuine choices. The People's Council made a genuine choice to pay less attention to Disneyland, and the council that succeeded it made a genuine choice to refocus the city's energy toward the theme park. Access to the tools of political power put these groups in positions to make these choices. The public perspective argues that cities can pursue redistributive policies, but it does not account for the tendency of business to reassert itself in the face of policies it opposes. The pro-Disney actors used financial power to retake the majority on the city council and reward allies like the chamber of commerce, Visit Anaheim, and the Angels.

Even though it no longer held the majority, the People's Council set boundaries for future actions taken by the city government. For example, Mayor Sidhu and the new council rejected direct government subsidies and tax benefits for corporate giants because they feared reprisal on the next election day. The new government leaders also emphasized how the seemingly neutral developmental policies that favored the resort district and the Platinum Triangle would benefit neighborhoods and labor. They learned that residents felt neglected by a city government that focused its attention on Disneyland. To improve the situation, Sidhu exercised relational power with Visit Anaheim and the chamber of commerce to identify neighborhood projects that needed governmental attention. The actions of the new mayor and council nevertheless suggest that their concerns for neighborhoods were more symbolic than substantive.

The partnership perspective pays considerable attention to coalitional composition, resources, and organizational capacity. The coalition that opposed Disneyland scored highly enough on these characteristics to defeat the corporate giant and get its policies passed into law. For a time, it had enough voting, relational, and financial power to set the agenda. Service unions made up the key addition to the pro-balance coalition because they enhanced the opposition's public outreach and mobilization. Access to authoritative institutions was the energizing ingredient allowing this new coalition to exercise policymaking power. Armed with government resources, the People's Council placed Measure L on the ballot, and the city attorney, with the support of the mayor and a majority of the city council, rejected Disney's attempt to move its hotel location and keep the tax subsidy. In the past, government had favored Disney. In this two-year period, that was no longer the case.

Sociologist Leland Saito, in his examination of Los Angeles politics observed a fragmentation of power, but, in Anaheim, Disney and its allies have maintained their dominant power position. Disney's leadership style changed over time, and its relational power slipped a bit, but the entertainment company still held concentrated power in the city. In the election after the one that brought the People's Council to power, Disney and its allies regained control of city government. Pro-Disney candidates exercised financial power by outspending their underfunded opponents and, except for Jose Moreno in District 3, won every race. The service union, a major force when the People's Council came to power, did not participate in the 2020 city council election. Reduced organizational capacity on the part of the pro-balance coalition in addition to deficient financial resources meant that this group could not continue to compete against Disney's power. The political order in Anaheim did not become a partnership between business and civil society. The most recent era shows that neighborhood and community concerns occupy one part of the order and Disney and its allies take up another. They do not partner with each other. The FBI investigation into Anaheim demonstrated that Disney's allies ran the city not just to create a favorable business environment (as determined by the local economy's biggest player) but to benefit and enrich their family members. Neighborhood concerns, living wages, and affordable housing represented obstacles to the Disney Political Order and not opportunities to partner with the excluded. Seniors, resort workers, and businesses in Little Arabia and Sunkist Plaza all bemoaned how the Disneyland Imperative ignored their interests. They were far from partners in this political order.

# Part III Conclusion

I n this most recent era (early 2010s to the present), political learning followed social learning. Latinos, Disneyland employees, and others came to
recognize that Disneyland's version of Anaheim didn't work for them. The
Two Anaheims meant that Disneyland and others received governmental giveaways as Latinos faced police brutality and the city suffered from a lack of
affordable housing, low wages, and other problems. Those marginalized by
the Two Anaheims had enough, but they needed to develop the political
capacity to defeat Disney. The election of the People's Council represented
the culmination of social and political learning for opponents of the Disneyland agenda. Social and political learning continued with the living wage
ordinance. Unions, workers, the city's electorate, and elected officials had
enough with Disney's low wages for rank-and-file workers and overcompensa-
tion of executive officials. They were fed up. With the inclusion of unions as
part of the pro-balance/antigreed coalition, advocates for the living wage ordinance accumulated enough power to defeat Disney.

Disney and its allies also went through social and political learning pro-
cesses during the People's Council period. They learned that voters rejected
subsidies and tax breaks and wanted more attention to neighborhoods and
the city as a whole. They also learned the power of unions. The result of this
learning was a baseball stadium and land deal that included neither a subsidy
nor a tax break, but it did emphasize community benefits such as a new city
park and additional low-income housing. The new power in city government attempted to balance development and attention to the Anaheim Resort District

(Disneyland) with representation of local workers, neighborhoods, and the overall community.

Even though Disney continued to exercise financial power through exorbitant campaign spending, it lost its majority on the city council in the first election after the implementation of district voting. During the People's Council's two years in office, Disney employed its standard political strategies but without the success these tactics produced in the past. It could no longer rely on relational power with city government to gain substantive representation. The pro-balance coalition exercised people and financial power through volunteer and voter mobilization efforts, protests when necessary, and campaign contributions that, at times, exceeded the amount spent by Disney.

Disney struck back with its massive financial power. The amount of money spent by Disney on the Anaheim elections became an issue in and of itself. Sidhu, the new mayor, a beneficiary of Disney's campaign contributions, defended himself on election night when he claimed, "I was elected by the voters."

Under a new mayor and city council majority, Anaheim government reestablished strong relational power with the chamber of commerce and Visit Anaheim, which assisted the city with business recruitment and retention and neighborhood input into the budget. The FBI would allege that this relational power was built on corruption, and Mayor Sidhu resigned as a result.

Disney attempted to remain in the shadows in the first city council term after the People's Council. It asked government for little but continued to act behind the scenes and contribute massive amounts of money to proresort actors.

Pro-balance actors bet on the value of democracy and authority. They believed that more democracy would empower them and transform their exclusion to inclusion. In the 1950s, sociologist Floyd Hunter challenged the idea that authority led to power, and many other commentators along the way have agreed that holding office may not result in elected officials governing.[1] The People's Council tested the extent to which authority allowed elected officials to exercise power.

The People's Council illustrated that government could say no to the corporate giant. Its council members argued that the election that brought them to power showed that voters wanted change. In the battle between democracy and capitalism, the People's Council scored a victory for government by the people. The living wage ordinance also illustrated a classic battle between democracy and the economy. Unions used the initiative and referendum process to get their interests represented. As they marched to raise awareness of the living wage ordinance, members of the unions chanted, "This is how democracy works." Disneyland and its allies want less democracy. They did not want the voters to decide on the living wage ordinance and instead asked for the various parties to settle the issue at the negotiating table.

The People's Council advanced new ideas. It focused on neighborhoods in direct ways through development projects in areas that had not seen government attention in decades. It promoted reform and government accountability to an extent that Anaheim had never seen. The People's Council and its allies also favored more democracy and greater citizen input than previous councils had. They established boundaries for future city leaders. For example, public policy needs to produce collective benefits and provide for residents' concerns.

Disney and its coalition partners continued to promote the ideas that Disneyland served the collective good and Anaheim's economic policies had worked to benefit the entire city. They also argued that pro-Disneyland policies allowed Anaheim to improve city services. A majority of the electorate may have disagreed, but the election results skewed by the disproportionate access to funds and other campaign resources returned a pro-Disney majority to the Anaheim City Council. In the post–People's Council period, pro-Disney forces walked a tightrope in which they respected the new terms of coexistence but advanced the familiar, though questionable proposition that economic development policies did address neighborhood concerns. Despite their public rhetoric to the contrary, members of the Disneyland Political Order took both legal and illegal steps to benefit themselves and their allies.

# Conclusion

*The Power Perspective*

This book started with a puzzle: How does a city balance the interests of private control of investment against those of the citizenry when the two conflict? To understand this puzzle in practice, we asked three questions about the relationship between a corporate giant and the medium-size city in which it is located: How have Disneyland and Anaheim coexisted? What were the terms of the coexistence? Under which conditions have the terms changed? Over time, the coexistence shifted from consensual to conflictual.

Anaheim was headed to becoming an unremarkable bedroom community but chose to become home to Disney, turning it into a midsize city shaped by a corporate giant. While Anaheim has profited from this relationship, some residents do not seem to be getting their fair share of the rewards. Over the years, various actors including a powerful union and some of Anaheim's public leadership have tried to upset the Disney-led status quo. Both sides have used various forms of power to advance their agendas. Disney doesn't exert complete power over Anaheim. The city thus serves as a case study of shifting power relations in urban development.

In the late 2010s, a group of city council members along with the union led an insurgency against the Disney-dominated city government, and this coalition enacted counterpolicies. Disney regained control over city government, but its dominance became restricted. Even though it no longer possessed authority in the city, the People's Council, the service union, and other traditionally excluded actors had set a boundary around Anaheim's public policy agenda, like the berm that rings Disneyland.

On the outside of this boundary sat tax rebates (like the ones offered to hoteliers), tax breaks (such as the ban on the gate tax for Disneyland), and so-called giveaways (like the deal Disney struck with the city for the building and ultimate control over the Mickey and Friends Parking Structure). Inside the boundary sat zoning changes and alterations that Disneyland asked for, and received, to the city's land-use policy to execute its newest project, DisneylandForward.

At one point in its time in Anaheim, Disney had hegemony, but that domination was subject to reversal and pushback. The coexistence between Disneyland and the people is more balanced now than it was then, even though Disneyland regained control. Now, even pro-Disney councils expect more from the corporate giant than previous ones did. These expectations include providing city parks and affordable housing with development.

One interesting aspect of this puzzle is that opponents of an agenda focused on Disneyland still want the park to succeed. The Walt Disney Company and the citizenry are not enemies. They are competitors, however, because Disney believes that a policy agenda skewed toward its interests will serve the city well. Residents in neighborhoods, service workers, Latinos, and others sought balance. The goal for the factions that want balance was not the elimination of Disneyland or even the harming of the parks. Instead, they wanted public policy to pay greater attention to them and less attention to Disney. Power dictated otherwise.

This book is about power. The conversation about power so far has been about whether cities have power over their residents or if elected officials need to create the capacity to govern. This book takes a different approach. Power comes in many forms including reputational, relational, financial, voting, people, landowning, and authority. The terms of coexistence skewed in Disney's favor because the company exercised financial, relational, reputational, and landowning power. The terms of coexistence changed, in part, because those who opposed the Disneyland Imperative developed various forms of power as a counterweight to Disney. Unions and Latinos produced change by deploying financial, relational, voting, and people power. When actors have access to and wield different forms of power, they can maintain the status quo or produce change. This conception of power as asymmetrical and multifaceted should change the way we conceive urban governance.

For most of the period, we have observed the terms of coexistence skewed in Disneyland's favor, which we refer to as the Disneyland Imperative. The entertainment powerhouse wanted favorable land-use and taxing decisions. It enjoyed tax breaks and rebates. Disney also sought control over its environment, which included inside its property and in the area around its resort. One observer of Disneyland and Anaheim politics asserted, "Disney wanted Anaheim built in the way they saw it." One pro-balance actor concluded, "Disney wants the flexibility to expand their park. They want freedom for their corporation without pushback from representatives. They will do that by contributing to campaigns that support other groups that will be supportive of their business." Disney seeks to be the dictator over the area in which its theme parks and businesses are located. If growth or development ran counter to Disney's interests, the business titan vigorously objected. And it won. Disney asked the government for infrastructure, and it wanted public entities to pay for it. Disney also wanted government and others to leave it alone. Its core concern was the bottom line.

Power dictated the terms of coexistence. To get the terms it wanted, the Disney Company worked hard to develop and exercise relational and reputational power. Walt Disney built, cultivated, and maintained relationships not only with the most powerful business leaders in the Anaheim area but also with those in positions of authority. He developed this relational power to leverage the city's postwar desire to attract businesses. To sustain these relationships, Disney provided park tickets, golfing and fishing trips, access to exclusive events, and substantial campaign contributions to the elite and powerful citizens of Anaheim. When necessary, Disney threatened the city. On some occasions, Disney mobilized its employees to pressure local officials. Disney's powerful surrogates and allies, such as the chamber of commerce and the Angels MLB team, supported Disney and won policy concessions that served the entertainment behemoth's interests.

For the most part, the actors who supported Disneyland did so because they believed that the theme park's private investment brought vital tax dollars to the city's treasury, allowing Anaheim to pay for the costs of city services. They legitimately believed that a successful Disneyland enriched the entire city. The original actors who pursued Disney believed that Disneyland would be another economic opportunity and potential industrial-type engine for the city. The pro-Disney actors we interviewed believe that the city would be in big trouble without the revenue that Disneyland provides.

The park tickets, drinking trips, and PAC money didn't compel the actors who received them to support Disneyland. Most of the people who received these gifts would have supported Disneyland regardless of the largesse. The gifts did create an even stronger bond between the company and the public and private actors who supported Disneyland.

Disney employed a social education that skewed terms in its favor. The company sold elites and residents alike on the value of the theme park to Anaheim. "As goes Disneyland, so goes Anaheim," was one mantra. Another was that the city shouldn't harm Disney in any way because you don't kill the goose that lays the golden eggs. Facts and figures about Disney's job creation and tax revenue undergirded this social education. The people learned and believed, at least in the early years.

Social learning helps explain the tension between Disney and the citizens of Anaheim over time. More residents realized that Disney received too much, and they didn't receive enough. They learned that Disney caused problems but avoided responsibility. People asked, If Disney is so great for us and the city, then why can't we get our sidewalks fixed? They believed both that Disneyland did not pay its fair share and that, over time, local inequality increased at their expense.

Democracy played a tenuous role in the Disneyland-Anaheim relationship. Disney preferred to keep the scope of political conflict as limited as possible. One person who followed Disney claimed that the company "applies a lot of pressure to city government. A ton." This observer also noted, "Disney doesn't like different voices. They prefer to be behind the scenes and not in the public eye." However, Disney did want more public participation when it was losing on an issue. Otherwise, Disney sought limited popular input and avoided political scientist E. E. Schattschneider's conclusion that expanding the scope of conflict endangers the current powerholders.[1]

Disney stayed away from most of the day-to-day issues that affect city government. According to one observer, "Disney only gets involved in issues that are relevant to them and making money. They'd like you to believe that they cared about everything, but they don't." Disney limited the scope of the local public agenda. It aspired to be like political scientist Peter Bachrach and economist Morton S. Baratz's second face of power, the one that restricts the public agenda items to issues without relevance to its interests.[2]

The terms of Disney's coexistence became less favorable to Disney over time. Disney had to expend more (and more varied) power to get less. When people's social learning did not match the lessons of day-to-day experience, the opportunity opened for change. People realized that Disneyland didn't benefit everyone and that the park came with negative consequences. Disney frustrated residents because the park seemed to get more from the city without paying its fair share. This transformation of the social learning was a key component to the change in the terms of coexistence.

Pro-balance actors learned how to defeat the political giant. They used lawsuits, a change in the city's method of election, initiatives and referenda, coalition building, and electoral politics to defeat Disney. The pro-balance coalition provided a social education of its own and highlighted that Two Anaheims existed, pro-Disney deals were crony capitalism and corporate giveaways, and Disney did not pay its fair share. People agreed. For one city council term, the so-called People's Council implemented policies opposed by Disney. In the next election, Disney used its vast financial resources to recapture a majority of city council seats, but the terms of local coexistence remain altered.

Three elements make up new terms of coexistence between city and corporate giant. First, Anaheim will not provide subsidies to Disney or anyone else. Second, tax breaks are also forbidden. Businesses, politicians, and the residents seem to agree to these terms. In fact, Disney asked the city for little while the People's Council was in power, and it emphasized that it did not want tax rebates. Third, any development needs to consider the effects on neighborhoods. The new narrative was that development should benefit neighborhoods. These three elements created a public policy boundary that Disney could not cross.

## Theoretical Touchstones Revisited

The coexistence between Disneyland and Anaheim refutes much, but not all, of Paul Peterson's *City Limits* and the private perspective. Structure played a role in Disney's power, but it was not determinative. Cities compete over economic development, as demonstrated by Anaheim's worries about the construction of a second Disney park in Long Beach and the allocation of Disney dollars to company properties in Paris, Orlando, and other far-flung locations. Peterson concludes that cities pursue an economic development imperative. Anaheim did not always follow an economic development imperative. A Disneyland Imperative dominated this city, and, at times, it conflicted with economic development and growth. In the case of building height restrictions, Disney opposed development and won. It also balked at certain kinds of development in the vicinity of the theme park. When an economic development imperative clashed with the Disneyland Imperative, the city pursued the latter.

From the outset, some residents and other actors opposed the Disneyland Imperative, but opposition was minimal at first. HOME lacked the power to defeat Disney, and most of the city still held the entertainment company in high regard. As people experienced an altered social education, they came to realize that what was good for Disneyland didn't always benefit them. With time, the opposition grew so powerful that it captured the mayor's office and a majority of the city council. It changed the terms of the Disneyland-Anaheim coexistence but lacked the power to defeat or even compete against the Disneyland Political Order on a permanent basis.

The private perspective touts the collective benefits of the economic development imperative. The Disneyland Imperative produced clear winners and losers. Disneyland was the chief benefactor of the political order that bears its name. It received preferential treatment from government, including favorable taxing and zoning policies. Many residents did not reap the benefits of the Disneyland Imperative. Traffic and noise and other kinds of pollution were some of the negative effects of the Disneyland Imperative. Disneyland employees, many of whom were working-class Latinos from Anaheim and the surrounding area, didn't earn a living wage as Disneyland prospered, and the conditions of their neighborhoods weren't better because of Disney's presence. For decades, whole swaths of the city lacked any kind of economic development. For one two-year span, a pro-balance majority on the city council emphasized quality of life issues and development for Anaheim's neighborhoods.

The private perspective undervalues the importance of politics. Cities deal with the starkest issues that affect people every day. Murder, police brutality, racism, other kinds of discrimination, housing, economic development, jobs, and schooling are some of the major issues confronting municipalities. These policy areas have immediate and long-lasting effects on the citizenry and are often the issues that pack council chambers. Anaheim's political choices advanced Disney but did not address many of these vital issues in the city.

Power determines a city's agenda. The corporate giant goes to great lengths to create, build, and reinforce relationships with those who hold authority in city government. The founding of the theme park, the imposition of height restrictions, and the gate tax ban show that Disneyland exercises its relational, financial, and reputational power. Any analysis that discounts or ignores how these explicit and implicit kinds of power affect municipal policy does not understand urban politics. Power affected the choices made by Anaheim city government. Disney used its financial power to elect candidates sympathetic to its cause. If elected officials wavered, Disney pressured them or supported other candidates. Pro-balance actors explained how difficult it is to compete against Disney. They struggled to find quality candidates to challenge pro-Disney candidates. Peterson's viewpoint, emphasizing the economic determination of local public affairs, doesn't account for these elements of political and economic power.

Cities make genuine choices, even in the face of a strong economic imperative. Our account of Anaheim demonstrates that a single-minded focus on economic development produces negative consequences for democracy. On many occasions Anaheim residents seemed to want one thing and Disney sought something else, and the economic titan won. Residents secured some victories over Disney—namely, the passage of a living wage ordinance—but those wins were infrequent. Voters and residents struggle to compete against Disney. This observation falls in line with other research that shows that defeating powerful interests is possible but takes time and comes with great difficulty.[3] The public perspective is correct about these elements of urban politics.

The public perspective argues that cities can pursue policies other than development. This perspective captures part of the Anaheim story but misses an important piece. The power necessary to set this agenda is critical, and the politics involved in deviating from what the economic and political colossus wants is a key variable. Cities can redistribute or take paths not preferred by powerholders, but power often prevents these policies. Law professor Schragger's work predicted that a progressive mayor, labor unions, and translocal networks would fight back against an economic powerhouse.[4] Resistance happened in Anaheim because the pro-balance coalition learned how to compete against the corporation, and they exercised people, voting, financial, and relational power to do it. Schragger and the public perspective do not tell us what happens next. Cities cannot prioritize redistribution (or any other policy for the public good) unless they exercise sustained policy execution oversight. Democracy is not enough.

When a new politics emerges, the financial power can beat it back in medium-size cities. It can more easily consolidate power in a medium-size city, like Anaheim, as opposed to a larger metropolis like Los Angeles. A redistribution of power in Los Angeles has made the partnership between the public and private more feasible. Major corporations exercise greater power in medium-size cities, which have fewer resources than the New Yorks or Chicagos. The exercise of corporate power is proportional to the institutional capacity of the private entity and the size of the city—the greater the corporation's institutional capacity, and the smaller the city, the more power the corporation wields. The ease with which large-scale multinational corporations can consolidate power decreases the likelihood of a partnership or balance.

The partnership perspective suggests that a balance between economic power and city is possible, but the relationship in Anaheim presents a puzzle. Can the interests of Disneyland (or any large business) be balanced with those of residents or the neighborhoods? Even some of Disney's fiercest critics say the city is better off with the financial powerhouse than without it. If given the opportunity to eject Disneyland from the city, they would not. Not everyone feels this way, of course. Some in the pro-balance coalition wish that Disneyland had disappeared after COVID-19 showed the dire consequences of a municipality's reliance on tourism and one theme park. We argue that residents in Anaheim want greater balance. Residents believed that the city catered too much to Disney to the exclusion of everyone else. The proper nexus and balance between a city and such an economic and political titan is quite difficult. Disney does not want balance. It cares about its business. Disney's power helped steer the city's policy agenda away from balance and toward company interests. In the new terms of coexistence, because of the People's Council, city leaders and large businesses like the Angels paid greater public attention to how development and any city decision affected neighborhoods. Whether this kind of attention was more symbolic than real remained to be seen but even under the new terms, Disney ruled.

## The Power Perspective

One contribution of this book is that we show how different powers are mobilized and exercised in ways not covered in previous scholarship. Our power perspective reconciles the differences among and the deficiencies within the public, private, and partnership perspectives. Each of these perspectives needs greater consideration of power, politics, and change. The private perspective misses the power dimension. The economic development imperative does not drive the urban agenda. Instead, power drives the public agenda, in this case, economic development. The public perspective does not discuss how power will affect actors' abilities to place redistributive policies on the agenda. It also misses how power maintains and changes the agenda. This perspective needs to consider how power makes it harder to change the agenda preferred by the corporate giant. The partnership perspective does not account for the effect of city size on power. While developers and big businesses may have lost some power in the largest cities, a different power dynamic has played out in medium-size cities, where economic powerhouses beat back the so-called new politics.

The exercise of power happens in every locality and public jurisdiction, and this book provides insights into how the status quo gets established and maintained, what opponents can do about it, and how powerholders respond to challenges. This book is about power and how a massive company and its allies exercise power to set and maintain a public agenda that favors them. Power determines a city's agenda. To understand how and why cities act, scholars need to locate powerholders and what those with power want from the city. Corporations like Disney develop and exercise various kinds of power. In Anaheim, Disney built and maintained relationships with the most influential businesses and leaders in the city and area, educated powerholders and residents about the company's value to them, offered massive funding to political campaigns, threatened to leave or allocate resources elsewhere, and mobilized residents and employees. Pro-balance actors exercised power through social education and learning, and they reformed institutions, mobilized at the grassroots, formed broad-based coalitions, and spent money on campaigns.

Power determines what a city does. Those who wield power determine the city's agenda. Cities have pursued economic development strategies because their powerholders advocated this agenda. They have moved away from a reliance on this agenda when the corporate regime's power waned. Cities with an economic titan or a dominant industry will often pursue an agenda that favors that company or a small circle of businesses because those with power and their allies want it this way. If people want the agenda to change, they need to develop the power to make it so.

Power imbalances also explain economic inequalities throughout the city. Disney exercised the most power, and people in the western part of the city had the least. The city responded to those who had power and ignored those who didn't. The power differential either created or exacerbated inequality. The terms of coexistence shifted when opponents of the status quo exercised greater power than those in charge. Inequality remains because the agenda still skews toward Disney. Power explains this outcome as well.

## Political Order

This book makes another contribution by offering a detailed expansion and improvement of regime theory with our use of political order. To understand how power operates in a city, a holistic perspective that includes public and private actors along with agenda setters, agenda supporters, the counter-agenda, and the marginalized is needed. The concept of political order allowed us to identify who set and supported the agenda, which actors opposed the agenda, and who lost because of the agenda. We also tracked fidelity toward the policy agenda in each area. Political order adds nuance to traditional urban regime theory because it provides an updated framework to understand governance in the context of an ever-changing and evolving setting. Political orders shift over time, and it is through longitudinal analysis that these shifts can be mapped.

The political motion across time as described in the coming pages explains how actors have set the local agenda and the ways in which opponents have changed governance. Critics have claimed that regime theory lacks this kind of explanatory power. A tracing of the political order and agenda fidelity across eras illustrates why and how change has occurred in Anaheim. The political order framework also overcomes another criticism of regime theory because it shows how governance typically marginalizes some sectors of society.

### *Period #1: 1950s–1990s*

The first era lasted from the time of the founding of Disneyland until the early to mid-1990s. During this time, the city and Disney had a peaceful coexistence. Some people opposed Disneyland, but, overall, the city and Disney enjoyed a solid partnership in this period with the city's agenda tilted toward the corporate giant. Anaheim tended to comply with whatever Disney wanted. A Disneyland Imperative dominated the city of Anaheim during this period. Favorable land-use decisions highlighted this era's terms of coexistence. To establish Disneyland in the first place, the city exercised its land-use powers to annex the unincorporated properties that became the theme park's site. Disney also asked the city for restrictive zoning ordinances to maintain the park's illusory apartness from its surroundings. These building height restrictions limited economic development not only near Disneyland but even miles away. The height restriction ordinance showed that Anaheim pursued a Disneyland Imperative as opposed to a broadly oriented economic development imperative. When the interests of Disneyland clashed with those of other developers, the city sided with Disney. The economic powerhouse also pushed for and received favorable taxing decisions. In particular, Anaheim exercised its taxing power and agreed not to levy a tax on Disneyland admissions.

Disney established its political dominance in this era. Walt Disney built relational power with the three biggest power wielders in Anaheim. His brother Roy cultivated relationships with hundreds of other political and business leaders. Walt, Roy, and the Disney Company directed social education at elites and residents alike, telling everyone that what was good for Disneyland would be good for Anaheim. Most believed. These social education lessons included facts like the number of jobs the park created and how much tax revenue Disneyland and affiliated businesses generated. This cultivation of relationships continued well after the theme park's founding. Disney provided park tickets, golfing and drinking trips, gifts, and large campaign contributions to maintain and advance its relationships and solidify its political power. The mayor, Anaheim administrators, city council members, and planning commissioners, possessing the land-use and taxation powers unavailable to Disney as a private entity, championed and enacted Disney's policies in this period.

If the Disney Company feared that its relational power and social education weren't enough, it employed other kinds of power. In the case of the height restriction, Disney used its reputational power to threaten that it would no longer invest in the park if the planning commission didn't protect Disneyland's illusory environment. It also mobilized its employees to put pressure on elected officials to not approve a gate tax. These tactics worked, and Disney received what it wanted.

A Disneyland Political Order ruled Anaheim during this era (see Figure C.1). Disney dictated the city's priority agenda, one that furthered Disney's interests and avoided what Disney did not want. Initially, Anaheim's mayor, city administrator, and chamber of commerce also occupied the center of that order, but their successors later moved into more auxiliary roles. Other supporters included the city and region's civic, political, and business lead-

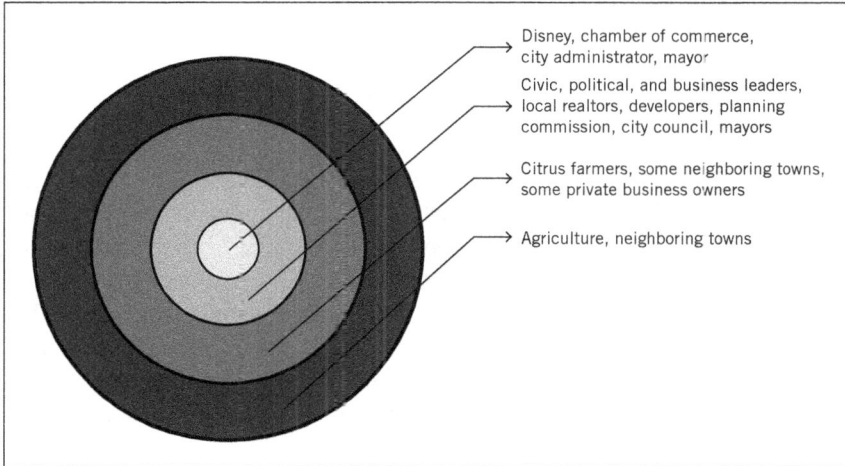

Disney, chamber of commerce, city administrator, mayor

Civic, political, and business leaders, local realtors, developers, planning commission, city council, mayors

Citrus farmers, some neighboring towns, some private business owners

Agriculture, neighboring towns

**Figure C.1** Political order, first era.

ership. The authority of the city council and planning commission codified Disney's agenda. Other members of the order's second tier, supporting and benefiting from the Disneyland Political Order, included the Angels, developers, local realtors, the convention center, and the visitors bureau. Those with an alternative agenda were quite few in this era. Developers who wanted to build vertically in the city clashed with the Disney Company, and they lost. Some private companies and neighboring towns opposed various aspects of the Disneyland project, but pro-Disney actors argued that these opponents actually desired a piece of the theme park's financial pie. In addition to certain developers, the citrus industry lost because of the Disneyland Political Order. Once the theme park was built and began to make money, the city and industry shifted away from citrus fields and toward businesses that profited from Disneyland's success. However, owners of the city's citrus farms did earn top dollar for their land (see Figure C.1).

Policy fidelity toward the Disneyland Imperative was quite strong and persistent in the park's first era. The founding of Disneyland aligned with the city's policy agenda advocating industry and growth. The height restrictions in Anaheim revealed that the city's policy priority was narrower than the advancement of growth in general, but rather to advance Disneyland's particular interests. In the case of the founding, growth and Disneyland overlapped, so the policy agenda appeared to be pro-growth. In regard to the height restrictions, however, Disneyland opposed growth and the city leaders chose Disneyland. The ban on a gate tax showed that the city wanted to protect Disney's bottom line and avoid any actions that might compromise park attendance. If people tried to mess with the goose that laid the golden eggs in this period, they lost. And they lost unequivocally.

### Period #2: 1990s–2010s

A contentious coexistence between Disney and pro-balance actors intensified from the early 1990s into the early 2010s. Disney asked for more from the city during this period, and it received what it wanted, but unlike the previous era, government and some sectors of society pushed back. At the start of this era, Disney sought to build a second theme park and wanted favorable zoning regulations, including the construction of a structure reaching three hundred feet in height. It also asked the government to pay for infrastructure and a parking garage, which Disney wanted built on its property. This proposed WestCOT expansion marked the first real pushback against Disney by the planning commission and residents, where both asked the company to modify its plans for the park. The city also balked at Disney's requests and wanted certain assurances from the company. Disney never built West-COT because the finances did not work in its favor.

In the aftermath of WestCOT, Disney asked for and received greater control over the area that surrounded the theme park. The city used its land-use power to create restrictive zoning ordinances that beautified the area. The Anaheim Resort District provided the kind of control over the neighborhood that Walt Disney wanted but had not achieved. The creation of this district changed how residents perceived the city's relationship with Disneyland. Before the Anaheim Resort District, both the city neighborhoods at some distance from and those adjoining Disneyland declined together. The resort district became a shiny, beautiful, and well-policed oasis while the outlying west side of Anaheim continued to decline. The district helped establish the idea that two cities of Anaheim existed, one for Disney and one for everyone else. This type of social lesson changed how residents viewed the coexistence between corporate giant and city. Labor unions and growing demographic power also facilitated long-term change that started in this period.

The deals that surrounded the construction of Disneyland's second park intensified the view among some that the city provided too much to the company and too little to the people. The terms of the second park included a city-financed parking garage on Disney's property, which the company would receive once Anaheim completed the bond payments. Disney pays a dollar per year to the city to lease the garage. Anaheim also provided infrastructure to the area and agreed to not tax a Disneyland ticket for decades.

Many observers and key players identified the fight over low-cost housing in the Anaheim Resort District as the turning point in the relationship between Disney and the city. Disney insisted on control over the resort district area. It rejected the construction of the housing. Disneyland workers and working-class people in and around city neighborhoods believed they had the right to live where they worked. They fought Disney and secured some victories along the way but lost in the end.

During this second era, Disney exercised power in some intense ways. For the WestCOT plan, it threatened to build a new theme park in Long Beach. During the affordable housing debate, Disney sued the city for the first time, pushed initiatives and referenda to overturn city decisions and prevent government influence on future projects, and even worked to disqualify a city council member from voting on the issue. The affordable housing issue showed that Disney could no longer rely on city authority to carry out its policy preferences. The corporate giant used democracy when necessary, and defeat at the city council inspired Disney to turn to the voters. This tactic was rare and noteworthy.

Disney and other developers stood to benefit from a new city policy that allowed for tax rebates in the construction of four-diamond hotels. Led by service unions and the mayor, at this point the public turned against Disney and the city. Residents went through a social learning process and, in turn, employed social education themselves. They voiced their frustration. As part of the social education, unions, Mayor Tait, and other pro-balance actors argued that the gate tax ban and the hotel subsidies represented corporate giveaways and crony capitalism. People wanted tax breaks, subsidies, and favorable deals for Disney to end, but they lacked the power to change the terms of coexistence.

The Disneyland Political Order remained intact during this second era although Disney lost some of its grip on the city agenda. Disneyland continued to set the public agenda, but, as the affordable housing conflict demonstrated, it no longer exercised complete control over public officials. Despite moments when they questioned or opposed Disney outright, the city council and planning commission remained part of the second tier of the Disneyland Political Order. They supported Disney's plans for a second park and championed favorable tax deals for the corporation. SOAR and WestCOT 2000, a coalition of the city and region's top businesspeople, the chamber of commerce, hoteliers, the convention center, the visitors bureau, and city staff also supported, benefited from, and implemented parts of the Disneyland Imperative in this era.

Disney lost some relational power in this period. During Walt Disney's lifetime, the company had a strong relationship with the city's political elite and that continued into the 1990s. Disneyland's leadership became more corporate and distant over time, and this change in leadership diminished the company's relational power. This decrease in relational power also helped change the Disneyland Political Order when it moved into the third period.

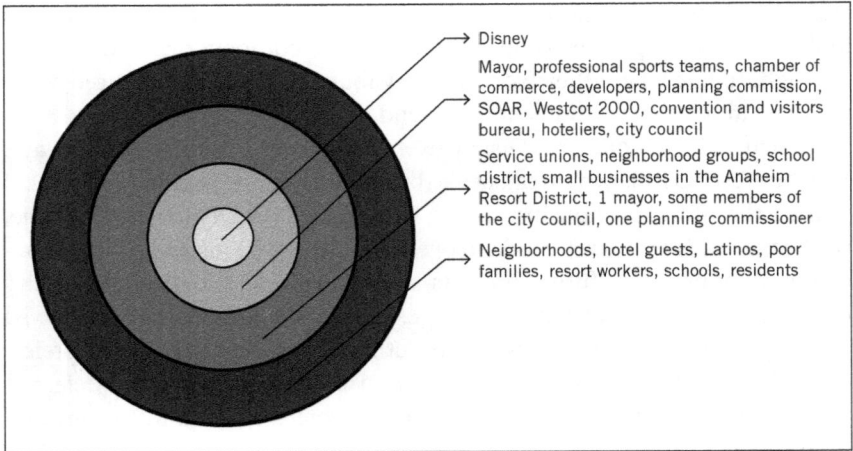

**Figure C.2** Political order, second era.

The political order changed as the pro-balance coalition grew larger and louder (see Figure C.2). A mayor, a member of the city council, Latinos, a homeowners group, the working class more generally, Disneyland employees and service unions, the school district, and small businesses in the Anaheim Resort District opposed elements of the Disneyland Imperative. They exercised relational power. Hotel guests, poor families, resort workers, and neighborhoods lost because of the Disneyland Political Order. The pro-balance coalition went through a period of social learning about the effects of the Disneyland Imperative, but it had yet to figure out how to defeat the economic titan. Fidelity toward the Disneyland Imperative remained concentrated, but it was not as unified as it had been during the first period.

### Period #3: Early 2010s–Present

The most recent period in the story of the coexistence between city and business colossus in Anaheim was as much about the pro-balance actors as it was Disney (see Figure C.3). The pro-balance coalition changed the terms of the coexistence, even though it held authority for a short period. Pro-balance actors included Latino activists, the Disneyland service workers union and its affiliates, and the ACLU. They created a broad-based coalition that defeated Disney at the polls and elected the so-called People's Council, a majority of whom believed that city government had done too much to advance Disneyland. This new council sought greater balance between the interests of Disney and of the rest of the city. Its reign was temporary. Its effects lasted longer.

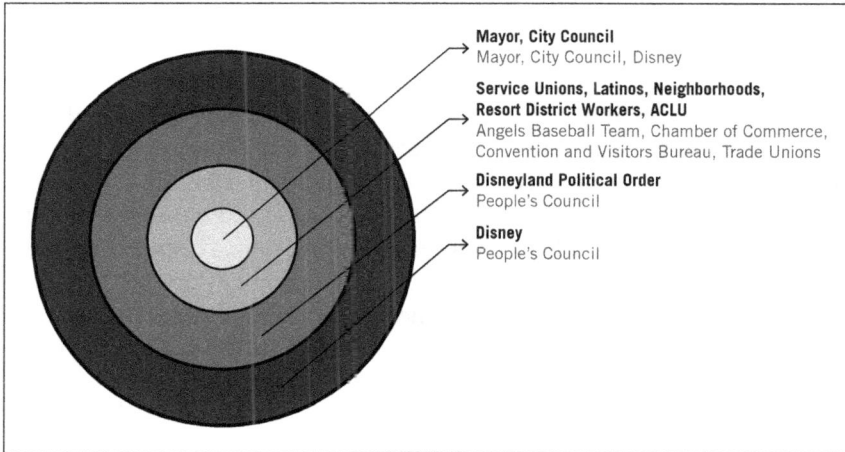

**Figure C.3** Political order, third era. *(Note: People's Council Order in Bold, Disneyland Political Order in Gray.)*

Social and political learning allowed the pro-balance coalition to change the terms of coexistence. While its social learning began in an earlier period, the pro-balance coalition went through political learning in this era. It learned how to defeat political and economic power. It exercised power through a politically sophisticated mix of lawsuits, institutional change, a broad and deep coalition, initiatives and referenda, and elections and office holding. Unions provided financial support and mobilization of voters, who elected a pro-balance council and passed a living wage ordinance. Without the service unions and voting power, the pro-balance coalition would have lost. Without the People's Council, the pro-balance coalition would have been unable to implement policy reform.

Awareness that Disney asked for too much and did not produce enough for the city was not the only reason for change. Service unions educated the public about the negative effects of Disneyland and the company's treatment of its employees. They brought financial power that allowed them to pass a living wage ordinance in the face of Disney's expressed objections. They galvanized people and voting power by going door-to-door. Because it was so difficult to compete against Disney, in a subsequent election, the city's main service union turned its attention away from Anaheim and to a neighboring city. The consequences of this shift were that Disney regained dominance over the city council and the union's candidates won the mayoralty and city council in Santa Ana. The use of people and voting power to produce change is quite difficult to sustain. Financial power comes with longer-lasting effects.

Latinos developed greater voting power, which helped them to compete against and, in some instances, defeat Disney. The social learning of Latinos was at the core of this group's voting power due to the experiences of extreme economic and political inequality. Latino organizations helped Latinos develop political capacity. They sued the city and pressed for affordable housing, political representation, and better treatment from the police. Mistreatment by the police broadened social learning as did the creation of the Anaheim Resort District. Latino voting and people power helped change the Disneyland Political Order.

The People's Council Order advanced new terms for the Disneyland-Anaheim relationship. Chief among these new terms were no tax deals, no government subsidies, and more attention to neighborhoods. The new council ended the luxury hotel tax rebate policy as soon as it could. During the two years of the People's Council, parts of the city received the kind of attention that they had not received for decades. Anaheim shifted from an exclusive focus on the Disneyland Imperative toward quality of life issues in neighborhoods. The council also passed governmental reform and placed the living wage ordinance on the ballot. At Disney's request, it also agreed to end the agreements that not only banned a gate tax on a Disneyland ticket for up to forty-five years but also allowed Disney to get a tax rebate for construction of a luxury hotel in Downtown Disney.

The People's Council reinforced Clarence Stone's point about the importance of authority.[5] Without the support of those with authority, the corporate giant no longer enjoyed public policies that favored it. With institutional authority on its side, neighborhoods received much more attention from government. The People's Council also supports Stone's point that cities can make choices and are not simply driven by economic factors. This new council thought that feeding the so-called economic engine didn't work for the city. According to one public official, "Disney is the engine, but you have to take your foot off the gas every once in a while." The People's Council chose a new direction and demonstrated that Anaheim was not path dependent. The People's Council's rise and brief time in the sun altered the local order sufficiently to create a new balance of forces and code of political conduct, leaving Disney as the chief political force but restricting some of its options and forcing institutional players to pay more attention to neighborhoods, the Latino population, and service workers.

Policy agenda infidelity and power diffusion were the hallmarks of this two-year period. The city no longer unified behind Disneyland. The Disney Company and city government were on opposite sides on a consistent basis for the first time. Multiple powerful coalitions advanced their agendas on the city and disagreed on the best course of action for Anaheim. Disney wanted an eastern gateway that never happened. Previous councils would have approved this project, but Disney abandoned the gateway because it needed the approval of the People's Council. Disney wanted to relocate its luxury hotel. It lost. Disney wanted a streetcar to drop people off at its gates. It lost. Disney opposed the living wage. It lost. Disney lost more in this two-year span than in the previous sixty years combined. The new political order moved toward an agenda that benefited others, in this case, low-wage workers and neighborhoods. It sought a greater balance between the interests of Disneyland and those of people in neighborhoods. Disney understood the new terms. It asked for little and made sure to avoid even a discussion about tax breaks or subsidies. Disney also fought back to regain control of the city's political order.

Disney used its financial power—namely, massive campaign contributions—to regain most of the city council seats and the mayor's seat in 2018. Two years later, the candidates supported by Disney won every council seat up for election. In two years, the People's Council went from holding four of the seven council seats to one. The service workers union, which helped make the People's Council possible, exercised its financial and people power elsewhere in 2020 and with great success. Its candidates captured a majority of the city council and the mayor's office in neighboring Santa Ana. The union's action showed how difficult it is to compete against Disney.

Even though it after regained control over the city council and mayor's office, Disney stayed quiet for a long period. The Angels baseball team served as a surrogate for Disney because it secured a favorable deal from Anaheim for the purchase of its stadium and land around that facility. The mayor and city council majority emphasized that the Angels received neither a tax break nor a government subsidy. They also highlighted how the Angels agreed to build green space around new construction for the benefit of Anaheim residents. The Angels deal showed the new terms of coexistence between the city and big business. Government subsidies and tax breaks were off the table. Furthermore, every development needed to pay attention—at least lip service—to how it served city neighborhoods and residents.

Disney worked behind the scenes to elect a mayor and city council partial to its interests. As revealed by an FBI investigation, Disney remained the city's power broker. The mayor also occupied the center of this new order. The chamber of commerce, Visit Anaheim, the Angels, the tourist sector, SOAR, and trade unions supported and benefited from this order. They sat in the second ring. The new order decimated the People's Council, which lost authority because of Disney's power. The legacy of the People's Council and its supporters was a new set of terms for the coexistence between the city and the Walt Disney Company. Gone were the days when Disney negotiated favorable tax deals or took advantage of government subsidies. The new terms forbade that. They also meant that all projects needed to pay attention to the effects on the neighborhoods. When Disney announced new plans for Disneyland in March 2021, it emphasized that it wanted zoning changes that would enhance city services. It stressed that it wanted neither government subsidies nor tax breaks.

## Why the Anaheim-Disneyland Relationship Matters

This book provides a practical application of the ways in which private capital and power affect public purposes. Disneyland affects Anaheim every day and in every way. It provides revenue every day. It causes traffic every day. It makes demands on the city in some fashion every day. This relationship presents a real-world problem: How does the government of a medium-size city balance the interests of private control over capital with those of the citizenry when the two conflict? The Anaheim government had to figure out how to solve this problem because both the content and the appearance of private and public interests diverged over time. At first, Disney had convinced most people that its interests coincided with the public good. Over time, people realized that this convergence didn't exist.

Cities operate in a context of scarce resources. While much of the urban politics scholarship has moved on from the regime politics concept, this part of urban regime theory remains true and important. Cities do not have the money to do whatever they please. As political scientist Clarence Stone asserts, cities must create the capacity to govern. Faced with scarcity of resources, cities must develop the power to govern; they do not have intrinsic power over those whom they govern.

The Anaheim experience shows how power affected a city's agenda. The city sided with private control over investment because Disney possessed an extensive tool kit of power. Walt Disney had created a political order that supported his agenda. He and his company have used social education to teach the most powerful people and residents about the benefits of his enterprise. Many believed, and some prospered. Social education and social learning represent an important part of the exercise of corporate power. To solidify and develop relational power, Disney took the city and region's most powerful on trips and provided them with free park tickets. When that largesse outlived its utility, Disney exercised its financial power through exorbitant campaign contributions. It also used threats, employee mobilization, lawsuits, and initiatives and referenda to exercise power. In every city, those who control private investment exercise these kinds of power. If the public at large wants change, they need to develop and exercise an array of political tools. To effect change, the people need more democracy; those who control private investment want less.

Pro-balance actors showed how to make democracy work, a lesson that change agents can use in a variety of settings. First, they gained awareness that private interests didn't provide for the collective good. This process took decades in Anaheim. Then, agents of change provided a social education to others that the status quo did not serve public purposes. They offset the corporate narrative. Grassroots organizing with a broad-based coalition helped agents of change compete against and even defeat champions of the status quo, but the road was hard.

Power determines the agenda. Cities have skewed toward an economic development imperative because proponents of that agenda exercise multiple powers. If the people in neighborhoods had millions to spend on campaigns, and corporations did not, government would favor their interests. People can set the agenda when they can develop and exercise power. That task is especially complicated and difficult in medium-size cities where one powerful corporation or business sector can more readily consolidate power than in a large city.

## The Fight for Balance

As he reflected on the Disney Company's role in the city of Anaheim, a member of the city council concluded that the relationship between these two institutions is a matter of philosophy. "It's a question of who owns the city. Who owns the democracy?" The pro-Disney answer to these questions is that public policy geared toward Disneyland and the resort district provides collective benefits. Consequently, Disney should have a major say in how the city is governed, especially when it comes to Disneyland and the company's interests. Residents provide a different answer, one that argues that Disney dollars rule the city and the people don't. They feel that their vote should matter more than Disney money, but it does not. While the people should rule in a democracy, cities operate in a context of scarce resources. Cities need investment dollars to survive. The real dilemma that faces government institutions and their occupants is figuring out what they can do to balance the interests of the people and large-scale businesses. The story of Disneyland in Anaheim encapsulates this conflict, and it is a tale of how to balance two competing forces, with one much more powerful than the other.

How can residents gain greater balance between their interests and those of a business power? The Disneyland experience provides some lessons. First, residents need to question the social education they have received from the large-scale business and its allies. The economic power practices social education that ends in social learning among the people. The education so internalized promotes the value of the corporation to the city and residents' lives. Citizens must ask whether the social education matches their reality. Once people unlearn this social education, they need to gain power. Social learning is not enough. To compete against an economic behemoth, those who oppose its agenda need to form a deep and broad-based coalition. While the corporate giant's main resource is money, the opposing coalition tends to respond with voting and people power.

To exercise that power, an alternative social education curriculum must be articulated. Grassroots insurgents must teach fellow residents and any potential allies that their reality differs from what the company claims. This social education can take place on the internet, at city council meetings, via demonstrations and protests, and through traditional media. Money can help counteract the financial resources held by the financial titan. In Anaheim, union financial resources helped elect pro-balance candidates and pass a referendum for a living wage. Lawsuits can also help opponents score victories against the dominant business interest. They provide a particular form of social education. The media often reports on lawsuits, and this coverage can teach residents about the plight of others, even when the lawsuits do not provide the desired relief.

Voting and institutional authority constitute ways for residents and opponents of the corporate political order to exercise power. Residents can elect mayors and members of the city council who either oppose the economic powerhouse or do not favor the corporate agenda as much as other candidates. Once in office, these city council members can support an agenda that advances interests other than those of the city's dominant economic entities.

The path to power is quite difficult for those who oppose a city's financial colossus. Grassroots organizing takes time and dedication. It often fizzles over time because it is so difficult to maintain. The path to power is also challenging because the economic titan possesses the institutional staying power—deep financial reserves, the political muscle represented by skilled attorneys and other professionals, long-cultivated personal ties to local elites—and rejects attempts to change its agenda. The fight between the people and corporate power tells an important story about democracy in America.

## The Corporate Giant and Democracy in America

The power of the corporate giant wilts democracy in America because it often subverts the will or interests of the people. The money that the corporation pours into local elections trumps people power. The candidates supported by the megabusiness can outspend their opponents by as much as 250–1. They often win elections because they have financial support and the name recognition that comes along with it. The most recent exercises of Disney's power show that campaign spending is not only a national or state issue;

in this medium-size city with an economic juggernaut, financial power in the form of campaign expenditures carried the day and crushed the opposition. Urban politics scholarship tends to miss this vital aspect of power.[6] Studies like those of global cities by political scientists Paul Kantor and Hank Savitch, while helpful in advancing our understanding of how cities govern, miss how one particular private actor has the opportunity to exert oversize influence in medium-size and smaller cities.

For the most part, the financial powerhouse opposes more participation. It likes to set the agenda with as small a circle as possible. Time and again, Disney won a public policy issue because a handful of elected or appointed officials sided with it. The business titan wants to play the role of Bachrach and Baratz's Second Face of Power.[7] It seeks to set what was and wasn't acceptable for the public agenda and remain in the shadows. When a relevant issue became public, the economic power galvanized its supporters, but, even then, it hoped to remain out of the public spotlight. It preferred to have others lobby for it and sought the intimacy of city council and city planning commission votes. It favored greater participation only when it lost in a limited participation venue. By contrast, the coalition that opposed the city's financial titan sought to use democratic channels and expand the scope of conflict to exercise its power. It achieved institutional and policy change through techniques such as initiatives and referenda. This coalition also opposed so-called reforms that were, in fact, procedural impediments imposed by the corporate giant–supported mayor requiring a third vote for a motion to be voted on and limiting public participation and comment at city council meetings.

Many citizens in Anaheim wanted a more balanced public policy agenda. They favored a balanced approach, one that paid attention to the demands and needs of the big business and residents. Others believed that a prosperous Disneyland benefited everyone in the city. City governments must figure out how to balance the interests of the corporate giant with those of the citizens when the two conflict. In Anaheim, the pro-balance actors created a public policy boundary, one that drew the line at tax breaks, tax rebates, and government giveaways. Disney learned not to cross that boundary. Power produced the boundary.

Disneyland politics is not only applicable to Anaheim, California; it occurs anywhere a dominant economic force exists. It also happens when a single industry or set of industries make claims on a polity. While citizens and elected officials might feel like they must comply with the requests and needs of the economic power or dominant industry, the reality is that they have a choice. That choice is difficult and requires social and political learning, but places and communities are not invariably path dependent. Politics and people matter, even in cities where corporate dollars appear to be the only thing that counts.

# Notes

## INTRODUCTION

1. Oh My Disney, "Walt Disney's College of Knowledge." In this book, we make a distinction between Walt Disney and the Disney Company. We refer to Walt Disney as Walt or Walt Disney, but not Disney. The Disney Company is referred to as Disney or the Disney Company.

2. Gennawey, *Disneyland Story*, 6.

3. "Officials Reveal Disneyland Details," 1.

4. Kilroy, "How Disney Chose OC," 1; Designing Disney, "Genesis of Disneyland"; D23, "Walt Disney's Proposed Theme Park."

5. Barrier, *Animated Man*, 233; "Walt Disney Make-Believe Project."

6. Details in this paragraph come from Snow, *Disney's Land*, 63; details can also be found in Korkis, "Real Story of the Mickey Mouse Park."

7. Several sources interviewed for this research agreed to speak on the condition of anonymity. We provide a general description for these informants throughout. This quote is from Anonymous informant #1, interview with author, October 7, 2020.

8. For various discussions of power to and power over, see Stone, *Regime Politics*; Stone, "Urban Regimes and the Capacity to Govern"; Camou, "Labor-Community Coalitions"; DeLeon, "Urban Antiregime"; Mossberger and Stoker, "Evolution of Urban Regime Theory" 5; Kühn, Bernt, and Colini, "Power, Politics and Peripheralization"; McGovern, "Analyzing Urban Politics"; Koch, "Bringing Power Back In"; Rast, "Governing the Regimeless City"; Bafarasat, "'Theorizing' Regime Theory"; Sandford, "Conceptualising 'Generative Power'"; Nicholls, "Power and Governance"; Fortner, "Racial Capitalism and City Politics."

9. Stone, "Poverty and Urban Social Reform," 851.

10. Savitch and Kantor, *Cities in the International Market Place*; Kantor and Savitch, "Can Politicians Bargain with Business?"

11. Kantor and Savitch, "Can Politicians Bargain with Business?" 240.

12. Ibid., 241.

13. Peterson, *City Limits*.

14. Schragger, *City Power*, 3; Sanders, *Convention Center Follies*; Rosentraub, *Major League Losers*; Swindell and Rosentraub, "Who Benefits from Professional Sports?"; Gross, "Legal Gambling"; D. Walker, "Casinos and Economic Growth"; Agha and Rascher, "Economic Development Effects"; Bradbury, "Sports Stadiums"; Eisinger, "Politics of Bread and Circuses."

15. Schragger, *City Power*, 16; details in the rest of this paragraph come from Schragger.

16. Saito, "Low-Income Residents Benefit"; see also Saito and Truong, "LA Live Community Benefits Agreement."

17. E.g., see Stone et al., *Urban Neighborhoods*; Joy and Vogel, "Beyond Neoliberalism"; Weaver, "Charting Change in the City"; Rast, "Urban Regime Theory"; McGovern, "Analyzing Urban Politics."

18. Details in this rest of this paragraph come from Saito, "Low-Income Residents Benefit," 131, 145, 146.

19. E.g., see Ward et al., "Urban Politics"; see also Cochrane, "Urban Politics beyond the Urban," 862–863; D. Martin, "Urban Politics as Sociospatial Struggles," 856–858; Ward, "Urban Politics," 864–865.

20. Lasswell, *Politics*.

21. For more on political order, see Stone, "Reflections on Regime Politics"; Burns and Thomas, *Reforming New Orleans*. Stone's *Regime Politics* argued that cities operate in a context of scarce resources and are governed by a stable and long-lasting regime that consists of public and private resource providers. For more on this argument, see Stone, *Regime Politics*.

22. McGovern notes that his mobilization-governance framework also attempts to improve on regime theory's inability to account for change in McGovern, "Analyzing Urban Politics"; see also Weaver, "Charting Change in the City"; Rast, "Urban Regime Theory."

23. In this book, we use the word "ring" to represent part of a political order. We do not mean a political ring, which Encyclopedia.com defines as "comparatively small group of persons, usually headed by a political boss, organized to control a city, county, or state, and primarily interested in deriving there from large personal monetary profit. Political rings became particularly notorious in American politics during the second half of the nineteenth century."

24. Stone, "Reflections on Regime Politics," 109.

25. McGovern, "Analyzing Urban Politics"; Stone, "Reflections on Regime Politics"; Kraus, "Significance of Race in Urban Politics"; Seamster, "White City."

26. Cohen, *Boundaries of Blackness*; Michener, "Power from the Margins"; Jones-Correa and Wong, "Whose Politics?"

27. Burns and Thomas, *Reforming New Orleans*.

28. McGovern, "Analyzing Urban Politics."

29. For competing views on political order, see Weaver, "Charting Change in the City"; Rast, "Urban Regime Theory."

30. For some exceptions, see Bowers and Rich, *Governing Middle-Sized Cities*; Perry, "Black Mayors in Non-Majority Black Cities"; Burns, *Electoral Politics Is Not Enough*.

31. Kumar and Stenberg, "Why Study Smaller Cities."

32. Ibid., 2026; Adler and Florida, "Geography as Strategy"; Malizia, "Economic Development."

33. For a similar argument made by geographers, see Bell and Jayne, "Small Cities?"

34. Kumar and Stenberg, "Why Study Smaller Cities," 2029.

35. For more on the value of a single case study, see Nicholson-Crotty and Meier, "Size Doesn't Matter."

36. Buntin, "Outside Disneyland."

37. Anonymous informant #1, interview with author, October 7, 2020.

38. City News Service, "Charter of the City of Anaheim."

39. Moreno v. Anaheim, Superior Court of the State of California, County of Orange, Case no. 394360–6 (2012).

40. City News Service, "Charter of the City of Anaheim."

41. City News Service, "Anaheim Municipal Code."

42. Lewinnek, Arellano, and Dang, *People's Guide to Orange County.*

43. U.S. Bureau of the Census, *Race and Hispanic Origin.*

44. Quote comes from Proposition 187. The summary of Proposition 227 comes from the League of Women Voters, "Proposition 227."

45. Harwood, "Struggling to Embrace Difference." The quote about Gigante being "specialized" came from the executive director of the city's redevelopment agency while a headline in the *Orange County Register* referred to the supermarket as being "too ethnic" for its location in Anaheim (351).

46. U.S. Bureau of the Census, *Median Household Income*; U.S. Bureau of the Census, *Hispanic or Latino Origin, 2013–2017.*

47. Lang and LeFurgy, *Boomburbs*; Lang and Simmons, *Boomburbs.*

48. Lang and Simmons, *Boomburbs*, 2.

49. For the complete list, see Maciag, "Population for U.S. Cities Statistics."

50. City-Data, "Anaheim: Economy."

51. Judd and Fainstein, *Tourist City*; also, in the same, see Judd, "Constructing the Tourist Bubble" (the table cited is on p. 42; Anaheim was seventh on this list).

52. E.g., see Weiner, "Great Big Beautiful Tomorrow"; Giroux, "Public Pedagogy and Rodent Politics"; Wills, *Disney Culture*; Wallace, *Mickey Mouse History*; Sperb, "Take a Frown, Turn It Upside Down"; Allen, "Disneyland"; Allen, "Seeing Double"; Allen, "A Town Called Celebration"; Aronstein, and Finke, "Discipline and Pleasure."

53. Wallace, "Mickey Mouse History," 33.

54. E.g., see Weiner, "Great Big Beautiful Tomorrow"; Wallace, *Mickey Mouse History*; Sperb, "Take a Frown, Turn It Upside Down"; Bemis, "Mirror, Mirror for Us All"; King, "Disneyland and Walt Disney World"; Watts, "Walt Disney"; Baber and Spickard, "Crafting Culture."

55. E.g., see Sorkin, *Variations on a Theme Park*; Zukin, *Landscapes of Power.*

56. Titizian, "Anniversary Day."

57. For exceptions and discussions of some of the Disneyland-Anaheim politics, see Findlay, *Magic Lands*; Gennawey, *Disneyland Story.*

58. Details in the rest of this paragraph come from Foglesong, *Married to the Mouse*, 3, 194.

59. Ibid., 124.

60. Florida Senate, *Parental Rights in Education—2022.*

61. Blair, "Disney Now Says."

62. Central Florida Tourism Oversight District, "About."

63. Maddaus, "Disney Reaches Settlement in Florida Lawsuit."

64. Ibid.

65. For more on the Reedy Creek Improvement District, see Foglesong, *Married to the Mouse*, 65, 75, 79, 139–145.

## CHAPTER 1

1. National Park Service, "Early History of the California Coast," available at https://www.nps.gov/prsf/learn/historyculture/spanish-period.htm.

2. Hicks, "Anaheim More Than an L.A. Suburb," 196–198; Hicks, "Anaheim in Pictures," 204–206.

3. Arellano, "Canto XLI."

4. Hicks, "Anaheim More Than an L.A. Suburb"; Hicks, "Anaheim in Pictures."

5. Details in the next two sentences come from "Early Anaheim: Early Settlers and Arts."

6. Details in the next two sentences come from Faessel, *Images of America*.

7. "Early Anaheim: Early Settlers and Arts."

8. Kindy, "Blacks Plan Boycott."

9. Daily Mail, "How Does It Feel?"

10. Details in the next two sentences come from LaTour, "Ku Klux Klan in Orange County."

11. Hoskins, "Klanaheim."

12. Lamb, "Yes on District Elections in Anaheim."

13. LaTour, "Ku Klux Klan in Orange County."

14. Details in the next two paragraphs come from ibid.

15. Details about Pearson, Moeller, and Murdoch come from Westcott and Simone, *Anaheim*; Avila, *Popular Culture* also makes the point that city leadership pursued economic development policies to replace orange groves with industry.

16. Westcott and Simone, *Anaheim*, 72.

17. Ibid., 71.

18. Ibid., 72.

19. Findlay, *Magic Lands*, 98; "Disneyland Celebrates Golden Anniversary."

20. "Early Anaheim: Early Settlers and Arts."

21. Westcott and Simone, *Anaheim*, 72.

22. "Early Anaheim: Early Settlers and Arts."

23. Westcott and Simone, *Anaheim*, 72–73.

24. Details in this paragraph come from ibid., 72.

25. Ibid.

26. "Early Anaheim: Early Settlers and Arts."

27. SRI International information comes from the Silicon Valley Historical Association.

28. Pierce, *Three Years in Wonderland*.

29. Disneyland Public Relations Department, "Building a Dream."

30. Kilroy, "How Disney Chose OC"; quote from Coker, "Looking Back at 1953"; Foglesong, *Married to the Mouse*, 46; Avila, *Popular Culture*.

31. Vintage Disneyland Tickets, "A Disney Preview." Avila, *Popular Culture*, 117.

32. Extinct Attractions, "Disney Legend Buzz Price." The focus on highway placement would also play a pivotal role in the site selection of Walt Disney World in Florida.

33. Ibid.

34. "Officials Reveal Disneyland Details," 1.

35. These sources are Kilroy, "How Disney Chose OC"; Pierce, *Three Years in Wonderland*.

36. Kilroy, "How Disney Chose OC."

37. Details in this paragraph come from Snow, *Disney's Land*, 77–78; the direct quote is on p. 78.

38. Watts, "Walt Disney," 96. This paragraph comes from Burns, Bieganski, Fueki et al., "Political Socialization and Disneyland."

39. Wallace, *Mickey Mouse History*, 161.

40. Avila, *Popular Culture*, first quote is on p. 121 and second comes from p. 124.

41. Watts, "Walt Disney," 96.

42. Coker, "How Disneyland Became Disneyland." Despite its glamour and appeal, Disneyland represented another revenue-generating industry for Murdoch. Like other industries, Disneyland would employ people, some of whom would perform difficult tasks, and it would increase pollution concerns within the area. The Disneyland industry would also add to city coffers. In 1954, Murdoch wasn't after an entertainment venue as much as he wanted tax-generating industries. Disneyland fell into that category for him.

43. Pierce, "1953 Halloween Festival."

44. Shultz, "Halloween."

45. Coker, "How Disneyland Became Disneyland."

46. Details in the rest of this paragraph come from Snow, *Disney's Land*, 77–78.

47. Details in this paragraph come from Westcott and Simone, *Anaheim*, 76; Sklar, *Dream It! Do It!* Rios, "Golden Legacy at the House of Mouse."

48. "Disneyland Comes Here."

49. Lang and LeFurgy, *Boomburbs*, 63.

50. Snow, *Disney's Land*, 79.

51. Coker, "How Disneyland Became Disneyland." The next two quotes in this paragraph also come from this source.

52. Westcott and Simone, *Anaheim*, 76.

53. "Fabulous 'Disneyland.'"

54. "Officials Reveal Disneyland Details," 1.

55. "Fabulous 'Disneyland.'"

56. "Disneyland Comes Here."

57. Reovan, "Theme Park in the City."

58. Details in this paragraph come from "Halt to Disneyland Annexation Sought."

59. Details about claims of gerrymandering come from ibid.

60. Westcott and Simone, *Anaheim*, 72.

61. Korkis, "Once Upon a Time in Anaheim."

62. Details of the settlement come from "Disneyland Row Ended."

63. Details in this paragraph come from "Officials Reveal Disneyland Details," 1.

64. Details in this paragraph come from "Disney Tells Planning on Big Playland."

65. "Officials Reveal Disneyland Details," 1.

66. Details in this paragraph and the next come from Loudon, "Disneyland."

67. "With High Hopes."

## CHAPTER 2

1. Dowd, "Remembering Disneyland's Disastrous Opening Day."

2. McGuinness, "68 Years Ago, Disneyland Opened."

3. City News Service, *City Scoop*.

4. Disneyland Public Relations Division, *Disneyland Report*.

5. Ibid.

6. Disneyland, "Happiness Industry," 11.

7. Details in this paragraph come from Disneyland, "Disneyland History."

8. "Thousands Jam Disneyland," 1.

9. "Disneyland Routes."

10. "Disneyland Keeps Police Busy," 1.

11. Westcott and Simone, *Anaheim*, 76.

12. Slater, "Traveling the Berm"; Pimentel, "From the Matterhorn."

13. Marling, "Imagineering the Disney Theme Parks," 83.

14. Some details about the height restrictions come from Gennawey, *Disneyland Story*, 187–189.

15. Quote comes from "Walt Disney Presents Views."

16. Details in this paragraph also come from Teague, "Planners Eye Height Limit."

17. Quoted from Pinkley, "Council Should OK Hotel."

18. Details in this paragraph come from "Planners Indicate Support"; "Anaheim Planners Delay Decision."

19. "Anaheim Planners Delay Decision."

20. "Readers Get Voice."

21. In *City Power*, Schragger refers to this as immobile capital, 128–130, 169–175.

22. Details in this paragraph come from "Planners Indicate Support"; "Anaheim Planners Delay Decision."

23. Ibid., "Height Hearing for D-Land Set"; the full report is from Economics Research Associates, "Economic Impact of Disneyland."

24. Teague, "Planners Eye Height Limit."

25. "Anaheim Planners Delay Decision."

26. According to Findlay, *Magic Lands*, 104, city government required the Sheraton to reduce its hotel to sixteen stories. The following source says the same thing: "Revised Plans Approved for Sheraton-Anaheim." This source states that the hotel will be fourteen stories: "New Hotel Plans Okay in Anaheim."

## CHAPTER 3

1. Walt Disney Company, *Gingerbread Man and the Golden Goose*.

2. Kevin Johnson, "Disney Warns," 1.

3. Kevin Johnson, "Anaheim Still Backs Tourism."

4. Gennawey, *Disneyland Story*, 269; Kevin Johnson, "Mickey's Style Can Get Nasty," A14.

5. Hernandez, "Disneyland at 40."

6. Gennawey, *Disneyland Story*, 269.

7. Ibid., quoted from Pack, "Anaheim Admission Tax."

8. Johnson, "Mickey's Style Can Get Nasty." Details and quotes in the next two paragraphs also come from ibid.

9. Kevin Johnson, "Disneyland," A1; Gennawey, *Disneyland Story*, 269; Johnson, "Mickey's Style Can Get Nasty."

10. Johnson, "Mickey's Style Can Get Nasty."

11. This quote and the next come from Johnson, "Disneyland."

12. This quote and the next come from Johnson, "Mickey's Style Can Get Nasty."

13. Serrano, "Anaheim Delays Action," B1.

14. Ibid.

15. Ibid.

16. Serrano, "Anaheim Delays Action."

17. This quote and the next come from Woo, "Amusement-Tax Supporters Drop Ballot," B3.

18. Johnson, "Anaheim Still Backs Tourism," A18.

19. Johnson, "Disney Warns."

20. Ibid., 1.

21. Details about the Anaheim Ichthyological, Sour Mash and Five-Card Draw Society in this paragraph and the next come from Johnson and Woodyard, "Disney Showers Gifts on Officials," 1.

22. Details in this sentence and the next come from Johnson and Woodyard, "Anaheim's Leaders Recall Largess," 1.

23. Kevin Johnson, "Free Tickets Not to Buy Influence," 1.

24. Johnson and Woodyard, "Anaheim's Leaders Recall Largess," 1; Kevin Johnson, "Disney Tickets."

25. Johnson and Woodyard, "Anaheim's Leaders Recall Largess"; Johnson, "Disney Tickets."

26. "Tickets to Ineffectiveness"; the quote comes from Harala, "Public Finance of Athletic Facilities," 51–52.

27. Johnson and Woodyard, "Disney Showers Gifts on Officials."

28. Details in this paragraph come from D. Miller, "One Election Changed Relationship."

29. This quote and the next two come from Johnson and Woodyard, "Anaheim's Leaders Recall Largess."

30. Johnson and Woodyard, "Disney Showers Gifts on Officials," 1.

31. This quote and the next two come from Johnson, "Free Tickets Not Meant to Buy Influence," B1.

32. Ibid.

33. Johnson and Woodyard, "Anaheim's Leaders Recall Largess," A14.

34. Ibid., A14.

35. Johnson and Woodyard, "Disney Showers Gifts on Officials."

36. Johnson, "Free Tickets Not Meant to Buy Influence," B1.

37. Johnson and Woodyard, "Disney Showers Gifts on Officials," A1.

38. Ibid., A1.

39. Johnson and Woodyard, "Anaheim's Leaders Recall Largess."

40. Johnson, "Disney Tickets."

41. "Tickets to Ineffectiveness," A10.

42. Details in this paragraph come from D. Miller, "One Election Changed Relationship."

43. Johnson and Woodyard, "Disney Showers Gifts on Officials."

44. Kevin Johnson, "*Times* Orange County Poll," 1.

45. Anonymous informant #2, interview with author, February 4, 2020.

46. The statistics in the next few sentences come from "No Such Thing as a Free Pass," B8.

47. Johnson, "*Times* Orange County Poll."

48. "No Such Thing as a Free Pass."

49. Details about the poll come from ibid.

50. Johnson, "Anaheim Still Backs Tourism."

51. Ibid.; Spencer, "Orange County Focus: Police Union," B3.

52. Details in the next two sentences come from Johnson, "Disneyland."

53. Johnson, "Anaheim Still Backs Tourism."

54. This information and the next quote come from ibid.

55. Tillman and Pimentel, "Why Disney Is Working Hard."

56. Details in this paragraph come from Marroquin, "Anaheim City Council Votes 3-2 to Extend Gate-Tax Ban," A1.

57. Elmahrek, "Anaheim Council Approves Protection."

58. Ibid.

59. Aguilar, "Anaheim Approves Tax Exemption"; Tso, "Disney Wins Extension."

60. Details in this paragraph come from Foxhall and Martin, "Tax Break Up for Renewal," C1.

61. Marroquin and Pimentel, "Disney Wants to Invest."

62. Foxhall and Martin, "Tax Break Up for Renewal."

63. Marroquin and Pimentel, "Disney Wants to Invest."

64. Throughout the book, we use the following terms that mean the same thing: admission/admissions tax, entertainment tax, entertainment gate tax, and gate tax. We do so because the actors at various times referred to this tax by these different names.

65. Peterson, *City Limits*, 15.

66. Glenn, "Two Schools of Political Development."

67. E.g., see Stone, "Urban Regimes and Capacity to Govern"; Stone, "Preemptive Power."

68. Westcott and Simone, *Anaheim*, C1.


## CHAPTER 4

1. "Disney Resort," B5.

2. Kevin Johnson, "Plan Unveiled for Huge Expansion," A1.

3. Fiore, "Disney Unveils Plans," B1.

4. "Disney Resort." An internet search indicates that many people spell WestCOT in different ways such as WESTCOT, Wescot, and WESCOT Center. In this book, we use WestCOT.

5. Rowe, "Disney Outlines $3 Billion Project," A1.

6. Young, "Disney's Big, BIG World," A1.

7. Young, "Study Doesn't Analyze Costs," A14.

8. This information and the rest of the quotes in this paragraph come from Shaffer, "'Enormous' Decision for Anaheim's Planners," B5.

9. Foglesong, *Married to the Mouse*.

10. Kevin Johnson, "Disney Warns."

11. Johnson and Woodyard, "Disney Chooses Anaheim," A1.

12. "Betting on Southern California," B5.

13. Woo, "More Disney Magic," A3.

14. Ibid.

15. Ibid.

16. Woo and Young, "WestCOT Draws Staunch Opposition," A1.

17. Rowe and Shaffer, "WestCOT," B1.

18. J. Miller, "Backers Shun Small Protest," B8.

19. Baldassare, *When Government Fails*.

20. This quote and the next come from Young, "WestCOT Center," B11.

21. Lait, "Disney Promises to Reduce Noise," A20.

22. Ibid.

23. Anonymous informant #3, interview with author, June 25, 2020.

24. "Reality Check in Fantasy Land," B14.

25. J. Miller, "WestCOT Backers Shun Small Protest."

26. Ibid.

27. Spencer, "Orange County Focus: Disney Expansion," B3.

28. Lait, "Disneyland Project Wins Key Vote."

29. Lait, "Disney Reaches Tentative Pact," OCB1.

30. Details in this paragraph come from the editorial, "Disney Dilemma," L4; Powers and Hilzenrath, "Disney's Hardball Reputation," A01.

31. Young, "Disney Plan Has a Housing Hitch," B1.

32. Lait, "Disney Reaches Tentative Pact."

33. "Disney Dilemma " L4.

34. Lait, "Disney Reaches Tentative Pact."

35. Young and Shaffer, "Disney Vow," B1.

36. "Disney Is Acting in a Neighborly Way," B8.

37. Shaffer, "Staff Gives WestCOT Conditional Approval," B4.

38. Rowe, "Disneyland Expansion Losing Momentum," A1.

39. Young, "Disney's Big, BIG World."

40. Ibid.

41. Shaffer, "White Spire Replaces Gold Sphere," B6.

42. Young, "Disney Shelves Plan for Park," B8.

43. Perlman, "U.S. May Be Asked to Pay," B1; Lait, "Disneyland Promises to Reduce Noise."

44. Lait, "Disneyland Promises to Reduce Noise."

45. Lait and Miller, "'Anaheim Problem' Has Happy Ending," A1.

46. Spencer, "Orange County Focus: Disney Expansion."

47. Rowe, "Disney Outlines $3 Billion Project."

48. Ibid.

49. Young, "Study Doesn't Analyze Costs."

50. Lait, "Unhappiest Place on Earth?" A1.

51. Associated Press and Frook. "Disney Studies Leaner WestCOT," 8.

52. Lait and Woodyard, "Plans Dim as Project Chief Resigns."

53. Reza, "U.S. Balks at Costs of Garage."

54. Ibid.

55. Fiore, "House Denies Funds," 32.

56. Reza, "OCTA Approves Funds," B4; Hernandez, "Senate Panel Oks $25 Million," B1.

57. Lait and Woodyard, "Disney Won't Decide for a Year," A1.

58. Dickerson and Hernandez, "Resort Funding Plan Outlined," A1; Woodyard and Hernandez, "Disney Cuts Anaheim Resort Plans," A1.

59. Hirsch, "Disney Lets Options Expire," A1.

60. Woodyard and Hernandez, "Disney Drastically Cuts Anaheim Resort Plans."

## CHAPTER 5

1. Foglesong, *Married to the Mouse*, 1–2.

2. Findlay, *Magic Lands*, 107, quoted from the *Orlando Sentinel*, November 28, 1965.

3. Foglesong, *Married to the Mouse*, 59.

4. E.g., see "Orange County Perspective," B10; Hernandez, "Anaheim's Beautification Plan," B1; M. Miller, "Disneyland-Area Rehab Ok'd," B1.

5. City News Service, *Disneyland Resort Specific Plan.*

6. City News Service, *Anaheim Resort Specific Plan.*

7. Hernandez, "'Anaheim Resort' Plan Public Hearing," B1; Hernandez, "Anaheim to Proceed with Revitalization Plan," B1.

8. Details in this paragraph come from Hernandez, "Anaheim to Proceed with Revitalization Plan."

9. Hernandez, "Anaheim's Beautification Plan."

10. M. Miller, "Disneyland-Area Rehab Ok'd."

11. Ibid.

12. Hernandez, "Anaheim's Beautification Plan."

13. Hernandez, "Anaheim to Proceed with Revitalization Plan."

14. Fisher, "Anaheim Takes Down Tacky Signs," B2.

15. Hernandez, "Sign of the Times," B2.

16. Fisher, "Anaheim Takes Down Tacky Signs."

17. Hernandez, "Sign of the Times."

18. Fisher, "Anaheim Takes Down Tacky Signs."

19. Details and quotes in this paragraph come from ibid.

20. Dickerson and Hernandez, "Anaheim Escalating Battle for Tourism," A1.

21. Fisher, "Expansion Passes First Hurdle," B1.

22. Fisher, "It's Not a Small World," A1; Marroquin and Pimentel, "Company Wants to Invest," A.

23. Macdonald, "Lands of Tomorrow," 3.

24. Ibid.

25. Hernandez and Hayes, "City Studying Disney-Related Improvements," B1.

26. MacDonald, "Lands of Tomorrow"; Dickerson and Hernandez, "Resort Funding Plan Outlined."

27. Ibid.

28. Ibid.

29. Fisher, "Disney Expansion Still Alive," C1.

30. Hayes, "500 Rally to Support Expansion," B3.

31. Hernandez, "$1.4-Billion Disneyland Expansion Approved," A1.

32. Foglesong, *Married to the Mouse*, xii.

33. Dickerson and Hernandez, "Resort Funding Plan Outlined."

34. Ibid.

35. Rowe, "Project Fares Better in Revised Report," B2.

36. Dickerson and Hernandez, "Resort Funding Plan Outlined."

37. Dickerson and Hernandez, "Anaheim Escalating Battle for Tourism."

38. Fisher, "Council Splits over Disney Plan," B1.

39. Hernandez and Hayes, "City Studying Disney-Related Improvements."

40. Fisher, "Council Splits over Disney Plan."

41. Ibid.

42. Hernandez, "$1.4-Billion Disneyland Expansion Approved."

43. Sanchez, "Orange County in Change," A1.

44. Ibid.

45. Fisher, "Big Day Nears for Disney," A22.

46. Ibid.

47. Ibid.

48. "Expanding to the Tune of $177 Million."

49. Fisher, "Big Day Nears for Disney."

50. Details in this sentence and the next come from D. Miller, "Is Disney Paying Its Share?" A1.

51. Fisher, "Big Day Nears for Disney."

52. Details in this paragraph come from H. Park, "Resort District Fee Angers Businesses," 3.

53. Tillman and Pimentel, "Why Disney Is Working Hard."

54. For more on Lindquist, see D23, "Disney Legends"; Lindquist and Combs, *In Service to the Mouse.*

55. Information on the Dominguez Tree comes from Duchess of Disneyland, "Dominguez Tree."

56. Anonymous informant #1, interview with author, October 7, 2020.

57. Anonymous informant #4, interview with author, October 7, 2020.

58. Information on Pressler comes from Reference for Business, "Paul S. Pressler."

59. Details in the next four paragraphs come from Sanchez, "Anaheim," A1.

60. Green, "Anaheim Hills."

61. Fisher, "Resort District's Coming Attraction," A1.

62. Carreon and Reckard, "City Council OKs Pointe Anaheim," B1; McKibben, "Disney Involved in GardenWalk Hotels," B7.

63. McKibben, "Land Sale Restarts Anaheim Project," B5.

64. Townsend and Ruiz, "2008: Top Stories of the Year."

65. Fisher, "Anaheim Eyes Disney Tax Deal," B1.


## CHAPTER 6

1. McKibben, "Anaheim Is Set for Wild Ride," B4; McKibben, "Housing May Be Approved," B3.

2. McKibben, "Anaheim Is Set for Wild Ride."

3. McKibben, "Housing May Be Approved."

4. City News Service, "Platinum Triangle"; McKibben, "Low-Cost Housing Plan," 4; "Anaheim's Platinum Triangle."

5. "Anaheim's Platinum Triangle."

6. Ibid.

7. Knight-Ridder Tribune Business News, "Anaheim Backs Lennar's Vision."

8. Ibid.

9. "From Potholes to Condos," 20.

10. McKibben, "Low-Cost Housing Plan."

11. McKibben, "Low-Cost Housing Plan"; McKibben, "Housing May Be Approved."

12. McKibben, "Disneyland Not Smiling," B1.

13. McKibben, "Low-Cost Housing Plan."

14. Ibid.; Orange County Communities Organized for Responsible Development (OCCORD), "About Us."

15. Quotes in this paragraph and the next come from McKibben, "Disneyland Not Smiling."

16. McKibben, "How Vote Went Disney's Way," B1.

17. Ibid.

18. Ibid.; McKibben, "Disney Sues Anaheim over Plan."

19. McKibben, "How Vote Went Disney's Way."

20. McKibben, "Disneyland Not Smiling."

21. Tully, "Anaheim Debates Land Use," Cover B.

22. McKibben, "How Vote Went Disney's Way."

23. Details in the rest of this paragraph come from Tully, "Anaheim Debates Land Use."

24. Tully, "Anaheim Debates Land Use."

25. McKibben, "How Vote Went Disney's Way."

26. Ibid.

27. McKibben, "Disney Sues Anaheim over Plan"; Tully, "Disney Sues Anaheim over Development."

28. McKibben, "How Vote Went Disney's Way."

29. Details in this sentence and the next two come from ibid.

30. McKibben, "Disney Wants Vote on Homes," B1.

31. Ibid.

32. Support Our Anaheim Resort Area (S.O.A.R.), "Overview."

33. Ballotpedia, "Save Our Anaheim Resort District Initiative."

34. McKibben, "How Vote Went Disney's Way."

35. Ibid.

36. McKibben, "Disney Wants Vote on Homes."

37. Quotes in this paragraph come from Tully, "Debate Grows over Subsidizing Housing."

38. McKibben, "Anaheim Will Reconsider Housing," B6.

39. McKibben, "Anaheim Is Set for Wild Ride."

40. Ibid.

41. Tully, "No Clear Direction."

42. Quotes in this paragraph come from Tully and Ortiz, "Mad about the Mouse."

43. Details in this sentence and the next two come from Haldane, "Disney Backers Plan Referendum," B5.

44. Tully, "Anaheim to Consider Referendum on Housing."

45. This quote and the next come from Haldane, "Disney Backers Plan Referendum."

46. This information and the next two quotes come from McKibben, "Defund Chamber of Commerce," 4.

47. Quotes in this paragraph come from Tully, "Police Enter Resort Fray," Cover B.

48. Ibid.

49. Details in this paragraph come from Lanser, "Word War II," Cover D.

50. Details in this paragraph come from Tully, "Revenue Figures Don't Match," Cover B.

51. Ibid.

52. Details in this paragraph come from McKibben, "Scope of Housing Dispute Broadens," B1.

53. Details in this paragraph come from McKibben, "Housing Deal May Be Dead," B3.

54. Ibid.

55. McKibben, "Resort-Area Housing Debate May Cool," B6.

56. "No Tomorrowland for Deal," Edit H.

57. Details in this paragraph come from ibid.

58. Details in this paragraph come from McKibben, "Disney Wins in Anaheim," B4.

59. McKibben, "Land Use Decision Likely on Ballot," B11.

60. Details in this paragraph come from McKibben, "Resort District Group's Main Backer," B1.

61. Ibid.

## CHAPTER 7

1. Marroquin, "Council OKs Hotel Subsidy."
2. Marroquin, "Tax Breaks to Attract Hotels."
3. Ibid.
4. Ibid.
5. Ibid., Vo, "Another Hotel Subsidy Deal."
6. Ibid.
7. Ibid.
8. Ibid.
9. Details in this paragraph come from Pimentel, "Anaheim Considers Tax Breaks."
10. Marroquin, "Subsidy Measure Won't Be on Ballot."
11. Details in this paragraph come from Pimentel, "Anaheim OKs Tax Incentives," B.
12. Pimentel, "Anaheim Considers Tax Breaks."
13. Ibid.
14. Ibid.
15. Peterson, *City Limits*.
16. Stone and Sanders, *Politics of Urban Development*.
17. Sanders, "Politics of Development in Middle-Sized Cities."

## CHAPTER 8

1. Details in this paragraph come from Serrano, "Hispanics Growing in Number, Not Power."
2. Hispanically Speaking News "¡No Mas!"
3. The 1980 data come from U.S. Bureau of the Census, *County and City Data Book 1983*. The 1990 data come from U.S. Bureau of the Census. *County and City Data Book 1994*. In 1980, the census used the category "Spanish Origin," and, in 1990, it used "Hispanic Origin."
4. The section on the Little People's Park Riot of 1978 borrows liberally from Arellano, "Little People's Park Riot."
5. Mickadeit, "Police Need Better Ties."
6. Schrader, "Fragile Balance Shaken."
7. Details in the next two paragraphs come from Arellano, "Little People's Park Riot."
8. Details in this paragraph come from ibid.
9. Serrano, "Hispanics Growing in Number, Not Power"; Elmahrek, "Can Anaheim Repair Broken Trust?"
10. "She Led Anaheim in Facing Injustice."
11. Serrano, "Hispanics Growing in Number, Not Power."
12. Arellano, "Canto XLI."
13. Arellano, "Little People's Park Riot"; SparkOC.com, "Memories of the Past."
14. Details in this paragraph come from Arellano, "Little People's Park Riot."
15. Elmahrek, "Can Anaheim Repair Broken Trust?"
16. Schrader, "Fragile Balance Shaken."
17. Hispanically Speaking News, "¡No Mas!"
18. Schrader, "Fragile Balance Shaken."
19. Ibid.
20. Hernandez, "INS Seeks to Exit Anaheim Jail."
21. Ibid.

22. Ibid.

23. Godines and Jolly, "Anaheim Urged to Boot INS."

24. Hernandez, "INS Seeks to Exit Anaheim Jail."

25. Godines and Jolly, "Anaheim Urged to Boot INS."

26. Schrader, "Fragile Balance Shaken."

27. Details in this paragraph and the next come from Schrader, "Fragile Balance Shaken."

28. Details about Martin's plan come from Carter, "Group Urges Anaheim"; Carter, "School Board Drops Proposal"; "Schools May Not Bill for Noncitizen Students."

29. Carter, "School Board Drops Proposal."

30. McKibben, "Police Didn't Spy on Activists."

31. Elmahrek, "Can Anaheim Repair Broken Trust?"

32. McKibben, "Police Didn't Spy on Activists."

33. Ibid.

34. Ibid.

35. This information and the next two quotes come from Elmahrek, "Can Anaheim Repair Broken Trust?"

36. David, "Dislocation of 200 Families"; Kopetman, "Anaheim"; Kopetman, "Face Lift Due."

37. David, "Dislocation of 200 Families."

38. Kopetman, "Proposal for Anaheim Development."

39. Ibid.

40. Details about the transformation of Jeffrey-Lynne to Hermosa Village come from Conley, "Effects of Revitalization on Crime"; Silber, "Jeffrey-Lynne Revitalization Heads to Council."

41. Schou, "Ethnic Cleansing."

42. Details about the transformation of Jeffrey-Lynne to Hermosa Village come from Conley, "Effects of Revitalization on Crime," 10.

43. Details about Gigante Grocery Store come from Harwood, "Struggling to Embrace Difference"; Holden and French, "Food Fight!"

44. Harwood, "Struggling to Embrace Difference," 361.

45. Holden and French, "Food Fight!" 86.

46. Details in this paragraph come from Elmahrek, "Can Anaheim Repair Broken Trust?"

47. McKibben, "Police Didn't Spy on Activists."

48. Hispanically Speaking News, "¡No Mas!"

49. Dobuzinskis, "Divisions Grip Anaheim."

50. Anton, "ACLU Lawsuit."

51. Dobuzinskis, "Divisions Grip Anaheim."

52. E.g., see Abott and Magazinnik, "At-Large Elections and Minority Representation"; Welch, "Impact of At-Large Elections"; Leal, Martinez-Ebers, and Meier, "Politics of Latino Education."

53. Dobuzinskis, "Divisions Grip Anaheim."

54. Ibid.

55. Vives, Santa Cruz, and Winton, "Police, Protesters Clash"; Dobuzinskis, "Divisions Grip Anaheim."

56. Santa Cruz, Goffard, and Winton, "Protests Reflect Deep Divisions," A10.

57. Dobuzinskis, "Divisions Grip Anaheim."

58. Hispanically Speaking News, "¡No Mas!"

59. Ibid.; Elmahrek, "Can Anaheim Repair Broken Trust?"

60. Vives, Santa Cruz, and Winton, "Police, Protesters Clash."

61. Ibid.

62. Ibid.; Dobuzinskis, "Divisions Grip Anaheim"; Brunell, Hurtado, and Martinez, "Latinos in California Seek Council Seat."

63. Vives, Santa Cruz, and Winton, "Police, Protesters Clash."

64. Ponsi, Mello, and Walker, "50 Protesters Gather Outside Disneyland."

65. Arellano, "Little People's Park Riot."

66. Dobuzinskis, "Divisions Grip Anaheim"; Vives, Santa Cruz, and Winton, "Police, Protesters Clash."

67. Details in this paragraph come from Velasco, "Gang Sweep Rubs Riots' Wounds."

68. Hispanically Speaking News, "¡No Mas!"

69. Details in this paragraph come from Dobuzinskis, "Divisions Grip Anaheim."

70. Hispanically Speaking News, "¡No Mas!"

71. Details in this paragraph come from ibid.

72. Wood, "Why Anaheim Erupted in Violence."

73. Santa Cruz, Goffard, and Winton, "Protests Reflect Deep Divisions," A1.

74. Elmahrek, "Can Anaheim Repair Broken Trust?"

75. Wood, "Why Anaheim Erupted in Violence."

76. Rojas and Santa Cruz, "City Council Rejects Proposal."

77. Ibid.

78. Orange County Registrar of Voters, "Full Text of Measure L—City of Anaheim."

79. Rojas and Santa Cruz, "City Council Rejects Proposal."

80. Details in this paragraph come from ibid.

81. Dobuzinskis, "Divisions Grip Anaheim."

82. Details in this paragraph come from ibid.

83. OCCORD, "More Jobs, Less Opportunity."

84. Marroquin, "Anaheim Election Trial."

85. Details in the rest of this paragraph come from City News Service, "Anaheim Settles Lawsuit with ACLU."

86. Marroquin, "Voting Districts Coming to Anaheim."

87. Ibid.

88. Details in this paragraph come from Marroquin, "Council Sets Voting Map."

89. Information from this paragraph comes from Krishnakumar, Miller, and Poston, "Disney Spent Heavily."

90. Information from this paragraph comes from ibid.

91. Pimentel, "New Anaheim Council Majority."

92. Anonymous informant #1, interview with author, October 7, 2020.

93. Anonymous informant #5, interview with author, September 20, 2020.

94. Details in this paragraph come from ibid.

## CHAPTER 9

1. Details in this paragraph come from Pimentel, "Council Derails Streetcar Project."

2. Statistics about support and opposition on the Anaheim City Council to the streetcar come from Orange County Register, "Anaheim Streetcar Making a Comeback."

3. Ibid.

4. Quote comes from Pimentel, "People's Council 'Eager.'"

5. Ibid.

6. Details in this paragraph come from Pimentel, "Disney to Present"; also see Pimentel, "Disney Neighbors Bad Feeling."

7. Pimentel, "Disney Neighbors Bad Feeling."

8. Details in this paragraph come from Pimentel, "Disney to Present."

9. Ibid.

10. Details in this paragraph come from Pimentel, "Disney Changes Directions," AA1.

11. Details in this paragraph come from Pimentel, "City to Move in New Direction," A1.

12. Vo, "City Manager Emery Resigns."

13. Details in this paragraph come from Puri, Popp, and Fleissig, *Economic Impact of Disneyland Resort*.

14. CSUF News Center, "Economists Quantify Disneyland's Impact."

15. Details in this paragraph come from Dunn, "Anaheim."

16. Details in this paragraph come from Tait, "Anaheim."

17. Details in this paragraph come from Murray, "Focused on Taxpayers and Neighborhoods."

18. For more on the importance of local media in urban politics, see Rubado and Jennings, "Political Consequences of the Local Watchdog."

19. Minow, "Changing Ecosystem of News," 500–502.

20. Gutsche, "Boosterism as Banishment."

21. Gerda, Vo, and Washburn, "Disney Breaks Own Spending Record."

22. Robinson, "Voters Make Change."

23. For more details, see J. Park and Robinson, "Anaheim Councilman Arrested."

24. Details in this paragraph come from City News Service, "Join Us and Shape the Future."

25. Details in this paragraph come from City News Service, "Community Center."

26. Details in this paragraph come from Pimentel, "Council Takes Aim at Lobbyists," AA1.

27. Details in this paragraph come from City News Service, "Anaheim Adopts Sunshine Ordinance."

28. "Thousands Sign Petition," BB1.

29. Graham, "County Plans to Clear Riverbed," BB13.

30. Graham, "Supervisors Nix Relocation Plan," AA1; T. Walker, "Where Anaheim Plans to Put Shelter."

31. Hunter-Gault et al., "Why Anaheim's Low-Wage Workers Struggle."

32. Details in this paragraph come from Gerda, "Nelson Had Homeless Camp Removed."

33. Details in this paragraph come from Do, "Homeless Surges in Disneyland's Shadow."

34. Details in this paragraph come from Graham, "County Plans to Clear Riverbed"; "Anaheim Shelter Plan"; Robinson, "Anaheim Picks Operator," AA10; T. Walker, "Where Anaheim Plans to Put Shelter"; Brazil, "Emergency Homeless Shelter"; Cunningham, "Council Approves Public-Private Partnership."

35. Details in this paragraph come from Honda Center, "Anaheim Sets Course"; Robinson, "Anaheim Signs Deal." Details about the name of the Angels baseball team come from Wikipedia, "Los Angeles Angels."

36. Ibid.

37. Details in this paragraph come from Pimentel, "'Big Splash' on Beach Boulevard"; Whitehead and Haire, "New Age for Beach Boulevard," AA1.

38. Pimentel, "'Big Splash' on Beach Boulevard."

39. Whitehead and Haire, "New Age for Beach Boulevard."

40. Ibid.

41. Robinson, "City to Buy Land along Beach Blvd," AA1.

42. Robinson, "Beach Boulevard Makeover."

43. Robinson, "City to Buy Land along Beach Blvd."

44. Whitehead and Haire, "New Age for Beach Boulevard."

45. Robinson, "City to Buy Land along Beach Blvd"; Pimental, "Anaheim's 'Sinkin' Lincoln' Site."

46. Details in this paragraph come from D. Miller, "Is Disney Paying Its Share?"

47. Details in this paragraph come from D. Miller, "One Election Changed Relationship"; D. Miller, "Is Disney Paying Its Share?"

48. Part II shows that the fissures between the city and the corporate giant emerged well before sixty years. The debate over WestCOT showed that the city was not going to give Disney everything it wanted without some resistance.

49. Details in this paragraph come from Elmahrek, "Councilwoman Criticized for Trip with Lobbyist."

50. Ibid.

51. Jack Spence, "Disney Policies—Then and Now."

52. Ibid.

53. La Ganga, "Disney Drops Policy."

54. Avila, *Popular Culture*, 197.

55. This quote and the next two come from Framke and Wilkinson, "Disney Blacklisting the *LA Times*, Explained."

56. Details in this paragraph come from the *Orange County Register* Editorial Board, "Does Disney Pay Its Fair Share?"

57. Ibid.

58. "A Note to Readers."

59. Details in this paragraph come from Framke and Wilkinson, "Disney Blacklisting the *LA Times*, Explained."

60. Details in this paragraph come from Ember and Barnes, "Disney Ends Ban on *LATimes*."

## CHAPTER 10

1. H. Martin, "Employees Surveyed Can't Afford Expenses."

2. Ibid., Drier and Fleming, "Working for the Mouse."

3. Drier and Fleming, "Working for the Mouse."

4. Details in this paragraph come from H. Martin, "Employees Surveyed Can't Afford Expenses."

5. Ibid.

6. Details in this paragraph come from H. Martin, "Unions Propose Ballot Measure."

7. Impacted companies would be required to increase the minimum wage to $15 per hour beginning on January 1, 2019, and continue to raise that wage by a dollar an hour through January 1, 2022. After the minimum wage reaches $18 per hour, annual increases would be linked to the cost of living.

8. Roosevelt, "Living Wage Ballot Drive," A3.

9. Details in this paragraph come from H. Martin, "Disneyland Workers Demonstrate."

10. Details in this paragraph come from Vo, "Council Discusses Disneyland Worker Wages."

11. Ibid.

12. Details in this paragraph are from Robinson, "Business Groups Launch Opposition."

13. Details in this paragraph come from Ortiz, "Orange County Workers United."

14. Goulding, "Unions Submit Living Wages Petition," 5.

15. Ibid.

16. The quotes in the next paragraph also come from ibid.

17. Details in this paragraph come from "Disneyland California Employees Demand Living Wage."

18. Vo, "Anaheim $18 Minimum Wage Initiative."

19. Margot Roosevelt, "Disney, Unions Agree on Contract," A3; the next two quotes also come from this source.

20. For details of this strike, see Public Broadcasting System, "Walt Disney"; Sito, "Disney Strike of 1941."

21. Walt Disney Family Museum, "Walt and the Goodwill Tour."

22. Details come from San Roman, "Strike Changed Magic Kingdom Forever." See also Smith and Eisenberg, "Conflict at Disneyland"; Koenig, "Strike II?"

23. San Roman, "Strike Changed Magic Kingdom Forever."

24. H. Martin, "Disney Promised a Luxury Hotel."

25. Hughes, "Disney Suspends Hotel Project."

26. H. Martin, "Disney Promised a Luxury Hotel"; KCAL News, "Dispute Suspends Construction."

27. The next three block quotes come from D'Amaro, "Letter to Mayor and City Council."

28. Bond, "Anaheim Ends Disney Subsidies"; H. Martin, "Disney Wants to End Tax Incentive."

29. This detail and the following quote come from ibid.

30. H. Martin, "Anaheim Puts End to Tax Breaks."

31. Ibid.

32. H. Martin, "Disney Cancels Plans for Hotel," C1.

33. Details about this paragraph come from ibid.

34. H. Martin, "Disney, Unions Open Wallets," C1.

35. H. Martin, "2018 Midterm Election," B2.

36. Details in this paragraph come from H. Martin, "Disney, Unions Open Wallets."

37. Ibid.

38. H. Martin, "Anaheim's 'Living Wage' Likely to Pass."

39. H. Martin, "2018 Midterm Election."

## CHAPTER 11

1. Vo, "Unprecedented Spending in Pivotal Election."

2. Malas, "In Disneyland's Hometown."

3. "Anaheim Mayor (Voters Choose One)," A4.

4. Ibid.

5. Pho, "Anaheim Mayoral Candidates Clash."

6. Ibid.

7. H. Martin, "2018 Midterm Election."

8. H. Martin, "Disney, Unions Open Wallets"; Vo, "Disney Pumps $600K into Election."

9. Ibid.

10. Vo, "Disney Pumps $600K into Election."

11. Details in this paragraph come from Robinson, "Did the Millions Spent Win Races?" AA3.

12. "Anaheim City Council, District 2," A4.

13. Ibid.

14. Vo, "Unprecedented Spending in Pivotal Election."

15. Moreno, Candidate Statement of Qualifications.

16. *Orange County Register* Staff Report, "City Council District 3 Candidates."

17. "Anaheim City Council, District 6," A9.

18. Ibid.

19. Vo, "Unprecedented Spending in Pivotal Election."

20. H. Martin, "Anaheim Council Races Tilt to Disney," A14.

21. Details in this paragraph come from "Anaheim Extends Angels at Stadium."

22. Robinson, "Angel Stadium."

23. Details about the Angels Stadium deal in the next two paragraphs come from City News Service, "The Big A"; Custodio, "Anaheim Announces $150 Million Stadium"; Brazil, "Angels to Stay in Anaheim"; Shaikin, "Anaheim Reduces Price of Angel Stadium," D1; Custodio and Bartusick, "Experts, Community Leaders Weigh In"; Custodio, "Anaheim Council Sells Angel Stadium"; Penaloza, "Did Anaheim Gift Stadium, Land to Moreno?"

24. Details in this paragraph come from "Anaheim Approves Historic Plan to Secure Baseball."

25. Details about the Angels Stadium deal in the next three paragraphs come from City News Service, "The Big A"; Custodio, "Anaheim Announces $150 Million Stadium"; Custodio, "Anaheim Council Sells Angel Stadium"; Custodio and Bartusick, "Experts, Community Leaders Weigh In."

26. Details in this paragraph come from Custodio and Bartusick, "Experts, Community Leaders Weigh In"; Custodio, "Anaheim Council Sells Angel Stadium."

27. Custodio, "Anaheim Council Sells Angel Stadium"; City News Service, "Anaheim City Council Approves Stadium Sale."

28. Details in this paragraph come from Custodio, "Anaheim Angel Stadium Sale Continues."

29. Details in this paragraph come from ibid.; Custodio, "Mayor Sidhu Unofficially Limits Discussion."

30. Disney Aspire, "Disney Aspire."

31. Mayor Harry Sidhu, "2019 State of the City Address," March 5, 2019, https://www.anaheim.net/DocumentCenter/View/25213/2019-Anaheim-State-of-the-City.

32. Collins, "Disney Donates to Help Housing for Homeless."

33. CHOC Walk, "Virtual CHOC Walk."

34. Disney News Desk, "Disney and KaBOOM!"

35. Details in this paragraph come from Macdonald, "Disneyland Takes First Step."

36. Details in this paragraph come from H. Martin, "Is Disneyland Getting City Subsidy?"; H. Martin, "Workers Sue for Living Wages," Business C1; Fruen, "Disney Is Sued."

37. Details about the 2019 suit and the class-action certification come from Brazil, "Judge Grants Class-Action Status "

38. Agustin, "Lawyer Plans to Appeal Decision."

39. Details in this sentence and the next come from San Roman, "Disney Loses Fight over Wage Law," B3.

40. Kyleigh Johnson, "Disneyland Resort Begins Multiyear Effort."

41. Unless otherwise noted, details about DisneylandForward come from the following sources: Hines, "What We Know about 'DisneylandForward'"; H. Martin, "New Plan

at Disneyland"; Stilwell, "Disneyland Announces DisneylandForward"; Vincent-Phoe-nix, "Disneyland Takes First Steps"; Kleiman, "DisneylandForward Initiative Seeks Community Support."

42. Kyleigh Johnson, "Disneyland Resort Begins Multiyear Effort."

43. Ibid.

44. Custodio and Pho, "Disney's Spending Pits Candidates against Critics."

45. Citizens United v. Federal Elections Commission 30 S. Ct. 876 (2010).

46. U.S. District Court for the Central District of California, Affidavit by FBI Special Agent Brad Adkins.

47. Ibid., e.g., see pp. 7, 8, 11, 14–15, 19, 21, 30, 52, 61, and 66.

48. Ibid., 11.

49. Ibid., 19.

50. Ibid., 19.

51. Ibid., 29.

52. Ibid., 29.

53. Details about the allegations against Sidhu come from People of the State of California and California Department of Housing and Community Development, a California State Agency v. City of Anaheim and City Council of the City of Anaheim, Ex Parte Application to Stay the Approval and Entry of the Proposed Stipulated Judgment; Declaration of David Pai in Support Thereof, Superior Court of the State of California, County of Orange, May 17, 2022. Case number 30-2022-01257462-CU-MC-CJC.

54. Staggs and Robinson, "Anaheim Mayor Resigns amid Investigation."

55. Ibid.

56. Elattar, "Anaheim City Council Rule Change."

57. Details in this paragraph come from Robinson, "Anaheim Council Nixes Ticket Tax."

58. Details in this paragraph come from Pho, "No Campaign Finance Reform for Anaheim."

59. Offices of City Attorney and City Clerk for the City of Anaheim, "An Ordinance of the City of Anaheim."

60. Gerda, "How Did Spending Vehicle Land in FBI Complaint?"

61. Gerda, "Disney Revs Up Campaign Spending after FBI Allegations."

62. Ibid.

63. Unless otherwise noted, details in the next six paragraphs come from Elattar and Leopo, "Vindication."

64. Details in the next couple of paragraphs come from Slaten, "How Far Has Anaheim Taken Reforms?"; quote that follows note 64 in text is from JL Group, "Administrative Investigation," 299.

65. JL Group, "Administrative Investigation," 307.

66. City News Service, "Anaheim Approves Campaign Finance Reforms."

67. Quotes in this paragraph come from Slaten, "Anaheim Mayor State of the City Address"; Slaten, "How Far Has Anaheim Taken Its Reforms?"; Nelson, "Opinion."

68. Details come from City of Anaheim, "City of Anaheim Approves DisneylandForward."

## PART III CONCLUSION

1. E.g., see Hunter, *Community Power Structure*; Domhoff, "Power Structure Research"; Domhoff, "Atlanta."

## CONCLUSION

1. Schattschneider, *Semi-Sovereign People*.
2. Bachrach and Baratz, "Two Faces of Power."
3. E.g., see Michener, "Power from the Margins."
4. Schragger, *City Power*.
5. Stone, *Regime Politics*.
6. For notable exceptions, see Krebs and Turner, "Following the Money"; Adams and Schreiber, "Gender, Campaign Finance, and Electoral Success."
7. Bachrach and Baratz, "Two Faces of Power."

# Bibliography

Abott, Carolyn, and Asya Magazinnik. "At-Large Elections and Minority Representation in Local Government." *American Journal of Political Science* 64, no. 3 (2020): 717–733.

Adams, Brian E., and Ronnee Schreiber. "Gender, Campaign Finance, and Electoral Success in Municipal Elections." *Journal of Urban Affairs* 33, no. 1 (2011): 83–97.

Adler, Patrick, and Richard Florida. "Geography as Strategy: The Changing Geography of Corporate Headquarters in Post-Industrial Capitalism." *Regional Studies* 54, no. 5 (2020): 610–620.

Agha, Nola, and Daniel Rascher. "Economic Development Effects of Major and Minor League Teams and Stadiums." *Journal of Sports Economics* 22, no. 3 (2021): 274–294.

Aguilar, Erika. "Anaheim Approves 30-year Tax Exemption Deal for Disney." LAist, July 8, 2015. Accessed September 14, 2024. Available at https://laist.com/news/kpcc-archive/anaheim-approves-30-year-tax-exemption-deal-for-di.

Agustin, Francis. "Lawyer Plans to Appeal Decision in Disneyland 'Fair Pay' Lawsuit." *Business Insider*, November 5, 2021. Available at https://www.businessinsider.com/labor-lawsuit-anaheim-disney-wages-appeal-disneyland-2021-11.

Allen, David. "Disneyland: Another Kind of Reality." *European Journal of American Culture* 33, no. 1 (2014): 33–47.

———. "Seeing Double: Disney's Wilderness Lodge." *European Journal of American Culture* 31, no. 2 (2012): 123–144.

———. "A Town Called Celebration." *European Journal of American Culture* 35, no. 3 (2016): 189–211.

"Anaheim Approves Historic Plan to Secure Baseball, Sell Stadium Site for $320 Million, Transform Land." *U.S. Fed News*, October 6, 2020.

"Anaheim City Council, District 2." *Chico Enterprise-Record*, October 4, 2018, A4.

"Anaheim City Council, District 6." *Chico Enterprise-Record*, October 4, 2018, A4.

"Anaheim Extends Angels at Stadium through 2020, Allowing Time for Discussions on New Lease." *U.S. Official News*, January 16, 2019.

"Anaheim Mayor (Voters Choose One)." *Chico Enterprise Record*, October 4, 2018, A4.

"Anaheim Planners Delay Decision on Disneyland Building Heights: Ruling Slated Aug. 17." *Orange County Evening News*, July 9, 1964.

"Anaheim Sets Course for Next 25+ Years of Great Sports, Entertainment at Honda Center." Plus Company Updates, November 22, 2018. Available at https://www.hondacenter.com/arena-info/press-releases/honda-center-celebrates-25th-anniversary/.

"Anaheim Shelter Plan: City Approves Site Purchase for Second Temporary Homeless Shelter." Plus Company Updates, December 6, 2018.

"Anaheim's Platinum Triangle Aims to Be OC's New Downtown." Multi-Housing News, 2005.

"Anaheim Streetcar Making a Comeback." *Orange County Register*, March 22, 2017. Available at https://www.ocregister.com/2017/03/22/anaheim-streetcar-making-a-comeback/.

Anton, Mike. "ACLU Lawsuit: Anaheim Council Elections Unfair to Latinos." *L.A. Now* (*Los Angeles Times*), June 29, 2012.

Arellano, Gustavo. "Canto XLI: A Timeline of Mexican Anaheim." December 8, 2018. Available at https://www.gustavoarellano.org/2018/12/506/.

———. "The Little People's Park Riot of 1978." *OC Weekly*, August 2, 2012. Available at https://www.ocweekly.com/the-little-peoples-park-riot-of-1978-6423524/.

Aronstein, Susan L., and Laurie A. Finke. "Discipline and Pleasure: The Pedagogical Work of Disneyland." *Educational Philosophy and Theory* 45, no. 6 (2013): 610–624.

Associated Press and John Evan Frook. "Disney Studies Leaner WestCOT." *Daily Variety*, December 13, 1993. Available at https://variety.com/1993/biz/news/disney-studies-leaner-westcot-116492/.

Avila, Eric. *Popular Culture in the Age of White Flight*. University of California Press, 2004.

Baber, Katherine, and James V. Spickard. "Crafting Culture: 'Tradition,' Art, and Music in Disney's 'A Small World.'" *Journal of Popular Culture* 48, no. 2 (2015): 225–239.

Bachrach, Peter, and Morton S. Baratz. "Two Faces of Power." *American Political Science Review* 56, no. 4 (1962): 947–952.

Bafarasat, Abbas Ziafati. "'Theorizing' Regime Theory: A City-Regional Perspective." *Journal of Urban Affairs* 40, no. 3 (2018): 412–425.

Baldassare, Mark. *When Government Fails: The Orange County Bankruptcy*. University of California Press, 1998.

Ballotpedia. "Save Our Anaheim Resort District Initiative (2008)." Available at https://ballotpedia.org/Save_Our_Anaheim_Resort_District_Initiative_(2008).

Barrier, Michael. *The Animated Man: A Life of Walt Disney*. University of California Press, 2007.

Bell, David, and Mark Jayne. "Small Cities? Towards a Research Agenda." *International Journal of Urban and Regional Research* 33, no. 3 (2009): 683–699.

Bemis, Bethanee. "Mirror, Mirror for Us All: Disney Theme Parks and the Collective Memory of the American National Narrative." *Public Historian* 42, no. 1 (2020): 54–79.

"Betting on Southern California." *Los Angeles Times*, December 14, 1991, B5.

Blair, Elizabeth. "After Protests, Disney CEO Speaks Out against Florida's 'Don't Say Gay' Bill." NPR, March 10, 2022. Available at https://www.npr.org/2022/03/08/1085130633/disney-response-florida-bill-dont-say-gay.

Bond, Paul. "Anaheim Ends $267 Million in Disney Theme Park Subsidies." *Hollywood Reporter*, August 28, 2018. Available at https://www.hollywoodreporter.com/business/business-news/anaheim-ends-267-million-disney-theme-park-subsidies-1138063/.

Bowers, James R., and Wilbur C. Rich, eds., *Governing Middle-Sized Cities: Studies in Mayoral Leadership*. Lynne Rienner, 2000.

Bradbury, John Charles. "Sports Stadiums and Local Economic Activity: Evidence from Sales Tax Collections." *Journal of Urban Affairs* 46, no. 1 (2022): 1–21.

Brazil, Ben. "Angels to Stay in Anaheim until at Least 2050 after Approval of Controversial Land Deal." *Daily Pilot*, September 30, 2020. Available at https://www.latimes.com /socal/daily-pilot/entertainment/story/2020–09–30/angels-to-stay-in-anaheim-until -at-least-2050-after-approval-of-controversial-land-deal.

———. "Emergency Homeless Shelter to Open Thursday in Anaheim." *Daily Pilot*, December 18, 2018. Available at https://www.latimes.com/socal/daily-pilot/news/tn-wknd -et-anaheim-shelter-20181220-story.html.

———. "Judge Grants Class-Action Status in Workers' Lawsuit against Disneyland." *Los Angeles Times*, July 21, 2021. Available at https://www.latimes.com/business/story/2021 –07–21/disney-lawsuit-workers-living-wage-moves-forward.

Brunell, Natalie, Jaqueline Hurtado, and Michael Martinez. "Latinos in California Seek Council Seat in Ongoing Tension with Anaheim Police." CNN.com, August 9, 2012.

Buntin, John. "Outside Disneyland, a Reminder for Governments to Be Careful What They Wish For." *Governing*, March 22, 2018. Available at https://www.governing.com /topics/mgmt/gov-disneyland-anaheim-incentives.html.

Burns, Peter F. *Electoral Politics Is Not Enough: Racial and Ethnic Minorities and Urban Politics.* State University of New York Press, 2012.

Burns, Peter F., Max Bieganski, Shunji Fueki et al. "Political Socialization and Disneyland." Paper presented at the Annual Meeting of the Western Political Science Association, San Francisco, CA, March 29–31, 2018.

Burns, Peter F., and Matthew O. Thomas. *Reforming New Orleans: The Contentious Politics of Change in the Big Easy.* Cornell University Press, 2015.

Camou, Michelle. "Labor-Community Coalitions through an Urban Regime Lens: Institutions and Ideas in Building Power from Below." *Urban Affairs Review* 50, no. 5 (2014): 623–647.

Carreon, Crystal, and E. Scott Reckard. "City Council OKs Pointe Anaheim." *Los Angeles Times*, June 23, 1999, B1.

Carter, Chelsea. "Anaheim School Board Drops Proposal to Make Students Prove Citizenship." Associated Press, October 26, 2001.

———. "Group Urges Anaheim to Let Police Arrest Suspected Illegal Immigrants." *San Diego Union Tribune*, January 24, 2001.

Central Florida Tourism Oversight District. "About the Central Florida Tourism Oversight District." Accessed September 14, 2024. Available at https://www.oversightdistrict .org/.

CHOC Walk. "Virtual CHOC Walk, Presented by Disneyland." CHOCWalk.org. Available at https://www.chocwalk.org/Static/event-info.

City-Data. "Anaheim: Economy: Major Industries and Commercial Activity." City-Data .com. Accessed July 11, 2020. Available at http://www.city-data.com/us-cities/The-West /Anaheim-Economy.html.

City News Service. "Anaheim Adopts Sunshine Ordinance, Brings Added Accountability to Local Government." August 18, 2017.

———. "Anaheim Approves Campaign Finance Reforms; Running Timeline." Accessed September 14, 2024. Available at https://www.anaheim.net/CivicAlerts.aspx?AID=2731.

———. "Anaheim City Council Approves Stadium Sale to Angels." September 30, 2020.

City of Anaheim. "DisneylandForward." Available at https://anaheim.net/5961/Disney landForward.

———. "Anaheim Municipal Code." 2024 S-26 Supplement. American Legal, 2024.

———. *The Anaheim Resort Specific Plan* "2.0 Planning Context," Section 2.2. Available at https://www.anaheim.net/DocumentCenter/Home/View/2482.

———. "Anaheim Settles Lawsuit with ACLU over Elections Process." *Press Telegram*, January 8, 2014. Available at https://www.presstelegram.com/2014/01/08/anaheim-settles-lawsuit-with-aclu-over-elections-process/.

———. "The Big A." Press release, November 23, 2020. Accessed September 14, 2024. Available at http://www.anaheim.net/5207/The-Big-A.

———. "Charter of the City of Anaheim." November 8, 2016.

———. *City Scoop*, 2, no. 6 (August–September 1956).

———. "Community Center, Parks, Streets, Public Safety Focus of Anaheim's Budget." June 20, 2017.

———. *Disneyland Resort Specific Plan*. June 21, 2024. Accessed September 14, 2024. Available at https://www.anaheim.net/1017/Disneyland-Resort-Specific-Plan.

———. "Join Us and Help Shape the Future of Anaheim Parks." April 23, 2017. Available at https://www.anaheimobserver.com/2017/04/23/help-shape-future-anaheim-parks/.

———. "Platinum Triangle." July 14, 2020. Accessed September 14, 2024. Available at https://www.anaheim.net/1072/Platinum-Triangle.

City of Anaheim. "City of Anaheim Approves DisneylandForward." Available at https://anaheim.net/5961/DisneylandForward.

Cochrane, Allan. "Urban Politics: An Interdisciplinary Dialogue." *International Journal of Urban and Regional Research* 35, no. 4 (2011): 853–871. Available at https://doi.org/10.1111/j.1468-2427.2011.01055.x.

———. "Urban Politics beyond the Urban." *International Journal of Urban and Regional Research* 35, no. 4 (July 1, 2011): 862–863. Available at http://oro.open.ac.uk/28979/.

Cohen, Cathy J. *The Boundaries of Blackness: AIDS and the Breakdown of Black Politics*. University of Chicago Press, 1999.

Coker, Matt. "Looking Back at 1953 and the Disneyland That Was Almost Not in Anaheim." *OC Weekly*, July 9, 2013. Available at https://www.ocweekly.com/looking-back-at-1953-and-the-disneyland-that-almost-was-not-in-anaheim-6473443/.

———. "Now-Deceased Anaheim City Manager Explains How Disneyland Became Disneyland." *OC Weekly*, May 28, 2013. Available at https://www.ocweekly.com/now-deceased-anaheim-city-manager-explains-how-disneyland-became-disneyland-video-6476619/.

Collins, Jeff. "Disney Donates $5 Million to Help Housing for Orange County's Homeless." *Orange County Register*, March 5, 2019. Available at https://www.ocregister.com/2019/03/05/disney-donates-5-million-to-help-fund-housing-for-orange-countys-homeless/.

Conley, Jamie Erin. "Spatial Analysis of the Effects of Revitalization on Crime in the Jeffrey-Lynne Community in Anaheim, California." Master of Arts Thesis in Interdisciplinary Studies, Cal State University San Bernardino, 2004. Available at https://scholarworks.lib.csusb.edu/cgi/viewcontent.cgi?referer=https://scholar.google.com/&httpsredir=1&article=3572&context=etd-project.

Cruz, Nicole Santa, Christopher Goffard, and Richard Winton. "Protests Reflect Deep Divisions in Anaheim." *Pittsburgh Post-Gazette*, July 30, 2012, A10.

CSUF News Center. "Titan Economists Quantify Disneyland's Impact on Southern California." Accessed September 14, 2024. Available at https://news.fullerton.edu/feature/disney-economic-impact/#:~:text=The%20economists%20found%20that%20in,made%20purchases%20from%20local%20businesses.

Cunningham, Matthew. "City Council Approves Public-Private Partnership to Build 200-Bed Temporary Emergency Homeless Shelter." Anaheimobserver.com, December 7, 2018. Available at https://www.anaheimobserver.com/2018/12/07/city-council-ap proves-public-private-partnership-to-build-200-bed-temporary-emergency-homeless -shelter/.

Custodio, Spencer. "Anaheim Angel Stadium Sale Continues No Matter Who's in Charge, Subsidy Critics Historically Sidelined." *Voice of OC*, September 29, 2020. Available at https://voiceofoc.org/2020/09/anaheims-bid-to-sell-angel-stadium-continues-no -matter-whos-in-charge-critics-of-subsidy-deals-historically-sidelined/.

———. "Anaheim Announces $150 Million Angel Stadium and Land Sale, Taxpayers Subsidize Housing and Park." *Voice of OC*, September 5, 2020. Available at https://voiceo foc.org/2020/09/anaheim-announces-bid-to-sell-angel-stadium-land-for-150-million -taxpayers-subsidize-housing-and-park/.

———. "Anaheim Council Sells Angel Stadium and Land for $150 Million, Subsidizes Housing and Park." *Voice of OC*, September 30, 2020. Available at https://voiceofoc .org/2020/09/anaheim-council-sells-angel-stadium-and-land-for-150-million-subsi dizes-housing-and-park/.

———. "Anaheim Mayor Sidhu Unofficially Limits Council Discussion." *Voice of OC*, May 9, 2019. Available at https://voiceofoc.org/2019/05/anaheim-mayor-sidhu-unofficially -limits-council-discussion/.

Custodio, Spencer, and Caitlin Bartusick. "Experts, Anaheim Community Leaders Weigh In on $150 Million Angel Stadium Deal." *Voice of OC*, September 28, 2020. Available at https://voiceofoc.org/2020/09/experts-anaheim-community-leaders-weigh-in-on -150-million-angel-stadium-sale/.

Custodio, Spencer, and Brandon Pho. "Disney's $1.5 Million Spending Pits Resort-Friendly Anaheim Council Candidates against Subsidy Critics." *Voice of OC*, October 22, 2020. Available at https://voiceofoc.org/2020/10/disneys-1-5-million-spending-pits-resort -friendly-anaheim-council-candidates-against-subsidy-critics/.

Daily Mail. "How Does It Feel That Your Life Was Just Saved by a Jewish Man?" February 29, 2016. Available at https://www.dailymail.co.uk/news/article-3468569/Jewish-man -tells-helped-two-KKK-members-away-mob-attack-Anaheim.html.

D'Amaro, Josh. "Letter to Honorable Mayor and City Council of Anaheim." August 21, 2018. Available at https://scng-dash.digitalfirstmedia.com/wp-content/uploads/2018 /08/josh-damaro-disney-letter.pdf.

David, Amin. "The Dislocation of 200 Families in Anaheim's Chevy Chase." *Los Angeles Times*, July 27, 1986. Available at https://www.latimes.com/archives/la-xpm-1986-07 -27-me-1600-story.html.

DeLeon, Richard E. "The Urban Antiregime: Progressive Politics in San Francisco." *Urban Affairs Quarterly* 27, no. 4 (1992): 555–579.

Designing Disney. "The Genesis of Disneyland: The 1951 'Riverside Drive Park.'" Accessed January 10, 2020. Available at https://www.designingdisney.com/parks/disneyland-re sort/genesis-disneyland-1951-riverside-drive-park/.

Dickerson, Marla, and Greg Hernandez. "Anaheim Escalating the Battle for Tourism." *Los Angeles Times*, July 11, 1996, A1.

———. "Disney Resort Funding Plan Outlined." *Los Angeles Times*, July 16, 1996, A1.

Disney Aspire. "Disney Aspire." Available at https://disney.guildeducation.com/partner? auth_redirect=true&gclid=CjwKCAjw1cX0BRBmEiwAy9tKHmYNB_mW4V6L -7qjBi6TgP9ryl8WbKNQG7iZSrvI1CdHXP8fFKZ5YBoCmosQAvD_BwE.

"The Disney Dilemma." *Orange County Register*, April 25, 1993, L4.

"Disney Is Acting in a Neighborly Way." *Los Angeles Times*, June 20, 1993, B8.

Disneyland. "Disneyland History." *News from Disneyland*, July 11, 1967.

Disneyland. "The Happiness Industry." *Anaheim Bulletin*, September 6, 1957, 11.

"Disneyland California Employees Demand Living Wage." *The Nation*, June 16, 2018.

"Disneyland Celebrates Its Golden Anniversary: With Its Sense of Security, the Park Transformed Surrounding City." *Grand Rapid Press*, July 10, 2005.

"Disneyland Comes Here: Fabulous Project Set for 160-Acre Playland." May 1, 1954. Article from Muzeo (Anaheim Archives). No publication source.

"Disneyland Keeps Local Police Busy." *Anaheim Bulletin*, July 18, 1955, 1.

Disneyland Public Relations Department. "Building a Dream." 1956.

Disneyland Public Relations Division. *Disneyland Report to Anaheim and Orange County*. 1958.

"Disneyland Routes." *Anaheim Gazette*, September 15, 1955.

"Disneyland Row Ended: Annexation Foes Reach Agreement with City." *Anaheim Bulletin*, December 28, 1954.

Disney News Desk. "Disney and KaBOOM! Bring 12th Playground to Anaheim's Julianna Park." Laughing Place, September 27, 2019. Accessed January 6, 2021. Available at https://www.laughingplace.com/w/news/2019/09/27/disney-and-kaboom-bring-12th-playground-to-anaheims-julianna-park/.

"Disney Resort." *Orange County Register*, December 13, 1991, B5.

"Disney Tells Planning on Big Playland." *Orange County Register*, 1954.

Do, Anh. "While Homeless Surges in Disneyland's Shadow, Anaheim Removes Bus Benches." *Los Angeles Times*, July 15, 2017. Accessed January 5, 2021. Available at https://www.latimes.com/local/lanow/la-me-ln-anaheim-bus-stops-20170715-story.html.

Dobuzinskis, Alex. "After Unrest, Divisions Grip Anaheim, Disneyland's Home." Reuters, August 11, 2012. Available at https://www.reuters.com/article/world/after-unrest-divisions-grip-anaheim-disneyland-s-home-idUSBRE87A0C8/.

"Does Disney Pay Its Fair Share? Yes." *Orange County Register*, October 14, 2017. Available at https://www.ocregister.com/2017/10/14/does-disney-pay-its-fair-share-yes/.

Domhoff, G. William. "Atlanta: Floyd Hunter Was Right." Who Rules America, 2005. Accessed September 14, 2024. Available at https://whorulesamerica.ucsc.edu/local/atlanta.html.

———. "C. Wright Mills, Floyd Hunter, and 50 Years of Power Structure Research." *Michigan Sociological Review* 21 (Fall 2007): 1–54.

Dowd, Katie. "Remembering Disneyland's Disastrous Opening Day." SFGate, July 17, 2022. Available at https://www.sfgate.com/disneyland/article/black-sunday-disneyland-opening-day-1955-15410291.php.

Drier, Peter, and Daniel Fleming. "Working for the Mouse: A Survey of Disneyland Resort Employees." Economic Roundtable and Urban & Environmental Policy Institute, February 2018. Available at https://economicrt.org/wp-content/uploads/2018/02/ERt-Disneyland-final-2-20-2018.pdf.

D23. "Disney Legends: Jack Lindquist." Accessed March 26, 2021. Available at https://d23.com/walt-disney-legend/jack-lindquist/.

———. "Walt Disney's Proposed Theme Park in Burbank." Accessed June 13, 2020. Available at https://d23.com/mickey-mouse-park-art-burbank-theme-park-disneyland/.

Duchess of Disneyland. "Dominguez Tree." Accessed March 26, 2021. Available at https://duchessofdisneyland.com/disneyland/the-dominguez-tree/.

Dunn, Lucy. "Anaheim: Instability Breeds Instability." *Orange County Register*, July 29, 2017. Available at https://www.ocregister.com/2017/07/29/instability-breeds-instability-in-anaheim/.

"Early Anaheim: Early Settlers and Arts." Muzeo (Anaheim Archives Exhibit). Accessed October 21, 2019.

Economics Research Associates. "Economic Impact of the Disneyland Recreation Complex on the City of Anaheim." June 30, 1964. Available at https://stars.library.ucf.edu/cgi/viewcontent.cgi?referer=https://www.google.com/&httpsredir=1&article=1155&context=buzzprice.

Eisinger, Peter. "The Politics of Bread and Circuses: Building the City for the Visitor Class." *Urban Affairs Review* 35, no. 3 (2000): 316–333.

Elattar, Hosam. "Anaheim City Council Rule Change Could Bring a Wave of New Policy Discussions." *Voice of OC*, June 22, 2022. Available at https://voiceofoc.org/2022/06/anaheim-city-council-rule-change-could-bring-a-wave-of-new-policy-discussions/.

Elattar, Hosam, and Julie Leopo. "Vindication: Anaheim Residents Sound Off on Concerns about Stadium Deal and City Council Members." *Voice of OC*, May 27, 2022. Available at https://voiceofoc.org/2022/05/vindication-anaheim-residents-sound-off-on-concerns-about-stadium-deal-and-city-council-members/.

Elmahrek, Adam. "Anaheim City Councilwoman Criticized for Trip with Disneyland Lobbyist." *Voice of OC*, August 7, 2015. Available at https://voiceofoc.org/2015/08/councilwoman-criticized-for-trip-with-disneyland-lobbyist/.

———. "Anaheim Council Approves Ticket Tax Protection for Disneyland." *Voice of OC*, July 8, 2015. Available at https://voiceofoc.org/2015/07/anaheim-strips-residents-of-power-to-tax-disneyland-for-up-to-45-years/.

———. "Can Anaheim Repair Broken Trust with Latino Community?" *Voice of OC*, August 1, 2012. Available at https://voiceofoc.org/2012/08/can-anaheim-repair-a-broken-trust-with-latino-community/.

Ember, Sydney, and Brooks Barnes. "Disney Ends Ban on *Los Angeles Times* amid Fierce Backlash." *New York Times*, November 7, 2017. Available at https://www.nytimes.com/2017/11/07/business/disney-la-times.html.

"Expanding to the Tune of $177 Million." *Orange County Register*, December 29, 2000.

Extinct Attractions. "Disney Legend Buzz Price Interview with David O'Neal—2." Video. Available at https://www.youtube.com/watch?v=lYn9C7RkPGY.

"Fabulous 'Disneyland' Termed Both TV Studio, Eighth Wonder of the World." United Press, n.d.

Faessel, Stephen J. *Images of America: Early Anaheim*. Arcadia, 2006.

Findlay, John M. *Magic Lands*. University of California Press, 1993.

Fiore, Faye. "Disney Unveils Plans." *Los Angeles Times*, August 1, 1990, B1.

———. "House Denies Funds for Disney's Parking Garage." *Los Angeles Times*, September 29, 1994, 32.

Fisher, Marla Jo. "Anaheim Eyes Disney Tax Deal." *Orange County Register*, October 1, 1996, B1.

———. "Anaheim Takes Down Its Tacky Signs." *Orange County Register*, April 22, 1999, B2.

———. "Big Day Nears for Disney." *Orange County Register*, October 6, 1996, A22.

———. "Council Splits over Meeting on Disney Plan." *Orange County Register*, October 2, 1996, B1.

———. "Disney Expansion Still Alive." *Orange County Register*, June 22, 1995, C1.

——. "Disneyland Expansion Passes First Hurdle." *Orange County Register*, August 20, 1996, B1.

——. "It's Not a Small World: Disneyland Plan Approved." *Orange County Register*, October 9, 1996, A1.

——. "Resort District's Coming Attraction." *Orange County Register*, December 28, 1998, A1.

Florida Senate. *Parental Rights in Education—2022: Bill Summaries*. 2022. Accessed September 14, 2024. Available at https://www.flsenate.gov/Committees/billsummaries/2022/html/2825.

Foglesong, Richard E. *Married to the Mouse: Walt Disney World and Orlando*. Yale University Press, 2001.

Fortner, Michael Javen. "Racial Capitalism and City Politics: Toward a Theoretical Synthesis." *Urban Affairs Review* 59, no. 2 (2023): 630–653.

Foxhall, Emily, and Hugo Martin. "Disney Tax Break Up for Renewal." *Los Angeles Times*, June 27, 2015, C1.

Framke, Caroline, and Alissa Wilkinson. "The Controversy over Disney Blacklisting the *LA Times*, Explained." Vox.com, November 8, 2017. Available at https://www.vox.com/culture/2017/11/7/16617394/la-times-disney-media-ban-blackout.

"From Potholes to Condos: Anaheim's Stadium Lofts Opens This Month." *California Construction Link*, June 1, 2006, 20.

Fruen, Lauren. "Disney Is Sued for 'Not Paying Hundreds of Workers at Their California Theme Park and Hotels a Living Wage—Forcing Many to Live in Their Cars or to Sleep on People's Couches.'" Daily Mail, December 11, 2019. Available at https://www.dailymail.co.uk/news/article-7781715/Disney-sued-not-paying-hundreds-workers-California-living-wage.html.

Gennawey, Sam. *The Disneyland Story*. Keen Communications, 2014.

Gerda, Nick. "Disney Revs Up Campaign Spending in Anaheim amid Calls to Curb Their Influence after FBI Allegations." *Voice of OC*, July 19, 2022. Available at https://voiceofoc.org/2022/07/disney-revs-up-campaign-spending-in-anaheim-amid-calls-to-curb-their-influence-after-fbi-allegations/.

——. "How Did Disneyland's Main Political Spending Vehicle Land in the Middle of an FBI Complaint?" *Voice of OC*, May 22, 2022. Available at https://voiceofoc.org/2022/05/how-did-disneylands-main-political-spending-vehicle-land-in-the-middle-of-an-fbi-complaint/#:~:text=The%20discussion%20of%20the%20Disney,how%20their%20%E2%80%9Cfamily%E2%80%9D%20operates.

——. "Shawn Nelson Had Homeless Camp Removed from Riverbed Near Honda Center, Emails Show." *Voice of OC*, March 22, 2017. Available at https://voiceofoc.org/2017/03/shawn-nelson-had-homeless-camp-removed-from-riverbed-near-honda-center-emails-show/.

Gerda, Nick, Thy Vo, and David Washburn. "Disney Breaks Its Own Spending Record in This Year's Anaheim Election." *Voice of OC*, November 1, 2016. Available at https://voiceofoc.org/2016/11/disney-breaks-its-own-spending-record-in-anaheim-election/.

Giroux, Henry A. "Public Pedagogy and Rodent Politics: Cultural Studies and the Challenge of Disney." *Arizona Journal of Hispanic Cultural Studies* 21, no. 1 (1998): 253–266.

Glenn, Brian. "The Two Schools of American Political Development." *Political Studies Review* 2, no. 2 (2004): 153–165.

Godines, Valeria, and Vik Jolly. "Anaheim Urged to Boot INS IMMIGRATION." *Orange County Register*, February 8, 2001.

Goulding, Susan Christian. "Unions Submit Living Wages Petition." *Orange County Register,* May 2, 2018, 5.

Graham, Jordan. "County Plans to Clear Riverbed." *Orange County Register,* January 5, 2018, BB13.

———. "Supervisors Nix Relocation Plan." *Orange County Register,* March 28, 2018, AA1.

Green, Susan. "Anaheim Hills: The Hills Are Alive in Anaheim." *Los Angeles Times,* October 13, 1988.

Gross, Meir. "Legal Gambling as a Strategy for Economic Development." *Economic Development Quarterly* 12, no. 3 (1998): 203–213.

Gutsche Jr., Robert E. "Boosterism as Banishment: Identifying the Power Function of Local, Business News and Coverage of City Spaces." *Journalism Studies* 16, no. 4 (2015): 497–512.

Haldane, David. "Disney Backers Plan Referendum on Housing." *Los Angeles Times,* April 27, 2007, B5.

"Halt to Anaheim Disneyland Annexation Sought: Excess Use of City's Powers Charged in Superior Court Suit." *Santa Ana Register,* September 18, 1954.

Harala, Larry. "Public Finance of Professional Athletic Facilities: Case Studies in Stadium and Arena Finance." University of Nevada, Las Vegas Theses, Dissertations, Professional Papers, and Capstones, 2000.

Harwood, Stacy Anne. "Struggling to Embrace Difference in Land-Use Decision Making in Multicultural Communities." *Planning, Practice & Research* 20, no. 4 (2005): 355–371.

Hayes, Bonnie. "500 Rally to Support Disneyland Expansion." *Los Angeles Times,* October 8, 1996, B3.

Hernandez, Greg. "'Anaheim Resort' Plan to Get Public Hearing." *Los Angeles Times,* September 19, 1994, B1.

———. "Anaheim's Beautification Plan Not without Flaws." *Los Angeles Times,* August 28, 1994, B1.

———. "Anaheim to Proceed with $172-Million Revitalization Plan." *Los Angeles Times,* February 3, 1995, B1.

———. "Disneyland at 40: Old Magic, New Wrinkles." *Los Angeles Times,* July 16, 1995. Available at https://www.latimes.com/archives/la-xpm-1995-07–16-mn-24616-story.html.

———. "In a Sign of the Times, 3 Hotels Spruce Up in City Face Lift." *Los Angeles Times,* August 2, 1995, B2.

———. "INS Seeks to Exit Anaheim Jail." *Los Angeles Times,* June 26, 1996. Available at https://www.latimes.com/archives/la-xpm-1996-06–26-me-18823-story.html.

———. "$1.4-Billion Disneyland Expansion Approved." *Los Angeles Times,* October 9, 1996, A1.

———. "Senate Panel OKs $25 Million for Transit Hub." *Los Angeles Times,* October 7, 1993, B1.

Hernandez, Greg, and Bonnie Hayes. "City Studying Disney-Related Improvements." *Los Angeles Times,* October 2, 1996, B1.

Hicks, Jerry. "Anaheim in Pictures." *Orange Coast Magazine,* September 2007, 204–206.

———. "Anaheim More Than an L.A. Suburb." *Orange Coast Magazine,* April 2006, 196–198.

Hines, Morgan. "What We Know about 'DisneylandForward.'" *USA Today,* March 26, 2021.

Hirsch, Jerry. "Disney Lets Options Expire." *Orange County Register,* January 31, 1995, A1.

Hispanically Speaking News. "¡No Mas! Say Anaheim Latinos on Their Fourth Day of Protests." Newstex, July 26, 2012.

Holden, Tracey Quigley, and Sandra L. French. "Food Fight! Gigante Grocery versus the City of Anaheim: The Battle for Legitimacy." *Journal of Business Communication* 49, no. 1 (2012): 74–94.

Hoskins, Kelsey. "Klanaheim." *Journal of Orange County Studies*, January 3, 2012. Available at https://orangecountystudies.wordpress.com/2012/01/03/klanaheim/.

Hughes, Paul. "Disney Suspends Hotel Project." *Orange County Business Journal*, August 16, 2018. Available at https://www.ocbj.com/tourism/disney-suspends-hotel-project/.

Hunter, Floyd. *Community Power Structure: A Study of Decision Makers*. University of North Carolina Press, 1953.

Hunter-Gault, Charlayne, William Brangham, Cat Wise, and Judy Woodruff, "PBS News-Hour for March 27, 2018." *PBS NewsHour*.

———. "Why Anaheim's Low-Wage Workers Struggle to Keep a Roof over Their Heads." *PBS NewsHour*, March 27, 2018. Available at https://www.pbs.org/newshour/show/why-anaheims-low-wage-workers-struggle-to-keep-a-roof-over-their-heads.

JL Group, LLC. "Administrative Investigation: Report of Findings in the Matter of the City of Anaheim Investigation." July 1, 2023. Available at https://www.anaheim.net/DocumentCenter/View/50673/Anaheim-redacted-independent-investigation-report-update-notice-8-3-23?bidId=.

Johnson, Kevin. "Anaheim Still Backs Tourism Growth but Frets about Costs: Attraction—More Than Half of Residents Favor Proposed Entertainment Tax to Keep the City's Economy Sound." *Los Angeles Times*, March 18, 1992, A18.

———. "Disneyland: It's the Mouse That Roared in Anaheim—Residents and Officials Overwhelmingly Approve the Image the Park Has Bestowed on Their City." *Los Angeles Times*, March 18, 1992, A1.

———. "Disney Tickets Could Bar Majority Vote." *Los Angeles Times*, April 2, 1992.

———. "Disney Warns Gate Tax Would Scuttle Resort." *Los Angeles Times*, September 5, 1991.

———. "Free Tickets Not Meant to Buy Influence, Disney Insists." *Los Angeles Times*, April 11, 1992, 1.

———. "Mickey's Style Can Get Nasty, Ex-Mayor of Anaheim Recalls." *Los Angeles Times*, June 30, 1991, A14.

———. "Plan Unveiled for Huge Disneyland Expansion; Parks: WestCOT Center Would Adjoin Existing Site. But Company Says Long Beach Is Still in the Running." *Los Angeles Times*, May 9, 1991, A1.

———. "The *Times* Orange County Poll: Anaheim's Residents Seek Political Reform." *Los Angeles Times*, March 17, 1992, 1.

Johnson, Kevin, and Chris Woodyard. "Anaheim's Leaders Recall Disney's Legacy of Largess." *Los Angeles Times*, June 30, 1991, 1.

———. "Disney Chooses Anaheim as Location for $3-Billion Resort." *Los Angeles Times*, December 13, 1991, A1.

———. "Disney Showers Gifts on Anaheim Officials." *Los Angeles Times*, June 27, 1991, 1.

Johnson, Kyleigh. "Disneyland Resort Begins a Multiyear Public Planning Effort to Allow for Future Integrated and Immersive Experiences." Disneyland Resort, External Communications Manager, March 26, 2021. Available at https://disneyparks.disney.go.com/blog/2021/03/disneyland-resort-begins-a-multiyear-public-planning-effort-to-allow-for-future-integrated-and-immersive-experiences/.

Jones-Correa, Michael, and Diane Wong. "Whose Politics? Reflections on Clarence Stone's Regime Politics." *Urban Affairs Review* 51, no. 1 (2015): 161–170.

Joy, Meghan, and Ronald K. Vogel. "Beyond Neoliberalism: A Policy Agenda for a Progressive City." *Urban Affairs Review* 57, no. 5 (2021): 1372–1409.

Judd, Dennis R. "Constructing the Tourist Bubble." In *The Tourist City*, edited by Dennis R. Judd and Susan S. Fainstein, 35–53. Yale University Press, 1999.

Judd, Dennis R., and Susan S. Fainstein, eds. *The Tourist City*. Yale University Press, 1999.

Kantor, Paul, and H. V. Savitch. "Can Politicians Bargain with Business? A Theoretical and Comparative Perspective on Urban Development." *Urban Affairs Quarterly* 29, no. 2 (1993): 230–255.

KCAL News. "Dispute Suspends Construction of New Disney Hotel in Anaheim." CBS Los Angeles, August 15, 2018. Accessed March 2, 2019. Available at https://losangeles .cbslocal.com/2018/08/16/dispute-suspends-construction-disney-hotel-anaheim/.

Kilroy, Mike. "How Disney Chose OC for His New Land." *Orange County Scene*, December 5, 1996, 1.

Kindy, Kimberly. "Blacks Plan Boycott of Anaheim Convention." *Orange County Register*, March 27, 1999.

King, Margaret J. "Disneyland and Walt Disney World: Traditional Values in Futuristic Form." *Journal of Popular Culture* 15, no. 1 (1981): 116–140.

Kleiman, Joe. "DisneylandForward Initiative Seeks Community Support for Changing Anaheim Municipal Code." InPark Magazine, March 28, 2021. Available at http:// www.inparkmagazine.com/disneylandforward-initiative/.

Knight-Ridder Tribune Business News. "Anaheim Backs Lennar's Vision." October 26, 2005.

Koch, Philippe. "Bringing Power Back In: Collective and Distributive Forms of Power in Public Participation." *Urban Studies* 50, no. 14 (2013): 2976–2992.

Koenig, David. "Strike II?" Mouse Planet, March 7, 2006. Available at https://www.mouse planet.com/7606/Strike_II.

Kopetman, Roxana. "Anaheim: Relocation Firm Hired for Chevy Project." *Los Angeles Times*, July 18, 1986. Available at https://www.latimes.com/archives/la-xpm-1986-07 -18-me-16612-story.html.

———. "Face Lift Due Anaheim Neighborhood." *Los Angeles Times*, July 2, 1986. Available at https://www.latimes.com/archives/la-xpm-1986-07-02-me-436-story.html.

———. "Proposal for Anaheim Development: Renovation Plan May Force Families Out of Apartments." *Los Angeles Times*, July 14, 1986. Available at https://www.latimes.com /archives/la-xpm-1986–07–14-me-19242-story.html.

Korkis, Jim. "Once Upon a Time in Anaheim." Mouse Planet, July 22, 2015. Accessed January 14, 2020. Available at https://www.mouseplanet.com/11098/Once_Upon_A_Time _In_Anaheim.

———. "The Real Story of the Mickey Mouse Park." Mouse Planet, September 4, 2019. Available at https://mouseplanet.com/the-real-story-of-the-mickey-mouse-park/7137/#:~ :text=In%20December%201951%2C%20Walt%20contacted,with%20the%20Gri ffith%20Park%20carousel.

Kraus, Neil. "The Significance of Race in Urban Politics: The Limitations of Regime Theory." *Race and Society* 7, no. 2 (2004): 95–111.

Krebs, Timothy B., and Fraser S. Turner. "Following the Money: The Influence of Campaign Finance Reform in the 2011 Chicago Mayoral Election." *Journal of Urban Affairs* 37, no. 2 (2015): 109–121.

Krishnakumar, Priya, Daniel Miller, and Ben Poston. "Disney Spent Heavily to Sway an Election in Anaheim—Did It Pay Off?" *Los Angeles Times*, September 24, 2017. Available at https://www.latimes.com/projects/la-fi-disney-anaheim-campaign-finance/.

Kühn, Manfred, Matthias Bernt, and Laura Colini. "Power, Politics and Peripheralization: Two Eastern German Cities." *European Urban and Regional Studies* 24, no. 3 (2017): 258–273.

Kumar, Tanu, and Matthew Stenberg. "Why Political Scientists Should Study Smaller Cities." *Urban Affairs Review* 59, no. 6 (2023): 2005–2042.

La Ganga, Maria L. "Disney Drops Policy Prohibiting Same-Sex Dancing." *Los Angeles Times*, August 14, 1985. Available at https://www.latimes.com/archives/la-xpm-1985 -08-14-me-2745-story.html.

Lait, Matt. "Disneyland Project Wins Key Vote." *Los Angeles Times*, June 23, 1993. Available at https://www.latimes.com/archives/la-xpm-1993–06–23-mn-6291-story.html.

———. "Disney Promises to Reduce Noise." *Los Angeles Times*, June 10, 1993, A20.

———. "Disney Reaches Tentative Pact in 1 of 2 Suits." *Los Angeles Times*, October 19, 1993, OCB1.

———. "Will Disney Make Anaheim Unhappiest Place on Earth?" *Los Angeles Times*, December 24, 1993, A1.

Lait, Matt, and Greg Miller. "'The Anaheim Problem' Has a Happy Ending." *Los Angeles Times*, July 18, 1996, A1.

Lait, Matt, and Chris Woodyard. "Disneyland Plans Dim as Project Chief Resigns." *Orange County Register*, December 21, 1993. Available at https://www.latimes.com/archives /la-xpm-1993–12–21-mn-4215-story.html.

———. "Disney Won't Decide on Resort for a Year at Least." *Orange County Register*, June 10, 1994, A1.

Lamb, Daniel. "Yes on District Elections in Anaheim, but the ACLU's Argument for Districts Was Wrong/Ahistorical." OC Politics Blog, January 10, 2014. Available at http:// ocpoliticsblog.com/2014/01/09/yes-on-districtselection-in-anaheim-but-the-aclus -arguement-for-districts-was-wrongahistorical/.

Lang, Robert E., and Jennifer B. LeFurgy. *Boomburbs: The Rise of America's Accidental Cities.* Brookings Institution, 2007.

Lang, Robert E., and Patrick A. Simmons. *Boomburbs: The Emergence of Large, Fast-Growing Suburban Cities in the United States.* Fannie Mae Foundation, Census Note 06, June 2001.

Lanser, Jonathan. "Disney, City Engage in Word War II." *Orange County Register*, May 27, 2007, Cover D.

Lasswell, Harold Dwight. *Politics: Who Gets What, When, How.* P. Smith, 1950.

LaTour, Jesse. "A Brief History of the Ku Klux Klan in Orange County: Notes on the Banality of Evil." *Fullerton Observer*, January 7, 2019. Available at https://fullertonob server.com/2019/01/07/a-brief-history-of-the-ku-klux-klan-in-orange-county-notes -on-the-banality-of-evil/.

League of Women Voters. "Proposition 227. English Language in Public Schools." Smart Voter. Available at http://www.smartvoter.org/1998jun/ca/state/prop/227/.

Leal, David L., Valerie Martinez-Ebers, and Kenneth J. Meier. "The Politics of Latino Education: The Biases of At-Large Elections." *Journal of Politics* 66, no. 4 (2004): 1224–1244.

Lewinnek, Elaine, Gustavo Arellano, and Thuy Vo Dang. *A People's Guide to Orange County.* University of California Press, 2022.

Lindquist, Jack, and Melinda J. Combs. *In Service to the Mouse: My Unexpected Journey to Becoming Disneyland's First President: A Memoir.* Neverland Media and Chapman University Press, 2010.

Loudon, Howard. "Disneyland: Friend or Foe." *Anaheim Bulletin*, July 2, 1955.

Macdonald, Brady. "Disneyland Takes First Step toward Building 12-Story Disney Vacation Club Timeshare Tower." *East Bay Times*, November 22, 2019.

———. "Lands of Tomorrow: Changes Will Give City Tourist Area New Look." *Orange County Register*, July 25, 1996, 3.

Maciag, Mike. "Population for U.S. Cities Statistics." *Governing*, November 29, 2017. Available at https://www.governing.com/gov-data/population-density-land-area-cities -map.html.

Maddaus, Gene. "Disney Reaches Settlement in Florida Lawsuit over Theme Park District." *Variety*, March 27, 2024. Available at https://variety.com/2024/biz/news/disney -settlement-florida-dont-say-gay-reedy-creek-1235953399/.

Malas, Nour. "In Disneyland's Hometown, Once Warm Relations Have Frozen." *Wall Street Journal*, September 24, 2018. Available at https://www.wsj.com/articles/in-dis neylands-hometown-once-warm-relations-have-frozen-1537801201.

Malizia, Emil. "Economic Development in Smaller Cities and Rural Areas." *Journal of the American Planning Association* 52, no. 4 (1986): 489–499.

Marling, Karal Ann. "Imagineering the Disney Theme Parks." In *Designing Disney's Theme Parks: The Architecture of Reassurance*, edited by Karal Ann Marling. Flammarion, 1997: 29–177.

Marroquin, Art. "Anaheim Council OKs $158 Million Hotel Subsidy." *Orange County Register*, May 14, 2013. Available at https://www.ocregister.com/2013/05/14/anaheim -council-oks-158-million-hotel-subsidy/.

———. "Anaheim Council Sets Voting Map for November." *Orange County Register*, February 11, 2016.

———. "Anaheim Election Trial Set for 2014." *Orange County Register*, July 31, 2013.

———. "Anaheim Public Hearing Considers Impact on Jobs and City Revenue." *Orange County Register*, July 8, 2015.

———. "Anaheim Will Offer Tax Breaks to Attract Luxury Hotels." *Orange County Register*, June 17, 2015. Available at https://www.ocregister.com/2015/06/17/anaheim-will -offer-tax-breaks-to-attract-luxury-hotels/.

———. "Hotel Subsidy Measure Won't be on Anaheim Ballot." *Orange County Register*, March 30, 2016. Available at https://www.ocregister.com/2016/03/24/hotel-subsidy -measure-wont-be-on-the-ballot/.

———. "Voting Districts Coming to Anaheim." *Orange County Register*, November 5, 2014. Available at https://www.ocregister.com/2014/11/05/voting-districts-coming-to -anaheim/.

Marroquin, Art, and Joseph Pimentel. "The Company Wants to Invest at Disneyland, California in Exchange for No New Gate Tax." *Orange County Register*, June 26, 2015, A.

———. "Disney Wants to Invest $1 Billion at Disneyland, California Adventure in Exchange for No New Gate Tax." *Orange County Register*, June 26, 2015. Available at https://www .ocregister.com/2015/06/26/disney-wants-to-invest-1-billion-at-disneyland-california -adventure-in-exchange-for-no-new-gate-tax/.

Martin, Deborah. "Urban Politics as Sociospatial Struggles." *International Journal of Urban and Regional Research* 35, no. 4 (2011): 856–858.

Martin, Hugo. "Anaheim Council Races Tilt to Disney." *Los Angeles Times*, November 7, 2018, A14.

———. "Anaheim Officially Puts an End to Tax Breaks for Disneyland Resort." *Los Angeles Times*, August 28, 2018. Available at https://www.latimes.com/business/la-fi-ana heim-disney-tax-break-20180828-story.html.

———. "Anaheim's 'Living Wage' Is Likely to Pass." *Los Angeles Times*, November 13, 2018. Available at https://www.latimes.com/business/la-fi-living-wage-measure-2018 1112-story.html.

———. "Disney Cancels Its Plans for Hotel." *Los Angeles Times*, October 11, 2018, C1.

———. "Disneyland Workers Demonstrate at Walt Disney Co. Meeting, Demanding Living Wages." *Los Angeles Times*, March 8, 2018. Available at https://www.latimes.com/business/la-fi-disney-shareholders-demonstration-20180308-story.html.

———. "Disney Promised a Luxury Hotel and Anaheim Offered $267 Million in Tax Breaks—But a Growing Feud Has Plans on Hold." *Los Angeles Times*, August 16, 2018. Available at https://www.latimes.com/business/la-fi-disneyland-hotel-subsidy-20180815-story.html.

———. "Disney, Unions Open Wallets for Election." *Los Angeles Times*, October 18, 2018, C1.

———. "Disney Wants to End Tax Incentive Deals with Anaheim in an Attempt to Improve Relationship with City." *Los Angeles Times*, August 22, 2018. Available at https://www.latimes.com/business/la-fi-disney-tax-agreements-20180822-story.html.

———. "Disney Workers Sue for Living Wages." *Los Angeles Times*, December 10, 2019, Business C1. Available at https://enewspaper.latimes.com/infinity/article_share.aspx?guid=65b1ab37-4f2a-429f-9e1f-9b2886ddccc6.

———. "Is the Disneyland Resort Getting a City Subsidy?" *Los Angeles Times*, December 9, 2019. Available at https://www.latimes.com/business/story/2019-12-09/is-the-disneyland-resort-getting-a-city-subsidy-union-lawsuit-pushes-court-to-decide.

———. "New Plan at Disneyland Calls for Squeezing in More Rides, Restaurants and Shops." *Los Angeles Times*, March 25, 2021. Available at https://www.latimes.com/business/story/2021-03-25/disneyland-forward-proposal-shops-attractions-parking-resorts.

———. "Three-Quarters of Employees Surveyed at Disney's Anaheim Resort Say They Can't Afford Basic Living Expenses." *Los Angeles Times*, February 28, 2018. Available at https://www.latimes.com/business/la-fi-disneyland-study-20180228-story.html.

———. "2018 Midterm Election: Anaheim Council Races Go Disney's Way." *Los Angeles Times*, November 8, 2018, B2.

———. "Unions at the Disneyland Resort Propose Ballot Measure to Raise Wages for Workers." *Los Angeles Times*, March 2, 2018. Available at https://www.latimes.com/business/la-fi-disneyland-wage-ordinance-20180302-story.html.

McGovern, Stephen J. "Analyzing Urban Politics: A Mobilization-Governance Framework." *Urban Affairs Review* 56, no. 4 (2020): 1011–1052.

McGuinness, Devan. "68 Years Ago, Disneyland Opened—And It Was a Laughably Horrible Mess." Fatherly.com, February 20, 2024. Available at https://www.fatherly.com/news/disneyland-opening-1955-bad.

McKibben, Dave. "Anaheim Housing May Be Approved." *Los Angeles Times*, January 24, 2007, B3.

———. "Anaheim Is Set for a Wild Ride over Housing." *Los Angeles Times*, April 23, 2007, B4.

———. "Anaheim Police Didn't Spy on Activists, Inquiry Finds." *Los Angeles Times*, July 1, 2005. Available at https://www.latimes.com/archives/la-xpm-2005-jul-01-me-anaheim1-story.html.

———. "Anaheim's Resort-Area Housing Debate May Cool." *Los Angeles Times*, November 10, 2007, B6.

———. "Anaheim Will Reconsider Resort District Housing." *Los Angeles Times*, March 21, 2007, B6.

———. "Defund Chamber of Commerce, Anaheim Official Says." *Los Angeles Times*, May 7, 2007, 4.

———. "Disney Involved in GardenWalk Hotels." *Los Angeles Times*, August 30, 2007, B7.

———. "Disneyland Not Smiling about Housing Plan." *Los Angeles Times*, February 13, 2007, B1.

———. "Disney Sues Anaheim over Plan." *Los Angeles Times*, February 27, 2007.

———. "Disney Wants Vote on Homes Issue." *Los Angeles Times*, March 20, 2007, B1.

———. "Disney Wins in Anaheim.' *Los Angeles Times*, March 6, 2008, B4.

———. "Housing Deal in Anaheim May Be Dead." *Los Angeles Times*, October 31, 2007, B3.

———. "How Vote on Housing Went Disney's Way." *Los Angeles Times*, February 15, 2007, B1. Available at https://www.latimes.com/archives/la-xpm-2007-feb-15-me-disney15-story.html.

———. "Land Sale Restarts Anaheim Project." *Los Angeles Times*, March 15, 2005, B5.

———. "Land Use Decision Likely to Stay on Anaheim Ballot." *Los Angeles Times*, February 21, 2008.

———. "Low-Cost Housing Plan in Resort Area Gets Anaheim's Initial OK." *Los Angeles Times*, August 24, 2006, 4.

———. "Resort District Group's Main Backer Is Disney." *Los Angeles Times*, March 3, 2008, B1.

———. "Scope of Housing Dispute Broadens." *Los Angeles Times*, July 9, 2007, B1.

Michener, Jamila. "Power from the Margins: Grassroots Mobilization and Urban Expansions of Civil Legal Rights." *Urban Affairs Review* 56, no. 5 (2020): 1390–1422.

Mickadeit, Frank. "Police Need Better Ties with Hispanics, Leaders Say." *Orange County Register*, June 6, 1988.

Miller, Daniel. "How One Election Changed Disneyland's Relationship with Its Hometown." *Los Angeles Times*, September 26, 2017. Available at https://www.latimes.com/projects/la-fi-disney-anaheim-city-council/.

———. "A *Times* Special Report: Is Disney Paying Its Share in Anaheim?" *Los Angeles Times*, September 24, 2017, A1. Available at https://www.latimes.com/projects/la-fi-disney-anaheim-deals/.

Miller, Jeffrey. "WestCOT Backers Shun Small Protest." *Orange County Register*, April 23, 1993, B8.

Miller, Martin. "Disneyland-Area Rehab OK'd." *Los Angeles Times*, August 30, 1994, B1.

Minow, Martha. "The Changing Ecosystem of News and Challenges for Freedom of the Press." *Loyola Law Review*, 64 (2018): 500–502.

Moreno, Jose F. Candidate Statement of Qualifications. City of Anaheim City Council. District 3.

Mossberger, Karen, and Gerry Stoker. "The Evolution of Urban Regime Theory: The Challenge of Conceptualization." *Urban Affairs Review* 36, no. 6 (2001): 810–835.

Murray, Kris. "Focused on Taxpayers and Neighborhoods." *Orange County Register*, August 13, 2017. Available at https://www.ocregister.com/2017/08/13/anaheim-is-focused-on-taxpayers-and-neighborhoods/.

National Park Service. "Early History of the California Coast." Available at https://www.nps.gov/nr/travel/ca/intro.htm#:~:text=Spanish%20colonization%20of%20%22Alta%20California,Coast%2C%20was%20established%20in%201769.

Nelson, Vern. "Opinion: Why Anaheim District 3 Should Recall Natalie Rubalcava." *Orange County Register*, June 6, 2024.

"New Hotel Plans Okay in Anaheim." *North Orange County Independent*, July 16, 1964.

Nicholls, Walter J. "Power and Governance: Metropolitan Governance in France." *Urban Studies* 42, no. 4 (2005): 783–800.

Nicholson-Crotty, Sean, and Kenneth J. Meier, "Size Doesn't Matter: In Defense of Single-State Studies." *State Politics and Policy Quarterly* 2, no. 4 (2002): 411–422.

"A Note to Readers." *Los Angeles Times*, November 3, 2017. Available at http://www.la times.com/entertainment/la-et-holiday-movie-preview-2017-times-note-on-disney -1509668978-htmlstory.html.

"No Tomorrowland for Deal." *Orange County Register*, November 29, 2007, Edit H.

Offices of City Attorney and City Clerk for the City of Anaheim. "An Ordinance of the City of Anaheim Adding New Sections and Amending Various Sections of Chapter 1.09 of Title 1 of the Anaheim Municipal Code Relating to Campaign Reform." June 21, 2022. Available at https://local.anaheim.net/docs_agend/questys_pub/34113/34143 /34145/34286/34340/Staff%20Report34340.pdf.

"Officials Reveal Disneyland Details: First Work to Begin Next Week." *Anaheim Bulletin*, June 11, 1954, 1.

Oh My Disney. "Walt Disney's College of Knowledge: Walt and Disneyland." Accessed January 9, 2020. Available at https://ohmy.disney.com/insider/2012/07/17/the-won derful-world-of-walt-walt-and-disneyland/.

Orange County Communities Organized for Responsible Development (OCCORD). "About Us." Accessed May 10, 2018. Available at https://www.occord.org/about.

———. "More Jobs, Less Opportunity: Economic Growth in Orange County." 2015. Avail- able at https://d3n8a8pro7vhmx.cloudfront.net/zacmaybury/pages/4240/attachments /original/1485909009/More_Jobs_Less_Opportunity.pdf?1485909009.

"Orange County Perspective: Anaheim Resort Plan: Questions Linger." *Los Angeles Times*, September 12, 1994. Available at https://www.latimes.com/archives/la-xpm-1994-09-12 -me-37676-story.html.

*Orange County Register* Editorial Board, "Does Disney Pay Its Fair Share? Yes," Orange County Register, October 14, 2017, https://www.ocregister.com/2017/10/14/does-disney -pay-its-fair-share-yes/.

*Orange County Register* Staff Report. "Anaheim City Council District 3 Candidates Share Their Priorities and Thoughts on Local Issues." *Orange County Register*, October 24, 2018. Available at https://www.ocregister.com/2018/10/24/election-2018-anaheim-city -council-district-3-candidates-share-their-priorities-and-thoughts-on-local-issues/.

Orange County Registrar of Voters. 2024. "Full Text of Measure L—City of Anaheim." Accessed September 7, 2024. Available at https://www.ocvote.com/fileadmin/user_up load/elections/gen2014/measures/8507.pdf.

Ortiz, Diane. "Orange County Workers United in Anaheim to Advocate for Living Wages and Celebrate International Workers Day." *Daily Titan*, May 1, 2018, 1. Available at https://dailytitan.com/news/local/orange-county-workers-unite-in-anaheim-to-advo cate-for-living-wages-and-celebrate-international-workers/article_8c7d0932-c83c -5ecd-8000-4b3444b28e1d.html.

Pack, Susan. "Anaheim Admission Tax Hit by Disneyland, Angels Officials." *Orange Coun- ty Register*, July 23, 1975.

Park, Haeyoun. "Resort District Fee Angers Businesses." *Orange County Register*, Novem- ber 4, 1999, 3.

Park, Jeong, and Alicia Robinson. "Anaheim Councilman Arrested in Civil Disobedience with Protesting Hotel Workers." *Orange County Register*, January 24, 2019. Available at https://www.ocregister.com/2019/01/24/anaheim-councilman-arrested-in-civil-diso bedience-with-protesting-hotel-workers/.

Penaloza, David Carrillo. "Did Anaheim Gift Stadium, Land to Angels Owner Arte More- no?" *Daily Pilot*, October 2, 2020. Available at https://www.latimes.com/socal/daily -pilot/news/newsletter/2020-10-02/timesoc-did-anaheim-gift-stadium-land-to-angels -owner-arte-moreno-timesoc.

Perlman, Jeffrey A. "U.S. May Be Asked to Pay for Parking Garage." *Los Angeles Times*, April 23, 1993, B1.

Perry, Ravi K. "Black Mayors in Non-Majority Black (Medium Sized) Cities: Universalizing the Interests of Blacks." *Ethnic Studies Review* 32, no. 1 (2009): 89–130.

Pho, Brandon. "Anaheim Mayoral Candidates Clash over Disney Campaign Spending and Minimum Wage Initiative.' *Voice of OC*, October 22, 2018. Available at https://voiceofoc.org/2018/10/anaheim-mayoral-candidates-clash-over-disney-campaign-spending-and-minimum-wage-initiative/.

———. "No Campaign Finance Reform for Anaheim." *Voice of OC*, July 14, 2022. Available at https://voiceofoc.org/2022/07/no-campaign-finance-reform-for-anaheim/.

Pierce, Todd James. "Disneyland and the 1953 Halloween Festival." Disney History Institute, October 29, 2012. Available at http://www.disneyhistoryinstitute.com/2012/10/disneyland-and-1953-halloween-festival.html.

———. *Three Years in Wonderland. The Disney Brothers, CV Wood, and the Making of the Great American Theme Park*. University Press of Mississippi, 2016.

Pimentel, Joseph. "Anaheim Considers Tax Breaks for 3 Luxury Hotels." *Orange County Register*, July 8, 2016. Available at https://www.ocregister.com/2016/07/08/anaheim-considers-tax-incentives-for-three-luxury-hotels-near-disneyland/.

———. "Anaheim OKs Tax Incentives for 3 Hotel Projects." *Orange County Register*, July 14, 2016, B.

———. "Anaheim's 'Sinkin' Lincoln' Site to Be Redeveloped into 30-Acre Mixed-Used Megaproject." Bisnow, August 5, 2019. Available at https://www.bisnow.com/orange-county/news/mixed-use/anaheim-sinkin-lincoln-site-to-be-redeveloped-into-mega-mixed-use-project-100197.

———. "'Big Splash' on Beach Boulevard." *Orange County Register*, February 16, 2017.

———. "Council Takes Aim at Lobbyists." *Chico Enterprise-Record*, August 3, 2017, AA1.

———. "Disney Changes Directions in Expansion Plans around Resort Cancels Eastern Expansion, Focuses on New Hotel and Parking on West Side." *Chico Enterprise-Record*, October 26, 2017, AA1.

———. "Disney Neighbors Have a Bad Feeling about Park's New Project." *Orange County Register*, December 10, 2016. Available at https://www.ocregister.com/2016/12/12/disneyland-neighbors-have-a-bad-feeling-about-parks-new-parking-bridge-project/.

———. "Disney to Present." *Orange County Register*, December 8, 2016.

———. "Does New Anaheim Council Majority Mean Less Attention for Disney, Angels, Resort District?" *Orange County Register*, December 1, 2016. Available at https://www.ocregister.com/2016/12/01/does-new-anaheim-council-majority-mean-less-attention-for-disney-angels-resort-district/.

———. "From the Matterhorn Ride to How It Was Built, Disneyland Was All about Innovations." *Orange County Register*, July 15, 2015. Available at https://www.ocregister.com/2015/07/15/from-the-matterhorn-ride-to-how-it-was-built-disneyland-was-all-about-innovations/.

———. "Mayor Says Time for City to Move in New Direction." *Orange County Register*, July 27, 2011, A1.

———. "New Anaheim Council Derails Streetcar Project, Chamber Funding." *Orange County Register*, December 22, 2016.

———. "People's Council 'Eager.'" *Orange County Register*, December 17, 2016.

Pinkley, Virgil. "Council Should OK Hotel Despite Disneyland Row." *Anaheim Gazette*, January 9, 1964.

"Planners Indicate Support for D-Land Height Limit Protection." *Anaheim Bulletin*, July 9, 1964.

Ponsi, Lou, Michael Mello, and Theresa Walker. "50 Protesters Gather Outside Disneyland." *Orange County Register*, July 29, 2012. Available at https://www.ocregister.com /2012/07/29/50-protesters-gather-outside-disneyland/.

Powers, William F., and David S. Hilzenrath. "Disney's Hardball Reputation; Officials Say to Expect a Tough Negotiator." *Washington Post*, November 21, 1993, A01.

"A Prudent Reality Check in Fantasy Land." *Los Angeles Times*, November 13, 1994, B14.

Public Broadcasting System. "Walt Disney: American Experience." August 29, 2017. Available at https://www.pbs.org/wgbh/americanexperience/films/walt-disney/.

Puri, Anil, Aaron Popp, and Adrian Fleissig. *Economic Impact of the Disneyland Resort*. Woods Center for Economic Analysis and Forecasting, California State University Fullerton, September 9, 2019.

Rast, Joel. "Governing the Regimeless City: The Frank Zeidler Administration in Milwaukee, 1948–1960." *Urban Affairs Review* 42, no. 1 (2006): 81–112.

———. "Urban Regime Theory and the Problem of Change." *Urban Affairs Review* 51, no. 1 (2015): 138–149.

"Readers Get Voice." *Santa Ana Register*, August 30, 1964.

Reference for Business. "Paul S. Pressler." Accessed March 26, 2021. Available at https:// www.referenceforbusiness.com/biography/M-R/Pressler-Paul-S-1956.html#ixzz6 qFXnZ4vu.

Reovan, Andrew. "Theme Park in the City: Disneyland and the Aesthetic of the 'Anaheim Resort.'" Honors Thesis for the Program in Urban Studies, Stanford University, May 19, 2009. Available at https://urbanstudies.stanford.edu/sites/g/files/sbiybj12071/f/reo vanthesis.pdf.

"Revised Plans Approved for Sheraton-Anaheim: 16-Story, $15 Million Hotel Will Have 780 Rooms and Penthouse Restaurant." *Los Angeles Times*, July 10, 1964.

Reza, H. G. "OCTA Approves Funds for Disney Garage." *Los Angeles Times*, April 12, 1994, B4. Available at https://www.latimes.com/archives/la-xpm-1994–07–16-mn-16255 -story.html.

———. "U.S. Balks at Costs of Garage Near Disneyland." *Los Angeles Times*, July 16, 1994. Available at https://www.latimes.com/archives/la-xpm-1994-07-16-mn-16255-story .html.

Rios, Delia. "A Golden Legacy at the House of Mouse." *Seattle Times*, July 17, 2005.

Robinson, Alicia. "Anaheim Council Nixes Proposed Ticket Tax on Disneyland, Other Large Venues." *Orange County Register*, July 20, 2022.

———. "Anaheim Picks Operator for Interim Homeless Shelter near Angel Stadium." *Orange County Register*, December 9, 2018. Available at https://www.ocregister.com /2018/12/07/anaheim-picks-operator-for-interim-homeless-shelter-near-angel-stadi um/.

———. "Anaheim Signs Deal to Keep Ducks." *Orange County Record*, November 21, 2018. Available at https://www.ocregister.com/2018/11/21/anaheim-signs-deal-to-keep-ducks -develop-land-around-honda-center/.

———. "Angel Stadium; Anaheim Mayor Weighs In on Priorities for Angels Lease Talks." *Orange County Register*, August 27, 2019. Available at https://www.ocregister.com/2019 /08/27/angel-stadium-anaheim-mayor-weighs-in-on-priorities-for-angels-lease-talks/.

———. "Beach Boulevard Makeover Takes Next Step with Anaheim's $14 Million Purchase of the Old Americana Motel and Neighboring Businesses." *Orange County Register*, January 4, 2018. Available at https://www.ocregister.com/2018/01/04/beach-boulevard

-makeover-takes-next-step-with-anaheims-14-million-purchase-of-the-old-americana
-motel-and-neighboring-businesses/.

———. "Business Groups Launch Opposition to Ballot Measure That Would Raise Minimum Wage for Disneyland Resort, Several Other Hotels." *Orange County Register*, March 23, 2018. Available at https://www.ocregister.com/2018/03/23/business-groups
-launch-opposition-to-ballot-measure-that-would-raise-minimum-wage-for-disneyland
-resort-several-other-hotels/.

———. "City to Buy 3.6 Acres of Land along Beach Blvd." *Chico Enterprise-Record*, January 11, 2018, AA1.

———. "Did the Millions Spent Win Races?" *Orange County Register*, December 2, 2018, AA3.

———. "Voters Make Change for the Anaheim City Council." *Orange County Register*, November 20, 2022. Available at https://www.ocregister.com/2022/11/20/voters-make
-change-for-the-anaheim-city-council/.

Rojas, Rick, and Nicole Santa Cruz. "Anaheim City Council Rejects Voting Districts Proposal." *Los Angeles Times*, August 9, 2012. Available at https://www.latimes.com/local
/la-xpm-2012-aug-09-la-me-0809-anaheim-20120809-story.html.

Roosevelt, Margot. "Disney, Unions Agree on Contract: Resort President Says Company Is Taking a Leadership Position on Wages in Orange County." *Chico Enterprise-Record*, July 28, 2018, A3.

———. "Disney Unions Launch Living Wage Ballot Drive." *Chico Enterprise-Record*, March 1, 2018, A3.

Rosentraub, Mark. *Major League Losers*. Basic Books, 1997.

Rowe, Jeff. "Disneyland Expansion Losing Its Momentum." *Orange County Register*, November 7, 1992, A1.

———. "Disney Outlines $3 Billion Project: Epcot-like Park Centerpiece for Anaheim Plans." *Orange County Register*, May 9, 1991, A1.

———. "New Disney Project Fares Better in Revised Report." *Orange County Register*, August 11, 1996, B2.

Rowe, Jeff, and Gina Shaffer. "WestCOT: Global Village: Tourism: In the First Detailed Update of the Proposed WestCOT Center, Disney Reveals Plans for Hotels within the Park." *Orange County Register*, April 23, 1993, B1.

Rubado Meghan E., and Jay T. Jennings. "Political Consequences of the Endangered Local Watchdog." *Urban Affairs Review* 56, no. 5 (2020): 1327–1356.

Saito, Leland T. "How Low-Income Residents Can Benefit from Urban Development: The LA Live Community Benefits Agreement." *City & Community* 11, no. 2 (2012): 129–150.

Saito, Leland T., and Jonathan Truong. "The LA Live Community Benefits Agreement." *Urban Affairs Review* 51, no. 2 (2015): 263–289.

Sanchez, Felix. "Anaheim: One City, Two Faces." *Orange County Register*, May 8, 2000, A1.

———. "Orange County in Change." *Orange County Register*, January 10, 2000, A1.

Sanders, Heywood T. *Convention Center Follies: Politics, Power, and Public Investment in American Cities*. University of Pennsylvania Press, 2014.

———. "The Politics of Development in Middle-Sized Cities: Getting from New Haven to Kalamazoo." In *The Politics of Urban Development*, edited by Clarence N. Stone and Heywood T. Sanders. University Press of Kansas, 1987.

Sandford, Mark. "Conceptualising 'Generative Power': Evidence from the City-Regions of England." *Urban Studies* 57, no. 10 (2020): 2098–2114.

San Roman, Gabriel. "Disney Loses Fight over Anaheim Wage Law; State High Court Rejects Appeal. Resort Workers Are Owed Raises and Back Pay." *Los Angeles Times*, October 27, 2023, B3.

———. "How the Disneyland Strike of 1984 Changed the Magic Kingdom Forever." *OC Weekly*, March 23, 2018. Available at https://www.ocweekly.com/how-the-disneyland-strike-of-1984-changed-the-magic-kingdom-forever/.

Savitch, Hank, and Paul Kantor. *Cities in the International Market Place: The Political Economy of Urban Development in North America and Western Europe*. Princeton University Press, 2002.

Schattschneider, E. E. *The Semi-Sovereign People*. Holt and Reinhart, 1960.

"Schools May Not Bill for Noncitizen Students." United Press International, August 20, 1999.

Schou, Nick. "Ethnic Cleansing." *OC Weekly*, July 8, 1999.

Schrader, Esther. "Fragile Balance Shaken in Anaheim Barrio." *Los Angeles Times*, April 14, 1997. Available at https://www.latimes.com/archives/la-xpm-1997-04-14-mn-48691-story.html.

Schragger, Richard C. *City Power: Urban Governance in a Global Age*. Oxford University Press, 2016.

Seamster, Louise. "The White City: Race and Urban Politics." *Sociology Compass* 9, no. 12 (2015): 1049–1065.

Serrano, Barbara. "Anaheim Delays Action on Admission Tax." *Orange County Register*, December 2, 1987, B1.

———. "Anaheim Hispanics Growing in Number, Not Political Power." *Orange County Register*, July 31, 1988.

Shaffer, Gina. "Anaheim Staff Gives WestCOT Conditional Approval." *Orange County Register*, May 19, 1993, B4.

———. "WestCOT an 'Enormous' Decision for Anaheim's Planners." *Orange County Register*, April 26, 1993, B5.

———. "White Spire Replaces Gold Sphere in Latest WestCOT Center Design." *Orange County Register*, April 23, 1993, B6.

Shaikin, Bill. "Anaheim Reduces Price of Angel Stadium: City Agrees to Take $175 Million Less to Get Moreno to Add Housing and a Park." *Los Angeles Times*, September 5, 2020, D1.

"She Led Anaheim in Facing Injustice: Josie Montoya Spent Her Time and Energy Fighting to Make Life Better for Hispanics." *Orange County Register*, March 19, 2002.

Shultz, Jason. "Halloween: The Holiday That Brought Disneyland to Anaheim." *Disneyland Nomenclature* (blog), October 31, 2009. Accessed September 14, 2024. Available at http://disneylandcompendium.blogspot.com/2009/10/halloween-holiday-that-brought.html.

Sidhu, Harry. "2019 State of the City Address." City National Grove of Anaheim, March 5, 2019. Available at https://www.anaheim.net/DocumentCenter/View/25213/2019-Anaheim-State-of-the-City.

Silber, Judy. "Jeffrey-Lynne Revitalization Heads to Council." *Los Angeles Times*, November 16, 1999.

Silicon Valley Historical Association. Available at https://www.siliconvalleyhistorical.org/sri-international-history.

Sito, Tom. "The Disney Strike of 1941." Animation World, July 19, 2005. Accessed September 14, 2024. Available at https://www.awn.com/animationworld/disney-strike-1941-how-it-changed-animation-comics#:~:text=Tom%20Sito%20revisits%20the%20Civil,course%20of%20animation%20and%20comics.&text=As%20Walt%20Disney%20turned%20his%20fashionable%20Packard%20roadster%20onto%20Buena%20Vista%20Blvd.

Sklar, Marty. *Dream It! Do It! My Half-Century Creating Disney's Magic Kingdoms.* Disney Electronic Content, 2013.

Slaten, Michael. "Anaheim Mayor Says City Has Turned to New Era at State of the City Address." *Orange County Register*, June 6, 2024. Available at https://www.ocregister.com/2024/06/06/anaheim-mayor-says-city-has-turned-to-new-era-at-state-of-the-city-address/.

———. "How Far Has Anaheim Taken Its Reforms?" *Orange County Register*, February 21, 2024. Available at https://www.ocregister.com/2024/02/21/how-far-has-anaheim-taken-its-reforms/.

Slater, Shawn. "Traveling the Berm." Available at https://disneyshawn.blogspot.com/2010/07/traveling-berm.html.

Smith, Ruth C., and Eric M. Eisenberg. "Conflict at Disneyland: A Root-Metaphor Analysis." *Communications Monographs* 54, no. 4 (1987): 367–380.

Snow, Richard. *Disney's Land: Walt Disney and the Invention of the Amusement Park That Changed the World.* Scribner, 2019.

Sorkin, Michael. *Variations on a Theme Park: The New American City and the End of Public Space.* Macmillan, 1992.

SparkOC.com. "Memories of the Past and Images of the Present." SparkOC.com. Accessed August 1, 2020. Available at https://www.sparkoc.com/public-art/memories-of-the-past-and-images-of-the-present/.

Spence, Jack. "Disney Policies—Then and Now." AllEars, April 21, 2014. Available at https://allears.net/2014/04/21/disney-policies-then-and-now/.

Spencer, Terry. "Orange County Focus: Anaheim: Disney Expansion Hearing Wednesday." *Los Angeles Times*, June 8, 1993, B3.

———. "Orange County Focus: Anaheim: Police Union to Urge Tax on Ticket Sales." *Los Angeles Times*, October 14, 1993, B3.

Sperb, Jason. "'Take a Frown, Turn It Upside Down': Splash Mountain, Walt Disney World, and the Cultural De-rac[e]-ination of Disney's Song of the South (1946)." *Journal of Popular Culture* 38, no. 5 (2005): 924–938.

Staggs, Brooke, and Alicia Robinson. "Anaheim Mayor Harry Sidhu Resigns amid Federal Investigation." *Orange County Register*, May 23, 2022. Available at https://www.ocregister.com/2022/05/23/anaheim-mayor-harry-sidhu-resigns-amid-federal-investigation/.

Stilwell, Andrew. "Disneyland Announces DisneylandForward." Coaster 101, March 25, 2021. Available at https://www.coaster101.com/2021/03/25/disneyland-announces-disneylandforward/.

Stone, Clarence N. "Poverty and the Continuing Campaign for Urban Social Reform." *Urban Affairs Review* 34, no. 6 (1999): 843–856.

———. "Preemptive Power: Floyd Hunter's 'Community Power Structure' Reconsidered." *American Journal of Political Science* 32, no. 1 (1988): 82–104.

———. "Reflections on Regime Politics: From Governing Coalition to Urban Political Order." *Urban Affairs Review* 51, no. 1 (2015): 101–137.

———. *Regime Politics: Governing Atlanta, 1946–1988.* University Press of Kansas, 1989.

———. "Urban Regimes and the Capacity to Govern: A Political Economy Approach." *Journal of Urban Affairs* 15, no. 1 (1993): 1–28.

Stone, Clarence N., and Heywood T. Sanders, eds. *The Politics of Urban Development.* University Press of Kansas, 1987.

Stone, Clarence N., Robert P. Stoker, John Betancur, Susan E. Clarke, Marilyn Dantico, Martin Horak, Karen Mossberger, Juliet Musso, Jefferey M. Sellers, Ellen Shiau, Harold Wolman, and Donn Worgs. *Urban Neighborhoods in a New Era*. University of Chicago Press, 2015.

Support Our Anaheim Resort Area (S.O.A.R.). "Overview." Available at http://soaranaheim .com.

Swindell, David, and Mark Rosentraub. "Who Benefits from the Presence of Professional Sports Teams? The Implications of Public Funding of Stadiums and Arenas." *Public Administration Review* 58, no. 1 (1998): 11–20.

Tait, Tom. "Anaheim: Change for the Good of All in Anaheim." *Orange County Register*, August 6, 2017. Available at https://www.ocregister.com/2017/08/06/change-for-the -good-of-all-in-anaheim/.

Teague, Jerry. "Planners Eye Height Limit." *Anaheim Bulletin*, July 6, 1964.

"There's No Such Thing as a Free Pass: Anaheim Officials Should Limit Gifts from Disney until Expansion Plans Are Final." *Los Angeles Times*, June 30, 1991, B8.

"Thousands Jam Disneyland at Preview Opening." *Anaheim Bulletin*, July 18, 1955, 1.

"Thousands Sign Petition to Clear Recreation Site." *Chico Enterprise-Record*, September 1, 2017, BB1.

"Tickets to Ineffectiveness: Three Anaheim City Councilmen Accept Too Many Free Disneyland Passes." *Los Angeles Times*, April 3, 1992.

Tillman, Jodie, and Joseph Pimentel. "Here's Why Disney Is Working Hard to Stop an Anaheim Gate Tax, and Why the City Needs It." *Orange County Register*, June 30, 2015. Available at https://www.ocregister.com/2015/06/30/heres-why-disney-is-working-to -stop-an-anaheim-gate-tax-and-why-the-city-needs-it/.

Titizian, Joseph. "Anniversary Day." The Walt Disney Family Museum, October 1, 2011. Accessed May 26, 2019. Available at https://www.waltdisney.org/blog/anniversary-day.

Townsend, Adam, and Rosalba Ruiz. "2008: Top Stories of the Year." *Orange County Register*, December 28, 2008.

Tso, Phoenix. "Disney Wins Extension of Tax Break in Anaheim, California." Reuters, July 8, 2015. Available at https://www.reuters.com/article/lifestyle/disney-wins-exten sion-of-tax-break-in-anaheim-california-idUSKCN0PI0RO/#:~:text=(Reuters)%20 %2D%20The%20Walt%20Disney,famed%20theme%20park%20complex%20there.

Tully, Sarah. "Anaheim Debates Land Use." *Orange County Register*, February 14, 2007, Cover B.

———. "Anaheim to Consider Referendum on Housing." *Orange County Register*, July 17, 2007. Available at https://www.ocregister.com/2007/07/17/anaheim-to-consider-ref erendum-on-housing/.

———. "Debate Grows over Subsidizing Housing for Disney Employees." *Orange County Register*, April 22, 2007. Available at https://www.ocregister.com/2007/04/22/april-22 -debate-grows-over-subsidizing-housing-for-disney-employees/.

———. "Disney Sues Anaheim over Development." *Orange County Register*, February 26, 2007. Available at https://www.ocregister.com/2007/02/26/feb-26-disney-sues-anaheim -over-development/.

———. "No Clear Direction on Resort Housing Vote." *Orange County Register*, April 24, 2007.

———. "Police Enter Resort Fray." *Orange County Register*, May 16, 2007, Cover B.

———. "Resort Revenue Figures Don't Match." *Orange County Register*, June 7, 2007, Cover B.

Tully, Sarah, and Erik Ortiz. "Mad about the Mouse." *Orange County Register*, April 26, 2007.

U.S. Bureau of the Census. *County and City Data Book 1983*. U.S. Department of Commerce, 1983.

———. *County and City Data Book 1994*. U.S. Department of Commerce, 1994.

———. *Hispanic or Latino Origin, 2013–2017 American Community Survey 5-Year Estimates*. U.S. Department of Commerce, 2017. Available at https://factfinder.census.gov /faces/tableservices/jsf/pages/productview.xhtml?pid=ACS_1 7_5YR_B03003.

———. *Median Household Income in the Past 12 Months (in 2017 Inflation-Adjusted Dollars), 2013–2017 American Community Survey 5-Year Estimates*. U.S. Department of Commerce, 2017. Available at https://factfinder.census.gov/faces/tableservices/jsf/pages /productview.xhtml?pid=ACS_17_5YR_B19013.

———. *Race and Hispanic Origin for Selected Cities and Other Places: Earliest Census to 1990*. U.S. Department of Commerce, 2005. Available at https://datausa.io/profile/geo /anaheim-ca#:~:text=Race%20and%20Ethnicity&text=55.7%25%20of%20the%20 people%20in,share%20of%20the%20total%20population.

U.S. District Court for the Central District of California. Affidavit by FBI Special Agent Brad Adkins in *United States of America v. Todd Ament*. May 16, 2022. Available at https://voiceofoc.org/wp-content/uploads/2022/05/Anaheim-Ament-loan-fraud -COMPLAINT.pdf.

Velasco, Schuyler. "For Latinos, Anaheim Gang Sweep Rubs Riots' Wounds." *Christian Science Monitor*, August 14, 2012. Available at https://www.csmonitor.com/USA/2012 /0814/For-Latinos-Anaheim-gang-sweep-rubs-riots-wounds.-Should-police-have -waited.

Vincent-Phoenix, Adrienne. "Disneyland Takes First Steps in Proposed Multi-Year Expansion Plan." MousePlanet, March 25, 2021. Available at https://www.mouseplanet .com/12897/Disneyland_takes_first_steps_in_proposed_multiyear_expansion_plan.

Vintage Disneyland Tickets. "A Disney Preview: Mickey Mouse's Fabulous New Playground." *Fortnight*. November 17, 1954, 18–19. Available at https://vintagedisneyland tickets.blogspot.com/2008/06/fortnight-august-1955-chaos-in.html.

Vives, Ruben, Nicole Santa Cruz, and Richard Winton. "Police, Protesters Clash as Tensions Roil Anaheim." *Los Angeles Times*, July 24, 2012. Available at https://www.latimes .com/nation/la-xpm-2012-jul-25-la-me-0725-anaheim-shooting-20120725-story.html.

Vo, Thy. "Anaheim City Manager Paul Emery Resigns." *Orange County Register*, July 11, 2017.

———. "Anaheim Council Approves Another Hotel Subsidy Deal." *Voice of OC*, June 17, 2015. Available at https://voiceofoc.org/2015/06/anaheim-council-approves-another -big-hotel-subsidy-deal/.

———. "Anaheim Council Discusses Disneyland Worker Wages." *Voice of OC*, April 12, 2018. Available at https://voiceofoc.org/2018/04/anaheim-council-discusses-disneyland -workers-wages/.

———. "Anaheim $18 Minimum Wage Initiative Advances to November Ballot." *Voice of OC*, June 21, 2018. Available at https://voiceofoc.org/2018/06/anaheim-18-mini mum-wage-initiative-advances-to-november-ballot/.

———. "Disney Pumps Another $600K into Anaheim Election; Tied with Unions at 1.5 Million." *Voice of OC*, October 18, 2018. Available at https://voiceofoc.org/2018/10 /disney-pumps-another-600k-into-anaheim-election-beating-its-2016-record-with -1-5-million-in-campaign-spending/.

———. "Unprecedented Spending in Another Pivotal Anaheim Election." *Voice of OC*, October 30, 2018. Available at https://voiceofoc.org/2018/10/unprecedented-spending -in-another-pivotal-anaheim-election/.

Walker, Douglas M. "Casinos and Economic Growth: An Update." *Journal of Gambling Business and Economics* 7, no. 2 (2013): 80–87.

Walker, Theresa. "Here's Where Anaheim Plans to Put a 2nd Homeless Shelter." *Orange County Register*, November 8, 2018. Available at https://www.ocregister.com/2018/11/07/heres-where-anaheim-plans-to-put-a-2nd-homeless-shelter/.

Wallace, Mike. *Mickey Mouse History and Other Essays on American Memory*. Temple University Press, 1996.

———. "Mickey Mouse History: Portraying the Past at Disney World." *Radical History Review* 32 (1985): 33–57.

"Walt and the Goodwill Tour." *Walt Disney Family Museum* (blog). September 8, 2016. Available at https://www.waltdisney.org/blog/walt-and-goodwill-tour.

Walt Disney Company. *The Gingerbread Man and the Golden Goose*. Golden Press, 1973.

"Walt Disney Make-Believe Project Planned Here." *Burbank Daily Review*, March 27, 1952.

"Walt Disney Presents Views on High-Rise Proposal." Disneyland Press Release, June 1964.

Ward, Kevin. "Urban Politics as a Politics of Comparison." *International Journal of Urban and Regional Research* 35, no. 4 (2011): 864–865.

Ward, Kevin, David Imbroscio, Deborah Martin, Clarence Stone, Robert Whelan, Faranak Miraftab, and Allan Cochrane. "Urban Politics: An Interdisciplinary Dialogue." *International Journal of Urban and Regional Research* 35, no. 4 (2011): 853–871.

Watts, Steven. "Walt Disney: Art and Politics in the American Century." *Journal of American History* 82, no. 1 (1995): 84–110.

Weaver, Timothy P. R. "Charting Change in the City: Urban Political Orders and Urban Political Development." *Urban Affairs Review* 58, no. 2 (2022): 319–355.

Weiner, Lynn. "'There's a Great Big Beautiful Tomorrow': Historic Memory and Gender in Walt Disney's 'Carousel of Progress,'" *Journal of American Culture* 20, no. 1 (1997): 111–116.

Welch, Susan. "The Impact of At-Large Elections on the Representation of Blacks and Hispanics." *Journal of Politics* 52, no. 4 (1990): 1050–1076.

Westcott, John, and Cynthia Simone. *Anaheim: City of Dreams—An Illustrated History*. Windsor, 1990.

Whitehead, Brian, and Chris Haire. "A New Age for Beach Boulevard Is Gaining Momentum." *Chico Enterprise-Record*, October 26, 2017, AA1.

Wikipedia. "Los Angeles Angels." Available at https://en.wikipedia.org/wiki/Los_Angeles_Angels.

Wills, John. *Disney Culture*. Rutgers University Press, 2017.

"With High Hopes: Disney Welcomes Young at Heart at Disneyland." *Disneyland News*, 1955.

Woo, Louise. "Amusement-Tax Supporters Drop Ballot Plans in Anaheim." *Orange County Register*, September 13, 1988, B3.

———. "More Disney Magic." *Orange County Register*, November 13, 1992, A3.

Woo, Louise, and Ricky Young. "WestCOT Plan Draws Staunch Opposition." *Orange County Register*, January 20, 1993, A1.

Wood, Daniel B. "Why Anaheim, Known for Disney and the Angels, Erupted in Violence This Week." *Christian Science Monitor*, July 26, 2012. Available at https://www.csmonitor.com/USA/2012/0726/Why-Anaheim-known-for-Disney-and-the-Angels-erupted-in-violence-this-week.

Woodyard, Chris, and Greg Hernandez. "Disney Drastically Cuts Anaheim Resort Plans." *Los Angeles Times*, January 31, 1995, A1.

Young, Ricky. "Disney Plan Has a Housing Hitch." *Orange County Register*, July 24, 1991, B1.

———. "Disney's Big, BIG World." *Orange County Register*, December 16, 1992, A1.

———. "Disney Shelves Plan for Park to Have Lakefront Retail Area." *Orange County Register*, April 23, 1993, B8.

———. "Study Doesn't Analyze Costs to Anaheim, Officials Say." *Orange County Register*, June 5, 1991, A14.

———. "WestCOT Center: Supporters Say Resort Might Be More Successful Than Disneyland." *Orange County Register*, December 15, 1991, B11.

Young, Ricky, and Gina Shaffer. "Disney Vow: Sue Us and WestCOT Dies." *Orange County Register*, April 27, 1993, B1.

Zukin, Sharon. *Landscapes of Power: From Detroit to Disney World*. University of California Press, 1993.

# Index

**Peter F. Burns** is Professor of Political Science at Soka University of America, author of *Electoral Politics Is Not Enough: Racial and Ethnic Minorities and Urban Politics*, and coauthor of *Reforming New Orleans: The Contentious Politics of Change in the Big Easy*.

**Matthew O. Thomas** is Professor of Political Science and Criminal Justice at California State University, Chico, and coauthor of *Reforming New Orleans: The Contentious Politics of Change in the Big Easy*.

**Max R. Bieganski** is an independent scholar and master's student in International Affairs at the School of Global Policy and Strategy at the University of California, San Diego. He received a BA in Liberal Arts and an MA in Educational Leadership and Societal Change from Soka University of America.

www.ingramcontent.com/pod-product-compliance
Lightning Source LLC
Chambersburg PA
CBHW030647270326
41929CB00007B/240